"George Burns shares wonderful stories that reveal his kindness and warmth while also providing engaging glimpses of true wisdom. Particularly impressive is how Burns promotes core values of decency and optimism while promoting insight and growth. Every reader will be a better therapist—and a better person—by absorbing the profound messages in this superb book."
—**Michael D. Yapko, PhD, clinical psychologist and author**
of *The Discriminating Therapist* and *Essentials of Hypnosis*

"In an engaging and lively style, George Burns takes the reader through a fascinating journey across different facets of the psychotherapeutic communication. This book shows readers how to collaborate with clients to build therapeutic strategies through use of metaphors and stories. Theoretically grounded in positive psychology, the approach focuses on the promotion of hope, mindfulness, personal strengths, and acceptance."
—**Antonella Delle Fave, MD, professor of psychology**
at the University of Milan, Italy

"Deploying the knowledge that stories can heal and enhance our lives, master storyteller and psychotherapist George Burns offers readers a wealth of inspiring stories covering specific facets of ourselves including empowerment, work and relationships. I warmly recommend this delightfully accessible book to anyone wishing to lead a happier and more fulfilled life."
—**Felicia Huppert, PhD, emeritus professor of psychology**
at the University of Cambridge, United Kingdom

101 Stories for Enhancing Happiness and Well-Being

Research shows us clearly *what* works in counseling and psychotherapy. Often by the time clients enter a therapist's office they have been told what to do—often soundly and sensibly—by well-meaning family, friends, and health professionals. The challenge for the effective therapist is *how* to communicate these same, sound messages in ways that the client is more likely to take on board, act on, and benefit from.

101 Stories for Enhancing Happiness and Well-Being harnesses the power of stories to translate the research from positive psychology into effective and practical therapeutic interventions. It communicates the core processes for enhancing happiness and well-being in ways that are easy to understand and incorporate into one's therapeutic practice and clients' lives.

George W. Burns is a clinical psychologist, adjunct professor of psychology at the Cairnmillar Institute of Psychotherapy and Counseling, and director of the Milton H. Erickson Institute of Western Australia. He conducts workshops worldwide, has authored 8 books, and volunteers as a psychologist in developing countries such as Bhutan.

101 Stories for Enhancing Happiness and Well-Being

Using Metaphors in Positive
Psychology and Therapy

George W. Burns

Routledge
Taylor & Francis Group

NEW YORK AND LONDON

First published 2017
by Routledge
711 Third Avenue, New York, NY 10017

and by Routledge
2 Park Square, Milton Park, Abingdon, Oxon, OX14 4RN

Routledge is an imprint of the Taylor & Francis Group, an informa business

Library of Congress Cataloging-in-Publication Data
Names: Burns, George W. (George William), author.
Title: 101 stories for enhancing happiness and well-being : using metaphors in positive psychology / George W Burns.
Other titles: One hundred one healing stories for enhancing happiness and well-being | One hundred and one healing stories for enhancing happiness and well-being
Description: 1 Edition. | New York : Routledge, 2017. | Includes bibliographical references and index.
Identifiers: LCCN 2016025776 | ISBN 9781138935822 (hardback : alk. paper) | ISBN 9781138935839 (pbk. : alk. paper) | ISBN 9781315672854 (ebook)
Subjects: LCSH: Happiness. | Well-being. | Metaphor—Therapeutic use. | Narrative therapy. | Positive psychology.
Classification: LCC BF575.H27 B877 2017 | DDC 150.19/88—dc23
LC record available at https://lccn.loc.gov/2016025776

ISBN: 978-1-138-93582-2 (hbk)
ISBN: 978-1-138-93583-9 (pbk)
ISBN: 978-1-315-67285-4 (ebk)

Typeset in Galliard
by Apex CoVantage, LLC

This one is dedicated to the two most
special boys in my life,
my grandsons,
Taran James and Oscar Cameron.

My deepest wish is that both of your lives will be
rich in stories of health, happiness, and love.

Contents

Acknowledgments

As I write, I look out from my window across the waters of the Shoalwater Islands Marine Park to Penguin Island. I see its lazy, elongated profile, its golden beaches at the ocean edge, its crumbling limestone cliffs, and its cap of green vegetation. I see the big picture image of the island but there is so much of the island that I don't see. From my window I don't see the Little Penguins resting in their burrows, the sleek Bridled Terns that migrate 5,000 miles before returning here to nest each year, or the world's most endangered sea lion that may have hauled out into the shade of a limestone cave. I don't see the community of people in the Hands Off Point Peron campaign who are fighting to protect this unique area from a proposed canal and housing estate on adjoining Point Peron and to preserve it as a coastal park for the people of the world forever. I see the island but I don't see all of what makes up the island.

As I view the island scene, I find myself reflecting on how, in a similar way, one may see a published book without seeing all that goes into making that book: the processes that went into its creation and, more importantly, the community of people behind its creation. Without them this book would not have found its existence and, hence, I am deeply indebted to and grateful for each and every one.

Generous friends have allowed me the opportunity of writing retreats in some of the most spectacular parts of the world. Dawa Penjor, Tashi Yangzom, and their family—who feel like my own family—gave me a room in the Tigers Nest Resort, Paro, Bhutan where I sat writing under the watchful eye of Taksang Gompa (Tiger's Nest Monastery) that hangs precariously from a cliff face 900 meters above the valley floor. From Namgay and Ugyen's Dochu La Resort, Bhutan, my writing was frequently distracted by the view of snowy Himalayan peaks (included the world's highest unclimbed mountain) and Ugyen's wall-to-wall art work. For such creative and inspirational writing environments, my deepest thanks, dear friends.

Stories have many sources and several of the stories and story ideas in this book have come from generous colleagues, friends, and clients: Thank you Emily Buehler, Ron Currie, Brian Egan, Lisa Kermode, Dr Rob McNeilly, Trapper Rick, Trulku Jamyang Rinpoche, Sultana Shamshi, Maree Smith,

Dr Helen Street, Dr Julie-Ann Sykley, Pema Tshering, Pema Wangchuk, Dr Michael Yapko, Taran, Oscar, Lucia, and the many wonderful clients with whom I have had the privilege of sharing stories.

It has been a pleasure to work with my editor, Anna Moore, my project manager, Kerry Boettcher, and all those behind the scene at Routledge. To have so many supportive people working with you in such a collaborative effort is a joy. Without them, this book simply would not now have been in your hands.

How can I write a book without mentioning Julie Nayda, my secretary, personal assistant, receptionist, and dear friend of 23 years who has been with me on every page of every book? I miss us sharing the same office and wish you a long, happy retirement.

Dr Keren Geddes has been my encouragement when inspiration failed and self-doubt invaded, proofing my writing, correcting my grammar, sharing kayak rides, sea lion swims, fun travels, sunsets and wine . . . and life itself. I am so grateful for the ways you—and Max—enhance my life with happiness, well-being, and love.

Fortunately, I don't need the research to tell me that, when it comes to the happiness stakes, family is tops. And I am privileged to have a top family. My life is so much richer and rewarding for the fact that you are part of it, Leah, Ian, Oscar, Taran, and Tom. I love you all.

PART ONE

 Orienting to Happiness-
Enhancing Stories

Introduction

If you change your story, you change your life, your experience, and your level of happiness. This is something I recently had confirmed for me by nine-year-old Lucia, the daughter of dear friends who travel a lot in the course of work, family, and vacations. Previously, Lucia had suddenly and inexplicably started to get anxious about getting on a plane. The anxiety developed with tension in her stomach and severe symptoms of vomiting and fainting when faced with an approaching flight. Terribly scary for a young child; terribly distressing for concerned parents.

In telling me the story of her recent trip back from England, she again began to experience the tension and feelings of nausea . . . and I was impressed. Simply by thinking about it and retelling the story, she could re-experience her feelings and experience them intensely. If the story was this powerful, I began to wonder, was it possible to change it to an equally powerful story of travelling comfortably and happily?

"I can't change it," asserted Lucia. "It is just there. It happens. I have tried. I can't do anything about it."

Lucia was stating something so many of us have said at times, including myself. When we have a strong, intense, extremely dominant thought or feeling, it is not easy to tell it to go away and expect that it will just disappear. And it may not be wise to. If you are in a situation of real threat or danger, it pays to give the situation highly focused attention. However, if you are in a low risk situation, such as flying is, then such thoughts are neither helpful nor functional. But how do you change them when, like Lucia, you believe you can't?

This is the sort of situation faced by many of our clients. Someone walks into your office and says, "I'm depressed." She tells you that well-meaning family and friends have told her, "Get out and exercise; Find a hobby or interest; Make some new friends; Do something for someone else; Look at the glass as half full," etc. You know this is scientifically sound and sensible . . . but she is no better for this sound advice. She continues her story, saying she consulted her physician who prescribed some antidepressants and advised her, "Get out and exercise; Find a hobby or interest; Make some new friends; Do something for someone else; Look at the glass as half full," etc.

Again you know this advice is well grounded in sound research from the fields of cognitive behavior therapy (CBT) and positive psychology but still it hasn't worked. What do you do? What more do you have to offer that has not already been offered? That the scientifically sound and sensible advice offered to your client has not been accepted or acted on previously means that, if you offer the same, you are likely to meet with the same response: yet another failure experience for your client. In turn, this is likely to create more feelings of helplessness for your client rather than hopefulness.

As therapists we are in the best possible time ever to be practicing our profession. Never before has there been so much research evidence about what works and what doesn't. However, people are still increasingly suffering psychological and mental health problems and, put simply, therapy doesn't always work. Why? Well, it is one thing knowing the research that shows us clearly *what* works in counseling and psychotherapy. It is another thing knowing *how* to effectively communicate that knowledge, skills, and strategies to the client. The science of our professions lies in knowing what works well. The art of our professions lies in knowing how to communicate that science, effectively and helpfully.

The real challenge for the effective therapist—once we know the interventions that research has demonstrated to be helpful—is *how* do we communicate those same, sound messages in ways that the client is more likely to take them on board, act on them, and benefit from them? One thing we know from the above—and all-too-common—case example is that direct and authoritarian advice does not always work. If it does, it is the simplest and quickest way to do therapy: tell someone once what to do and they do it. But how often, as with our depressed client above, does that actually work?

It is here that metaphors and therapeutic stories come to the fore. Stories can, have been, and are used in psychotherapy as metaphors, or indirect suggestions, to help effectively communicate a therapeutic message that will commonly provide the means or pathways to facilitate a client resolving their problems. Therapeutic stories can help bypass resistance, particularly when the therapeutic metaphors are generated by the client, come from the client's own story, or are built collaboratively with the client (Burns, 2001, 2007).

What Do I Mean By *Metaphor*?

I confess to deliberately being vague in my definition of metaphors throughout this book. I do not want to draw pedantic lines between metaphors, anecdotes, analogies, similes, and stories—as one might in a pure literary sense—but rather see their commonalities as symbolic forms of effective communication, especially in therapy.

Metaphors are far more common in our everyday language than most of us are aware. They fall off our tongue, they color our language, they trigger associations—and each of these previous phrases is a metaphor. They may be a single word, a phrase, a sentence, or a longer story. Some may be explicit and conscious while others may be more implicit and unconscious. However, in a broad stroke of the definition brush (which is also a metaphor!), the term *metaphor* in the original Greek meant "to carry something across" or "to transfer." In literature it refers to carrying one image or concept across to another. It is the comparison of two unrelated concepts or images based on a resemblance or similarity (such as the broad stroke of a brush and vague definition above).

Metaphors are used in language and literature for creating beauty, polish, emphasis, and—importantly for us as therapists—engaging the listener at a more symbolic and different cognitive level. They are thus an expressive, creative, perhaps challenging, and powerful form of communication. As therapy is a language-based process of healing, heavily reliant on the effectiveness of communication between client and therapist, the use of metaphor in therapeutic stories can link with familiar language structures of the client and assist the client's process of change.

Why Use Metaphors in Therapy?

Metaphors and stories are efficient and meaningful methods for communicating about experience. They are a way of sharing what we have learnt with others in a manner that will, hopefully, make someone else's journey easier and more enjoyable. Thus, a therapeutic metaphor is usually offered to a client with the express purpose of assisting that person to reach their goals in the most effective and efficient way. It is about filling the experiential gap between what is or has been, and what can be.

Even a brief look at history will show that every culture, since the time we humans began communicating through language, has used stories to communicate values, morals, and standards. In fact, even before language we painted our stories on cave walls. It is therefore little wonder that the world's greatest teachers chose stories, parables, and metaphors as their preferred medium of education. Buddha, Jesus, Mohammed, and Loa Tsu did not lecture. They told stories. They did not quote facts, statistics, or evidence-based data but told tales of life. They offered a parable or story that opened the range of experiences and interpretations available to their followers. Their stories have lived on for as long as two and a half thousand years, and are still retold by their followers. They knew that stories are a means of communicating *par excellence*. Not only do we learn from stories, but we *love* them.

As therapeutic teaching tools, stories are engaging and interactive. They teach by attraction, bypass resistance, nurture imagination, and elicit search-for-meaning processes in the listener. They develop problem-solving skills, create outcome possibilities, and invite independent decision-making.

The impact of stories was recently demonstrated for me when I was conducting a workshop on using stories in therapy at an international conference. The day before one of my colleagues presented a keynote lecture on his research, with several slides of data projected onto a large screen. At one stage, he illustrated a point with a story about his family dog. The next day I asked my audience of about 500 people if they remembered his fifth slide and what it was about. Not a single hand went up. However, when I then asked who remembered the story he told about his family dog, almost every hand went up.

As well as being lovers of stories, we are also all storytellers. We reconnect with our loved ones at the end of a day by relating the tales of what happened to us at work, home, or school. We share our experiences, our trials and tribulations, our joys and triumphs, and our humorous encounters through stories. We get home and say, "You'll never guess what happened to me today." . . . And launch into a story.

Why This Book?

First, I have a long-standing interest in stories and their ability to communicate important life messages—and want to share with you both that love and the therapeutic effectiveness I have found in using stories. Not only are stories able to communicate those important life messages but they also have the power to communicate them effectively when other styles of communication may not. This is illustrated in the example given of my colleague who gave the keynote lecture at an international conference. Attendants remembered the story of his family dog. They did not remember the scientific data on his fifth slide.

Second, not many of us like to be told what to do. Direct and authoritarian forms of communication tend to trigger resistance and rebellion, but tell a story and a person is not being treated in an authoritarian way. They are simply being offered a story about which they have a choice of accepting or not. A story is not just a more user-friendly way of communicating an important message, it is also an empowering way for someone to choose whether to take on board a message . . . or not.

Finally, I just love stories. I guess I have loved them from that early age when my mother sat on my bedside and read me night-time stories that had me slipping into a peaceful slumber. It was not just the stories but also the process of listening to, being absorbed in, learning from and engaging with the teller that aroused in me a lingering curiosity. Why do we love stories? Why do we feel engaged in them? How can we use stories helpfully and meaningfully to enhance our well-being? Well, it's that very curiosity of this that led me to working with stories in my professional life as a therapist and, in turn, putting together this book that you now hold in your hands.

What Does This Book Offer?

First, I am a practitioner of therapy. I enjoy books and strategies that are simple, practical, and essentially usable. I want to offer you some of the beneficial things that I have learnt over a life time of being a therapist in ways that are pragmatic and applicable.

Second, with this purpose in mind, I have presented 101 examples of thera-peutic, metaphoric stories arranged in 17 chapters reflecting 17 core areas of life concerns that therapists commonly encounter. The 17 chapters also are themed on positive outcomes and grounded in interventions that research from the fields of positive psychology and cognitive behavior therapy have shown to be effective.

Third, each chapter commences with a brief introductory description of, and evidence-base for, the theme of the therapeutic outcome stories of that chapter. While I want to give you the evidence base, I don't want to distract your attention from the stories with interruptive referencing and notes and so have avoided these as much as possible in the text, opting instead to provide a section at the end of the book with my resources and potential future reading opportunities for you.

Fourth, each story is prefaced with its Happiness-Enhancing Characteristics that summate the:

Problems addressed
Resources developed
Outcomes offered

for that particular story.

I have provided these (a) to assist you to see the therapeutic characteristics inherent in each story, (b) to show you the processes I go through in creating stories for an individual client, and (c) help familiarize you with a process by which you may go about creating your own therapeutic stories for your own clients. Just as my ultimate goal in therapy is to empower my clients to live their lives well and independently, so in this book my ultimate goal is to help empower you to become an effective, independent metaphor therapist.

Finally, each chapter is shadow-tabbed on the page edge to allow you to quickly access a chapter or story when working with a client toward a particu-lar therapeutic goal.

What Is the Link between Positive Psychology, CBT, Mindfulness, and Metaphors?

Positive psychology, cognitive behavior therapy and mindfulness are among our most researched and evidence-based approaches to psychology and psy-chotherapy. As well as containing many scientifically sound strategies and interventions, they take a practical and positive orientation to resolving life issues by facilitating healthy functioning through happiness, enhancement, and well-being.

As such, there is little need for me to describe the history, underlying phi-losophy, or specific interventions of these approaches. They are already well documented elsewhere in the literature. However, as I mentioned at the begin-ning of this introduction, knowing *what* works is one thing. Communicating that effectively to an individual client is another. In this latter area, most of our major approaches to therapy have been lacking. Consequently, I want to offer methods for communicating essential therapeutic interventions in ways that work. Let me illustrate with an example.

Two strategies that are well-founded in the positive psychology research are that exercise and gratitude serve as preventatives to depression, reduce the rate, severity, and length of depression, and facilitate greater levels of happiness. Great. It seems simple: tell a client to go home and exercise daily or record three things they can be grateful for at the end of each day, and their depression will be fixed. But how often has that actually worked for you or your clients? If it does, it is obviously the simplest and quickest way to do therapy. However, my experience has been that it is not the most probable outcome. People need to have their story heard and to be offered new stories of how things can be different. They need stories that connect to them and their problem, show strategies, means, or pathways they can follow to bring about change, and offer hope that it is realistically possible. Here metaphors can effectively and helpfully communicate the powerful evidence-based interventions of therapy.

So that is why I have written this, my eighth book, my fourth on metaphors. That is what this book is about. And that reminds me of why I began to tell you the story about Lucia who believed she could not change her fear of flying.

I asked Lucia, "What do you do for fun?"

As she began to relate stories about swimming, dancing, and ice-skating, there was a noticeable shift in her mood, body, expression, and conversation. She became more animated and more relaxed. Her facial expression shifted from stress to joy. She was more alive in the stories she told of happy times.

I asked her what she noticed about the ways she was now feeling and acting. "I am feeling happier," she said.

"Yes," I agreed. "How have you done that? How have you shifted from thoughts of sadness to thoughts of happiness?" I enquired.

"I don't know," she answered.

"Maybe it is not necessary to know how," I added. "Maybe it is just enough to know you can. Tell me too, when do you feel most relaxed?"

"Having a spa bath."

I asked her to close her eyes and imagine having a spa bath. We talked about all the relaxing sensations, the sights, the sounds, the smells, the tactile feelings. As expected, she had the same power to experience these positive sensations as she did the negative ones in her anticipatory story about flying. I asked her to think about these fun and relaxing things if scary thoughts of flying came back because she now knew she could change them even if she didn't know how.

As Lucia and I only had this one chance to speak in person before her next flight, I asked her to phone me the morning of her flight. I spoke to her mother first who said Lucia, in contrast to recent past experiences, slept well the night before and had eaten breakfast that morning. When I spoke with Lucia, there was still tension in her voice as we talked about the flight but when I directed conversation to having a spa bath and ice-skating, her mood quickly shifted. I asked her to practice this on the plane.

She said, "I am looking forward to seeing the movie, The Witches, in flight." She had found something positive to focus on and anticipate.

As requested, she also phoned me from the airport just prior to boarding. "I am feeling good," she said, "but my stomach is feeling a bit tight."

"Can you accept that your stomach might feel a bit tight, that this might not all change at once, and go on enjoying the rest of you that feels good?" I asked.

I later had a text message from Lucia's mother saying, "I look forward to telling you how incredibly Lucia managed her flight." I looked forward to hearing it from Lucia.

I wish, at the age of nine, I had known what Lucia knows: Change your story and you change your life.

The PRO Approach for Assessing Outcomes

If clients are to change their stories in ways that change their experience and life, where and how can we therapists begin to facilitate that process of change? Simply put, it begins at the beginning: the moment we meet a client for the first time and how we go about assessing that client for change and outcomes. It begins not so much with the history and causes of the presenting problem as with the client's desired outcomes and the processes, skills, resources, pathways, or strengths necessary to get them there.

One of the major contributions that positive psychology has brought to psychology and psychotherapy is a major paradigm shift. For a long time most—but certainly not all—psychological and psychotherapeutic models have focused on what's wrong with a person rather than with what's right with the person (Erickson, 2010). Positive psychology has shifted that previous emphasis to look more at a person's strengths, abilities, and resources (Biswas-Diener, 2010a; Linley, 2008; Linley & Burns, 2010).

In doing so, positive psychotherapy holds happiness, well-being, strength utilization, and goal attainment as the desired outcomes for our individual clients. To achieve these a therapist does not necessarily need to explore a person's pathology or lengthy past history. As the ultimate goal of positive psychotherapy is to assist a person to move from where they are to where they want to be, to enhanced happiness and well-being, the PRO approach that I have described in previous works provides a process of doing this (Burns, 2001, 2005, 2007, 2010). PRO is an anagram standing for the:

- Problems a person wishes to address;
- Resources, strengths, pathways, and abilities they need to access and develop in order to reach their desired therapeutic outcomes; and
- Outcomes they wish to achieve through the therapeutic process.

Let us look at each of those components of the PRO Assessment in turn.

Problems Addressed

Our clients will commonly bring us stories that are very problem-focused and even problem-saturated. After all, it is the problem—and a person's lack of success, thus far, in finding a solution—that has brought them into our office in the first place. Hearing such stories over and over again—especially if our professional training has primarily had us looking for and diagnosing problems—makes it easy for the therapist to also become caught in the very problem-focused and problem-saturated content of those stories. It is the *content* in which clients commonly become stuck as if sinking in quicksand. It doesn't help for us to jump in the quicksand with them and begin to ask *why* they are stuck or sinking.

As a therapist, we need to respectfully and empathically hear the content of those stuck stories while being mindfully focused on the necessary *processes* of *how* a person can move out of the quicksand, of how they can transition from being stuck and unhappy to unstuck and happy. For the sake of the client's successful outcomes and well-being, as well as our own well-being, therapists will therefore want, and need, to keep their focus clearly and strongly on the client's desired outcomes. Consequently, we may want to initiate our conversation with hopeful, outcome-oriented questions like:

• Given that you have been feeling so (depressed, anxious, angry, etc.), what are you hoping to achieve from therapy?
• What are the outcomes that you are wanting to achieve from our conversations?
• How would you like to see life different from what it is at the moment?
• When you have got to where you want to be how will things have changed for you?

However, even if we start by trying to guide clients with such outcome-oriented questions, they are still likely to tell us their problem-based stories. Those stories of their problem/s need to be heard . . . and heard respectfully. It is important to remember that the beginnings of a positive relationship between you and your client will hinge on how empathically or not we hear those stories.

Dr Christopher Peterson was one of the one founding fathers of positive psychology and also one of the top 100 most cited psychologists in history. He has defined positive psychology as the scientific study of what makes life most worth living. He said that psychological science and practice should be as concerned with strength as with weakness; as interested in building the best things in life as in repairing the worst; and as concerned with making the lives of all people fulfilling as with healing pathology (Peterson, 2008).

Nowhere in his definition did he say or imply that psychology should ignore or dismiss the very real problems that people experience. Problems are a part of our life. We don't live our three score and 10 years without having them. However, the client does not need to dwell on them or be saturated by them. Doing so is a surefire way to hopelessness, helplessness, and depression. Similarly, the therapist does not need to dwell on the details, specifics, or origins of the problems as this is likely to simply validate those feelings of hopelessness, helplessness, and depression for the client. Our therapeutic orientation is best focused on the processes that will be useful in helping the client move beyond the problems to greater levels of happiness and well-being.

Let us keep in mind that a person's presenting problem is merely the starting point. It is like the starting blocks that athletes use to launch themselves on the track toward their goal of the finishing line. It is the starting point from which we can offer the client a therapeutic story or, indeed, any other therapeutic intervention.

Resources Developed

Dr Rick Snyder has spoken of the need for people to have clear, defined, and practical *pathways* if they are to develop hope, hopefulness, and goal attainment (Cheavens & Gum, 2010; Snyder, 1994, 2002). Dr Alex Linley has emphasized the need to recognize and utilize our individual strengths and abilities to create and maintain happiness and well-being (Linley, 2008; Linley & Burns, 2010). Dr Tayyab Rashid has presented the Strengths-Based Assessment as a means to identify, measure, and build strengths that nurture resilience and well-being (2015). Over the years I have sought to define, examine and work with developing the resources, abilities, strengths, and pathways necessary for a person to achieve their therapeutic outcomes of enhanced well-being (Burns, 2001, 2005, 2007, 2010). I believe there are more commonalities than differences in the language that we are all using. What we are saying is that the person has to have the means and abilities to get from point A to point B, to have the skills and strengths to move from anxiety to tranquility, from depression to happiness, from anger to calm. And we as therapists need to offer every possible assistance for them to both recognize and employ those resources effectively toward their goals.

I love the delightful story of the Zen master who, after being away teaching for the day, came home to find his humble hut burnt down. He stopped, looked at the hut, and thought to himself, *At last I have an uninterrupted view of the sky at night.*

The story has a very clear problem (the master's hut has burnt down) and a clear outcome (he has an uninterrupted view of the sky at night) but what the story does not provide is the pathways, strengths, or resources that are needed to get from the problem into the outcome—unless you perhaps happened to be an enlightened Zen master.

So how do we explore the resources and abilities our clients need to get from the problem to the outcome? Here Seligman's PERMA model of five core components that contribute to happiness provides a useful format for asking resource-seeking questions (Seligman, 2011). Below I have listed those five components followed by some sample questions to assist both therapist and client in their search for and discovery of resources in each area.

Pleasure and Positive Emotions

- What do you do for fun?
- When do you feel at your happiest?
- What brings you pleasure and enjoyment?
- What helps lift your mood?
- When you are happy what are you doing?
- When you are happy what are you thinking?
- When you are happy what are you feeling?
- What everyday things do you enjoy doing?

Engagement, Mindfulness, and Flow

- What tasks of challenge or skill do you engage in?
- What do you do that demands a high level of concentration?
- When do you experience yourself engaged in deep, effortless involvement?
- In what sort of activities do you lose all sense of self?
- When do you find that time appears to stand still or vanish for you?
- What types of mindfulness, meditation, or focused awareness do you practice?

Relationships

- What relationships enhance your sense of well-being?
- What is it about those relationships that benefit your well-being?
- How do your social relationships contribute to your happiness?
- What ways do work relationships enhance your well-being?
- What aspects of family relationships enhance you?
- How do your intimate relationships help you to feel happier?
- What are the contributions that you make to relationships that have you feeling better?

Meaning and Purpose

- What gives you a sense of meaning and purpose in life?
- What are the values that guide you through life?
- If you have a purpose in life what would you say that is?
- Do you have a vision for the future? How would you describe that?
- What are you most looking forward to in the future?
- What causes are you currently engaged in or can see yourself engaged in in the future?

Accomplishment and Achievements

- What do you consider you are good at?
- When you are at your best, what are you doing?

- What do you enjoy doing most?
- What would you describe as your most significant accomplishment or achievement?
- Tell me about the best experience you have had.
- What are the most energizing things that you do?
- What gives you the greatest sense of feeling authentic, of feeling who you really are?

One of my peer reviewers, having read the above section, asked, "But what if you have a client who doesn't come up with anything, who puts up roadblocks?" First, as the 34 sample questions above cover five core areas of well-being, it is most unlikely that a client will not connect with at least one question in one area.

Second, you will note the above questions are carefully crafted. They do not ask 'why.' Anyone who has ever had or worked with teenagers will know that if you ask why an adolescent did something the answer will inevitably be, "I don't know." 'Why' questions tend to be past-oriented and do not necessarily illicit searching for and communication of answers. Nor do the above questions invite simple yes or no responses such as in, "Do you have any strengths?" If you ask such a question, you risk getting "No" as an answer and thus bringing a quick stop to both conversation and therapy. Instead, the above style of questions (a) presupposes that people have certain strengths, abilities, and skills and (b) invites them to discuss and share those resources. Simply put, it is harder not to respond—and not to respond constructively— to these presuppositional style questions.

Third, the sample questions provided tend to be in the present tense. If you are meeting with a person who is currently depressed you might expect that a question like, "What do you do for fun?" will receive an answer something like, "Nothing." If this is the case, it may be helpful to shift the tense into the past as in, "If you are currently not doing anything for fun, what have you done for fun in the past?" And if this fails to result in a useful response, it may assist the client to look forward with a question such as, "When you are feeling happier what will you be doing for fun then?"

Is there a guarantee that you will never get a client who blocks you at every move? No there isn't. However, it is most unlikely if you follow these guidelines, carefully craft your enquiries as open-ended, presuppositional questions, and assist your client to explore those questions in both present, past, and future tenses. Utilizing these guidelines will enhance the probability of finding resources and strengths in even the most reluctant client.

Outcomes Offered

For a person to move forward in therapy, as in life, they need clear goals and directions. An important part of the therapist's role, therefore, is to help a person to define those goals and directions—for both client and therapist. This is not rocket science. If you get in your automobile, you need to know where you want to go if you are to have any chance of arriving at your destination. The same principle applies in therapy.

Below are some process steps and brief guidelines to help define a client's desired therapeutic outcome. Sometimes, simply in the process of defining their desired outcomes, clients begin to find their own solutions but if not you will have clear, specific, and practical goals with which to work with the client in therapy.

1 Take an Outcome-Oriented Assumption, Attitude, and Approach

It benefits both therapist and client if the therapist has an outcome-oriented assumption. By that I mean that if the client comes in to my office and says, "I am depressed," I hold the assumption they are not wanting to know more about depression but more about happiness. If a client says, "I am feeling anxious and stressed," my assumption is that they are not wanting to know more about anxiety but more about relaxation, calmness, and tranquility.

In addition, we know that when a therapist holds a positive attitude or belief about the client's ability to overcome their problems and reach their desired goal, generally they do. If the therapist believes the client is able and either has or can develop the necessary resources, then generally they do. It is, therefore, important for the therapist or counselor to have (a) an outcome-oriented assumption and attitude that incorporates hopefulness and a positive expectation about the client's ability to achieve their goal as well as (b) an approach that works toward having that happen.

2 Enquire About the Client's Desired Therapeutic Goal

It may sound simple enough but if we're wanting to help our clients move towards a desired goal we need to discover what that goal is, what steps the person needs to take towards achieving it, and how they will know once they have attained it. This is one of the basic paradigm shifts of Positive Psychotherapy in which the therapist will be more interested in, and direct attention toward, the client's desired goals and their attainment than towards the problem and its causes. To help do this you may ask questions like:

- What are your goals in coming to therapy?
- What do you want to achieve out of this discussion with me?
- What do you hope to gain from our sessions together?
- In what ways would you like to see life improving for you?
- When you have stopped (using substances, feeling depressed, being so stressed, etc.) how will life be better?
- At the end of our time together what differences would you like to have happened?

3 *Shift the Negative to the Positive*

It is not uncommon for clients to express their desired goals in the negative: *I don't want to be feeling depressed anymore; I don't want use drugs anymore; I don't want my relationship to continue in this direction.* If that is so, we need to help them shift the goals into the positive. Positive goals (where a person is moving toward a desired objective)—in contrast to negative goals (where a person is trying to stop or avoid something they have not so far been able to stop)—are much easier to (a) set, (b) achieve, (c) maintain, and (d) be motivated toward attaining. To help facilitate the shift from negative to positive goals the following style of questions may assist:

- If you don't want to be feeling depressed, how do you want to feel?
- If you don't want to be taking drugs/alcohol, what do you want to be doing?
- If you don't want to feel anxious, how would you rather feel?
- If you are not happy with the directions in your relationship how will it be when things are going well again?

4 *Question a Global Goal*

Clients will often reply, stating a global or generalized goal like: *I want to be happier, sober, more relaxed, or in a better relationship.* Such global goals are diffuse and therefore hard to target and achieve. What does happier, sober, more relaxed, or a better relationship mean for that particular individual? This we—and they—need to know more clearly and specifically. So, if that is the case, our role becomes one of helping the client be more specific with questions like:

- When you are happier, how will you be thinking, feeling, and acting?
- When you are sober, what will be different in your thoughts, feelings, and behavior?
- When you are more relaxed, what do you think is the first thing you will notice that is different?
- When your relationship has improved what specific changes will you and your partner see?

5 *Explore Specific Outcomes*

Then get even more specific. As therapists, we may not be able to give someone a handful of happiness that lasts for the rest of their lives in any given session of counselling or therapy but we may be able to help them take at least some small steps towards greater happiness and well-being. Therefore, let us help them find those first, specific, small, and achievable steps.

- If you will be thinking differently (when you are happy, dry, relaxed, or whatever) what particular thoughts will you be thinking?
- When you are feeling happier, clean, more relaxed (or whatever goal your client has specified), what are the feelings you will be experiencing?
- As you move towards that goal, what will you specifically be doing differently?

Once you have clear, specific, defined, and achievable goals, it is easier to assist your client to explore the pathways towards achieving them.

6 Anticipate a Positive Outcome

When you realistically and hopefully anticipate that your client can and will achieve their goal it helps to provide hope and positive expectations for the client. Thinking something like, *As this client has relapsed several times, it seems unlikely they will ever recover,* sets a negative expectation for the client. After all, if their professional therapist doesn't expect them to get better where is the hope for them? On the other hand, consider the difference in thinking and saying something like: *I know it is a great struggle to stay on track but the fact that you have relapsed several times is a clear indication that you have also gotten on top of that problem several times. How can you help make those times longer and stronger?* In other words, if you want your client to focus on achieving a positive outcome, you also need to be looking for and seeing that positive outcome.

7 Reinforce Any Steps Toward the Outcome

It is important to validate, reinforce, and ratify any and all steps—no matter how small—that a person makes towards their desired goal. Even the smallest step forward is a step in the right direction, so congratulate your client on each step. Ask a client to keep a record of their dry days, happier moments, times of relaxation, etc., as this helps confirm the progress. Ask them to send a letter, email, text message, or phone to update you on their progress. This helps confirm it for them. Once one small goal is attained and affirmed it builds hope and confidence to move on to the next step or goal.

Applying the PRO Assessment for Outcomes

The PRO assessment is not meant or intended to be a diagnostic tool, manual, or formulaic approach but rather a guiding framework for pragmatically exploring the strengths, pathways, and goals that will help a person move toward greater levels of happiness and well-being.

PRO ASSESSMENT

Having undertaken the PRO assessment, both you and your client will have a clearer understanding of the:

(a) Problems they wish to address,
(b) Resources they have in the core component areas of happiness that both they and you can utilize for reaching their desired goals, and
(c) Outcomes they wish to achieve.

In sum, it will provide you with a specific and practical framework on which to base your therapeutic interventions and build therapeutic metaphors. Examples of the PRO Approach for developing healing stories are given in the following chapters. Each therapeutic metaphor is prefaced by its Happiness-Enhancing Characteristics under the headings of the Problems Addressed, the Resources Developed, and the Outcomes Offered.

A Gratuitous Opening Story
The Power of Stories

In a distant kingdom in a distant past, aware of the value of stories, a wise king appointed a royal storyteller whose sole job was to tell stories to the royal court but especially to the somewhat spoilt and precocious young princess. As an only child and hence the only heir to the throne, the king and queen bent over backwards for her, appointing an army of attentive servants to immediately satisfy her every wish and whim—one of whom was the storyteller.

Like all good storytellers, he knew full well the power of stories to entertain, inform, and educate us. He knew that they can teach us values, show us how to solve problems, and provide experiential learning where we may not have actually had the experience. He knew that stories can heal and change; that they could add light to darkness, joy to despair, and peace to distress. Proof of his knowledge came one day as the princess had been playing in the royal garden.

Catching sight of her own reflection in the clear, still garden pool, she vainly leaned closer to better admire her beauty. In doing so her royal crown, encrusted in precious jewels, slipped from her head, fell into the water and sunk to the bottom. The princess screamed, the servants ran, and plunged into the pool to retrieve the crown. The more that plunged in, the more that thrashed and splashed around, the more the mud was stirred up and the more the waters grew murkier and murkier. The chances of recovering her crown seemed to be diminishing rapidly. The princess screamed louder, the servants in fear and panic continued to thrash and splash . . . and the crown continued to remain hidden at the bottom of the pond.

Quietly the storyteller walked into the confusion, approached the anxious, agitated princess, and said, "Your Highness, let me tell you a story."

"Get away, you old fool," she yelled. "This is no time for your childish stories. Can't you see what has happened? Your tales won't get my crown back."

As if she hadn't spoken, the storyteller began, "Once upon a time . . ."

It wasn't long before the princess started to alternate her attention between the pond and the story. A short while later she sat down beside the storyteller, absorbed and engrossed in his tale. She could see herself in the characters and places he wove into his story. Intrigued, the servants gave up on their thrashing and splashing, climbed from the pond and sat listening to where the story took them.

Both princess and servants were entranced. As they listened, their breathing slowed, their muscles relaxed, and their minds calmed. No longer were they panicky about the sunken crown. In fact, if truth be known, they probably weren't even thinking about it at all. By the time the storyteller came to the end of his tale, a calmness prevailed not only in the listeners but also in the pond. The time they had spent listening quietly to the story had allowed the mud to settle—perhaps metaphorically as well in reality—and the crown was now clearly visible on the bottom.

The storyteller arose, took a clean dive into the clear water, and emerged holding the crown. Offering it to the princess, he said, "Sometimes stories help enhance our clarity and enable us to find what we want."

PART TWO
 Happiness-Enhancing Stories

1 On Being a Goal-Setter and Goal-Achiever

> If one does not know to which port one is sailing, no wind is favorable.
> Lucius Anneaus Seneca, Roman Philosopher

Introduction

Personal life goals are crucial to both our existence and our well-being. In fact, it is hard to imagine life without goals. If we didn't have a goal to go to work in the morning, care for our family, engage in a weekend sporting pursuit, socialize with friends, or whatever, we may never get out of bed. Life would end up very purposeless, hopeless, and depressed.

Having, striving towards, and achieving appropriate goals benefits our well-being on both a day-to-day and long-term basis. Goals help us to find meaning and purpose in life. They enable us to be in touch with our strengths and resources, they facilitate greater self-understanding and they have even been associated with living a longer and healthier life. For life to be meaningful and happy we need to have goals not only that we have achieved but that we can look forward to achieving.

However, it is not as simplistic as just having goals. It is the *type* of goals we have that makes a difference to our well-being. The pursuit and attainment of goals that have inherent worth and value are more likely to contribute to our happiness.

In addition, it is not just goal attainment but also the *process* or *path* of moving toward a particular goal that helps enhance our well-being. Confirming the old proverb that says "It is better to journey than arrive," researchers have shown that the process of moving toward a goal may actually be more important to happiness than attaining the goal itself.

Dr Rick Snyder (1994, 2002) has found that as well as having specific goals we also need (a) clear, definable pathways to be able to reach those goals and (b) the reasons or intrinsic motivation—that he calls *agency*—if we are going to successfully apply ourselves to their achievement and our happiness.

The stories in this chapter are designed to help explore personal goals, set the type of goals that are most helpful, and follow processes by which those personal goals can be achieved. They provide step-by-step strategies for defining, setting, and attaining goals that are likely to enhance a person's quality of life and well-being.

Story 1

Do You Follow the Goal or the Path?

Happiness-Enhancing Characteristics

   Problems Addressed

      Being solely goal-directed
      Striving too hard
      Missing the subtle messages

   Resources Developed

      Listen to those who have sought similar goals
      Learn from those who have sought similar goals
      Look for the pathways by which to attain your goals

   Outcomes Offered

      Keep your goal in mind
      Keep sight of the pathways and processes to get there

There is a Zen story I like of a young student who was keen to attain enlightenment and to do so as quickly as possible. As a result, he approached his teacher and asked, "If I work hard and diligently, how long will it take for me to become enlightened?"

His teacher contemplated this question for a while, as Zen masters are prone to do, then replied, "Ten years."

"Ten years!" exclaimed the student. "What if I dedicate myself to it, work *very* hard and *really* apply myself to learn fast? How long will it take then?"

With even further contemplation, the teacher gave his considered reply, "Then it will take twenty years."

Confused and thinking the master had misunderstood him—*How could working harder double rather than shorten the time?*—the student rephrased his question. "If I dedicate myself *solely* to it, if I work *very, very* hard and if I *really, really* apply myself to learn fast? How long will it take then?"

Obviously, this needed even more consideration and the student waited eagerly for the teacher's answer. Eventually he gave it. "In that case," he said, "it will take thirty years."

"Thirty years!" exclaimed the confused student, struggling to contain his disappointment and frustration. "I don't understand. Each time I say I will work harder, you reply that it will take me longer. How can that be? Why do you say that?"

"Well," replied the teacher, "when your eyes are set solely on the goal, you have none for the path."

Story 2

Taking It Step-by-Step

Happiness-Enhancing Characteristics

Problems Addressed

> Facing a big, enormous, or formidable task
> Dealing with things you *should* be doing
> Finding purpose or direction

Resources Developed

> Finding what you *want* to do
> Discovering *intrinsic* rewards
> Utilizing personal strengths
> Finding pathways toward goal achievement
> Applying yourself to the task
> Just doing it
> Taking it step-by-step
> Learning to train and practice the required skills

Outcomes Offered

> Reaching your goal
> Achieving your objective
> Reaping the rewards

People often ask me, "How do you get to write a book, let alone eight?" Their question has me thinking, *How do you get to do anything? How do you get out of bed in the morning? How do you get a career? How do you build recreational skills? How do you form a relationship? How do you overcome a problem?*

In the process of writing this new book, I have paused to ask myself, *How do I do it?* It is interesting to reflect on that process of how we go about achieving something in our lives.

The first thing for me is that I *wanted* to. I enjoy telling and writing stories. I thought about how it might be helpful to share my thoughts and experiences with colleagues and how, in turn, it might be helpful to the people they work with. I have enjoyed the emails from readers of my previous books saying how they have been beneficial. In other words, I began to find many reasons why I *wanted* to do it.

Tackling a task, like writing a new book, holds *intrinsic* or inbuilt rewards for me. It wasn't going to work well for me, for my publishers, or for you, the reader, if I hated the task and felt I *should* be doing it just to fulfill my author's contract. Fortunately, I love writing. It provides me with pleasure seeing ideas turn into words and words turn into something as solid and tangible as a book. It has me engaged, totally absorbed, when I am working on it and thinking about the best way to present or write the next story. It adds meaning and purpose to my life by producing something that I hope will contribute to the happiness and well-being of others. I can look at it as a worthy and worthwhile task.

Given that I want to write this book and that the task has intrinsic rewards for me, I still need to know *how* to do it. If I can't see the path from point A to point B, I am not likely to get there. I need to know the pathways, to see the map, to have a practical plan. But as well as the path the book will take, I also need to know the path *I* will take. *How* can I set aside the time? *When* can I set aside the time? How do I need to organize myself, my life, and my relationships with those close to me to achieve my goals?

Then I need to *apply* myself, to make the commitment to the task, and to get on with doing it. At first I had self-doubts. I was contracted to write 101 stories in 100,000 words. It seemed like a formidable task. Would I be able to do it? What if I ran out of ideas? What if I couldn't fulfill the contract? *I can write one story*, I reminded myself. *If I can write one, I can write another.* And so I began to take it one step at a time. The more I did, the easier it became, and the more ideas came to mind. I was training my thinking and my actions in the directions I wanted them to go.

So when people often ask me, "How do you get to write a book, let alone eight?" I want to reply, "How do you get to do anything?" Ask anyone how they do something well and you are likely to find similar answers. "How do you get to be a recording artist, a film star, a sporting hero, a successful business operator, a good worker, a confident parent, a skilled therapist, or a happy person?" They are likely to answer, "I just did it."

If you are really curious about the process and press it further, you may hear: "It was something I *wanted* to do. I found *intrinsic* rewards in doing it. I *applied* myself. I took it *step-by-step*. I *trained* and I *practiced*."

Whether writing a book, running a race, studying for a degree, wanting to be a better parent, or seeking a happier life, the processes for getting there are much the same.

Story 3

Finding and Building Hope

Happiness-Enhancing Characteristics

Problems Addressed

Feelings of hopelessness
Feelings of helplessness
Depression

Resources Developed

Setting of goals
Find practical, achievable pathways
Generating and maintaining motivation and agency

Outcomes Offered

Hopefulness
Helpfulness
Improved physical and psychological health
Enhanced happiness

HOPE disappeared today. I watched as it pulled out of the driveway, turned into the street, and disappeared down the road. An interesting metaphor, I thought, given that my neighbor has a personalized registration plate on her automobile: HOPE.

At times hope can seem to disappear. If experienced intensely and for a long period, feelings of hopelessness and helplessness are almost a guarantee of depression. So, when I speak of hopelessness and helplessness, what do I mean? Well, hopelessness is what we feel when we don't see any joyful or happy future. It is when we think, *My life is terrible and I can't see it getting any better.* Helplessness is when we think similar pessimistic thoughts about ourselves: *I am terrible and I can't see* myself *getting any better.*

Researchers tell us that these thoughts and feelings can be learnt. They speak of learned helplessness and learned hopelessness and this, for me, is the light at the end of the tunnel. If we can learn helplessness, is it not logical to assume we can learn helpfulness? If we can learn hopelessness, is it not equally as possible to learn hopefulness? The question really is not *if* I can but rather *how* I can become more hopeful and helpful.

We are fortunate that many people have studied this very question. One of these, Dr Rick Snyder, says that hope has three elements. Hopeful thinking, first, incorporates the setting of *goals*, of seeing where you want to go, of how you want life to be different or better. Second, it incorporates the belief that you can find practical, achievable ways and means to reach your desired goals or outcomes. This he calls *pathways*. Finally, hope incorporates the belief that you can generate and maintain the necessary motivation and energy to reach your desired goal. This is referred to as *agency*.

The good news is that we all commonly employ these three elements in our lives. To do anything as simple as going shopping, you set a goal (I want to buy food for supper), you find the pathways (do I drive, walk, or take a bus, and which route will I follow to get the supermarket?) and you have the agency (I am hungry and want to eat).

All three elements are essential if you want high hope. You might, for example, have a goal of wanting to eat supper but if you don't have the pathways to get to the shops or the agency to do it, you are not likely to do it and thus feel rather hopeless—as well as hungry. You may know how to get to the shops (the pathways) but if you don't have the goal to go or the motivation to do it, again you are not likely to get there. Finally, you could have the agency (feeling hungry) but if you don't have a goal to satisfy it or see how you can get some food (the pathways), once more it may not happen and you will be left feeling both hungry, helpless, and hopeless.

People who are low in hopeful thinking often have difficulty knowing exactly what they want in their futures. They have poorly defined goals (low goal-setting skills). They struggle to think of ways to reach their goals (low pathways), and/or find themselves lacking the drive to move forward toward their goals (low agency). This is often at the basis of many of the life struggles we encounter. If we continue to experience goal-failure after goal-failure, it is understandably easy to give up, avoid new goal-setting situations, and slip into depression.

But that is the problem side. What about the positive side? If the lack of these three elements (goals, pathways, and agency) can lead to learned hopelessness, how can we use those elements to learn greater hopefulness?

First, Dr Snyder would say, set your goals. Maybe it might help in a quiet moment to take a pen and paper to jot down your answers to some goal-oriented questions like:

> *How do I want my life to be different?*
> *How do I want to be feeling?*
> *How do I want to be thinking?*
> *What do I want to be doing more of?*
> *Where do I want my life to be in the future?*

Then Dr Snyder might suggest you find the pathways with questions like:

> *What do I need to do to reach that goal or goals?*
> *What are the steps I need to take?*
> *What are the practical things I can do to get there?*

Finally, you need to look for what gives you agency or purpose with questions such as:

> *What is going to inspire or motivate me?*
> *How is this going to benefit me?*
> *What am I going to gain?*
> *How can I just commit myself to do it?*

When we have high levels of hope—goals that we want to achieve, pathways that will get us there, and the agency to do them—we are more likely to be successful in whatever we do, be it work, study, relationships, athletics, or recreational pursuits as well as in both our physical and psychological health. The more hopeful we are the less depressed we are and, perhaps even more importantly, the happier we are.

This evening I was happy to see HOPE returning down the street, turn into my neighbor's driveway, and arrive home.

Story 4

Setting SMART Goals

Happiness-Enhancing Characteristics

Problems Addressed

Lack of awareness
Lack of knowledge
Lack of helpful goals

Resources Developed

Setting specific or targeted goals
Setting measurable goals
Setting attainable goals
Setting relevant goals
Setting goals in a time frame

Outcomes Offered

Ability to set SMART goals
Openness to learn new things

I find it interesting how teachers can learn from their pupils. Over the several terms I have served as a volunteer psychologist in the remote and tiny little Himalayan Kingdom of Bhutan, one of my roles has been teaching counseling skills to the local health workers. During the initial course I conducted, I put emphasis on how one role of effective counseling is to help people set clear goals for counseling and, indeed, for life.

"Ah, you mean SMART goals," several of my students said almost in unison.

I don't know if you have ever heard of them but when I later came to research more about them, I found the anagram for S.M.A.R.T. goals had been around for several decades but for me it was new.

"What are SMART goals?" I asked my students. As it appeared that they had been taught about SMART goals in a previous course, here was a chance for them to revisit what they knew, adapt their knowledge into the context of what we were doing . . . and for me to learn something new.

One young man got up, walked to the whiteboard, took up a felt pen and wrote a large 'S'. Beside it he wrote the word 'specific' and said, "If a goal is specific or targeted, you have a much greater chance of achieving it than if it is general or ambiguous."

Someone else added, "You have to ask yourself, 'What do I want to accomplish?' and if it is too general, like 'I want to get a degree,' then you have to break it down to specifics such as 'What subjects do I want to study?' or 'Which university will I apply for?'"

His fellow student at the whiteboard then wrote a large 'M' beneath the 'S' and beside it put the word 'measurable.' He explained, "You have to be able to measure your progress toward the attainment of each goal that you set. Otherwise, how will you know if you have reached it or not? Measurability helps you keep on track, see your progress, reach your target dates, and then celebrate the joy of achievement."

A capital 'A' was added beneath the 'S' and the 'M' with the word 'attainable' beside it. "It's pointless setting a goal," he said, "if it's not possible for you to achieve it."

Yes, I thought, *while it is good to have goals that stretch us a bit if they are too high or too low they become meaningless.* There is also evidence that setting unachievable goals or asking for things we can't realistically have only leads to us feeling frustrated or even depressed. On the other hand, contentment, satisfaction, and self-confidence can come from reaching practically attainable goals.

His next letter, 'R,' began 'relevant.' Even as he was writing up the word, someone else began to describe it. "If you see a goal as being relevant, useful or meaningful for you," she said, "you are going to be more willing, able, and motivated to work toward it. It will be one you truly believe can be achieved and, therefore, will be more likely to achieve it."

Finally, next to the capital 'T' he spelt out 'timely' and explained, "A goal needs to be set within a time frame or have a target date. We all know what happens if we say, 'I will get round to doing it someday.' We simply don't ever get around to getting it done. However, if we say, 'I'll do it this weekend, before the end of the month or by a specific date' we are more likely to be successful. Goals without timelines tend to be overridden by the day-to-day issues that invariably arise, whereas commitment to timelines parallels goal attainment. Why do lecturers set timelines for assignments or bosses set them for work tasks? Simply because they know that way they will get done."

From what they taught me, I now like to think SMART when setting goals.

Isn't it interesting where and from whom you might learn new things at times?

Story 5

To Reach a Port

Happiness-Enhancing Characteristics

Problems Addressed

Feeling insecure
Feeling aimless, directionless, or rudderless

When things are not going as hoped
When things are 'bad' in one's life

Resources Developed

Learning to set your course or goal
Learning to move on
Preparing self for what might lie ahead
Making the commitment to do it
Finding the energy or motivation to do it

Outcomes Offered

Enjoying the journey
Reaching the desired goal or port
Regaining feelings of security and direction

"To reach a port, you have to sail," said Ron. His metaphor didn't surprise me. Ron was an old salt, a lover of the sea and everything nautical. He had spent a good part of his life in the navy and owned his own sailboat. After the orderly structure of naval life, he felt insecure and aimless in himself. As I am sure we have all experienced at some stage or another, when things go bad in one area, they also tend to go bad in others. When the proverbial hits the fan it tends to get scattered around. When the muck starts to pile up, a molehill can quickly become a mountain—and that is just how it felt for Ron.

We began to discuss what goals he wanted to achieve in therapy. *Now that directions have changed for you, what new directions do you want to see yourself taking? How do you want to see your life evolving from here? What would be your most desired outcomes from this current situation?* It was as we examined these questions that he made the comment, "To reach a port, you have to sail."

Wanting to join him in his own metaphor, in his image and experience, I asked, "If you were master of the vessel how would you go about doing that?"

"To begin with, you have to know your destination, what port you are sailing for. Only when you know where you want to go can you pull out the charts and plot a course to reach your destination. There's no point in just lying at anchor, unless you've dropped the pick in the bay of a tropical island and just want to hang out for a while . . . but even then you have to eventually move on."

"How do you think it might feel to be sitting at anchor, not having a port to go to?" I asked.

"It would be like being cast adrift, like being without sail or direction, like being rudderless. Sometimes it is pleasant just to drift for a while but it is fraught with dangers. You can't drift forever. Eventually you are going to run aground, get washed onto a reef, be smashed against the rocks, or be swamped by the seas."

"So what would the master need to do to ensure he, his vessel, and those he is responsible for didn't get into this situation?" I pressed.

"First, he would have to set his course," he said. "Then he would need to prepare himself and the vessel for what might lie ahead. Of course, you don't know exactly what the winds, seas, and tides might throw at you but a good captain is one who looks ahead, prepares for the worst case scenario, and is ready to deal with challenges that may arise. He has to set out from the safety of where he has been at anchor, knowing that there may be risks before him. If he is not willing to take the risks, he would just sit there and go nowhere."

"Given that, how is he now going to get to his destination?" I asked.

"He needs to set sail. He needs to make the commitment and give the orders to raise the sail for power, haul up the anchor that has been keeping him fixed in one point, and set the course so that he is no longer directionless. On the way he may be sailing with the wind at times and against it at others. He needs to choose when to run with it, when to alter course, and when to make compromises like tacking into the wind. It's not always the most direct course that gets you to your destination."

"When you said earlier," I reflected, "that to reach a port, you had to sail, to me it sounded like there had to be some power, some driving force, some energy or some motivation there behind you."

"Yes," he added reiterating in a more thoughtful way what he had already said, "To reach a port, you have to sail."

Story 6

Setting Your Own Outcome Goals

Happiness-Enhancing Characteristics

Problems Addressed

> Wanting to learn new skills
> Wanting life to be better or happier
> Wanting an improved quality of life
> Losing sight of your goals

Resources Developed

> Learning to set outcome-oriented goals
> Learning to focus attention on the goal
> Learning to shape positive goals
> Learning to set specific goals
> Learning to implement goals

Outcomes Offered

> Experiencing the rewards of goal achievement

When my grandson was learning to ride a tricycle I escorted him on a ride. His goal was, for the first time, to cycle to the neighborhood park. Observing him along the way had me mindful of a question I almost invariably ask people when they come to see me professionally.

It is not a specific question but rather a type of question. It is a question that has assumptions built into it and maybe it helps to explain some of those assumptions. The first assumption is that a person has come to see me, as a psychologist, because they want life to be better or happier. The second assumption is that if someone says to me "I feel depressed" I assume they don't want me to talk to them a lot about depression but rather about how to be happy. If a person says to me "I feel anxious" I assume they don't want me to talk about anxiety as much as about feeling relaxed. If someone says "We are having relationship problems" I assume that they want to know more about relating happily and lovingly. The third assumption I hold is one of hope and expectation that we are capable of working toward, and achieving, an improved quality of life for ourselves.

With this in mind, I ask the type of question that goes something like this, *What would you like to gain out of our conversation today? How would you like to see your life improve in the future? If you could take just one step toward making life happier, more relaxed, or more enjoyable what would that step be?*

You will notice that my questions are very deliberately biased. They don't ask about the past because it seems to me that no matter how traumatic, how unpleasant, or even how pleasant the past might have been, it cannot be changed. While we may be able to change our attitudes about the past we cannot change the things that have happened to us. On the other hand, we are able to plan, shape, and create a future, and in doing so we are able to feel a sense of empowerment. So, as a therapist, I really want to know what direction a person wishes to go.

As a grandfather, I wanted to know the direction my grandson wished to travel. Setting off, he initially steered a course toward the park, focusing his attention on me walking ahead of him. Then a neighbor called out from behind us to say hello. He looked behind, in her direction, automatically turned the handlebars that way, and took a tumble, fortunately, onto the grassy verge. After getting back on the tricycle he again fixed his gaze on me and started to steer straight ahead. Soon after, on the opposite side of the road, a dog ran to its enclosing fence boundary and started to bark. As my grandson shifted his attention to the dog so he again began to steer in that direction.

It reminded me that where we put attention tends to determine the direction we go. When driving a car it would be fatal to keep turning around and looking behind to see where you have been. To drive safely and get to your destination you need to focus your attention ahead, on where you are going. As we need to do in life.

However after decades of asking about where people want to go, I have noticed that they often respond in the negative, telling me where they *don't* want to go. *I don't want to be depressed anymore; I don't want to be feeling anxious or stressed; I don't want these feelings of anger; I don't want to be in an unhappy relationship.*

When this happens I aim to help them reshape their goals into the positive with questions like: *If you don't want to feel depressed any more, how do you want to feel? If you don't want to be feeling anxious or stressed, what would you rather be experiencing?*

Over the years it has been interesting to observe a common pattern in people's responses. Most people respond in a very general or global way by saying things like, *I want to be happy. I want to be relaxed. I want to have a loving, caring relationship.*

Unfortunately, such global goals are hard to achieve simply by the fact that they are too big and too distant. They are like my grandson, while learning the rudimentary skills of riding a tricycle, saying I want to instantly be an Olympic cycling champion. This is not to say that such a goal is unachievable but rather that there are many specific steps you would need to take along the road to ultimately reach that goal.

Therefore I want to invite people to be specific. *When you are feeling happier how are you going to be thinking, feeling, and doing? What is the first small step you can take towards feeling more relaxed? What are the times in the past when you have experienced even momentary periods of loving and caring in your relationship? What were you thinking and doing at those times?*

If my grandson had the goal to become a competitive cyclist, he would first need to learn each of the specific skills of pedaling, steering, balancing, and attending to where he is going on his tricycle before he moved on to learn the specific skills for riding a bicycle with trainer wheels, then a bicycle without trainer wheels, then even more advanced cycling skills. It is a step-by-step process that begins with a specific starting point.

Once a person has defined a goal that is outcome-oriented and specific in an immediately achievable way, it is then much easier to find the pathways to attain the goal. In fact, often just clearly exploring the goal is enough to enable a person to implement it and experience the rewards of their achievement.

So I am wondering, *How do you want your life to be in the future? What positive goal or goals would you like to achieve in regards to your personal well-being? And what is the first specific step you can take toward achieving that?*

Once my grandson saw the park, once he had his goal or destination in sight, his steering did not waiver, his little legs rotated the pedals with a new-found energy, and he made an unswerving b-line toward the swings.

2 On Finding and Using Strengths

The artist is nothing without the gift, but the gift is nothing without work.
Emile Zola, French Novelist, (1840–1902)

Introduction

All of us have things that we are good at and things that we are not so good at. All of us have strengths—the things that we do well, are accomplished at, or skilled in. Often these are overlooked as parents, teachers, bosses, and psychiatric labels point out our weaknesses, assumedly, in the unfounded hope that awareness of our faults will result in a development of strengths.

However, we are who we are because of our strengths rather than our weaknesses. We have achieved what we have achieved in work, relationships, sport, arts, or life because of our strengths. Our strengths define who we are, give us meaning and enjoyment, fuel our energy and passions, and fill us with a sense of self-worth. Our strengths are potentials for excellence.

Acknowledging and using our personal strengths builds resilience against the onset of mental health problems like depression and can significantly reduce depression if it is present. More positively, the awareness and employment of our strengths is correlated with greater levels of self-esteem and self-efficacy. People who make good use of their personal strengths report experiencing higher levels of psychological well-being, life satisfaction, and positive affect. For these reasons alone, recognizing and developing your personal strengths is an appropriate if not essential process in the creation of greater happiness and personal well-being.

In a school-wide approach in the United Kingdom, a program entitled Celebrating Strengths helps students recognize and build their personal strengths. Children are taught to spot strengths in themselves, in their fellow students, and in stories they are told that highlight different particular strengths. Results from this project report an increase in student confidence and self-esteem as well as social and emotional intelligence. But it is not just the students who benefitted. As a side benefit, the teachers also gained through increased teacher engagement, work enjoyment, and resilience (Fox Eades, 2008; Fox Eades, Proctor, & Ashley, 2013).

In this chapter, the stories provide sample metaphors about how to help identify, develop, and use strengths. This is because the research shows that it is not enough just to know your strengths. The full benefits come when a person is effectively and meaningfully making use of those strengths. Three of the stories are based on a real life tale that illustrates various stages of strengths development. If you wish to follow the whole case story and see how it was adapted into three metaphors in this chapter, see Linley & Burns (2010).

Story 7

The Art of Strengthspotting

Happiness-Enhancing Characteristics

Problems Addressed

> Having negative, self-recriminatory thoughts
> Giving ourselves a hard time
> Engaging in self-rebuke
> Putting ourselves down
> Being self-critical
> Feeling hopeless or useless

Resources Developed

> Learning to identify one's core strengths
> Listening for the special sounds of strengths
> Listening and looking out for the strengths in others
> Enquiring about your own strengths
> Finding ways to use your strengths

Outcomes Offered

> Greater levels of well-being
> Greater levels of self-esteem
> Greater levels of self-efficacy
> Greater achievement of goals when using personal strengths

A colleague of mine in the United Kingdom, Dr Alex Linley, has coined a term that I really like. He calls it 'strengthspotting.' Generally we are pretty good at giving ourselves a hard time, engaging in self-rebuke, and putting ourselves down. Who hasn't, from time to time, chastised themselves, been unnecessarily self-critical, or even thought *I'm hopeless* or *I'm useless*? Most of us would agree that such negative thoughts seem to come all too easily, naturally, or frequently.

Spotting, acknowledging, and using our strengths for some reason doesn't always come so readily to most of us—but doing so may be important, first, in reducing the risk of depression, second, in diminishing depression if it does occur, and, third, in increasing our levels of well-being.

Dr Linley asked an important question: Is using strengths associated with greater levels of well-being, self-esteem, and self-efficacy? Researching this question, he found that people who used their strengths more had higher levels of self-esteem, self-efficacy, subjective well-being, psychological well-being, and vitality. In fact, whatever a person's current level of self-esteem and self-efficacy, using strengths is likely to lead to that person experiencing increased levels of well-being. People also achieve their goals more effectively when they are using their strengths and experience significant and sustained decreases in depression.

So, if being aware of and making use of our strengths can be so beneficial, how can we do that? First, says Dr Linley, is to listen to the special sounds of strengths. With a class he taught by telephone to participants from half a dozen countries around the world, he asked participants to initially speak for five minutes about a weakness, or about something with which they were struggling. Then he asked them to spend five minutes talking about a personal strength or about when they are at their best. Because the exercise was conducted by telephone there were no visual cues like body language or facial expressions.

Other participants in the course were asked to observe and describe the responses. Not surprisingly, when people are talking about weaknesses, they are more negative, hesitant, and disengaged. On the other hand, when talking about strengths, they are more positive, energetic, and engaged. They sound happier, more confident, and more relaxed. There is a passion in their tone, their conversation is free flowing, and they explain things graphically. We not only sound but feel more alive when engaged with strengths.

Second, says Dr Linley, is what he calls day-to-day strengthspotting. Listen and look out for the strengths in others as you share a meal with a spouse, discuss a project with a colleague, listen to a child recounting the events of a day at school, stand in a queue at a supermarket check-out, or hear a sportsperson being interviewed on television. Hopefully, you may begin to discover how strengths can come to the fore at any time, from anyone—possibly even from unlikely people in unlikely places.

Third, Dr Linley suggests, is to enquire about your own strengths and he has even suggested some questions that may help:

> *What sort of everyday things do I enjoy doing?*
> *What would I describe as my most significant accomplishment?*
> *When I feel at my best, what am I doing?*
> *What are the most energizing things that I do?*
> *What am I doing when I feel most invigorated?*
> *What am I most looking forward to in the future?*

STRENGTH-SPOTTING

If I think about the coming week, what will I be doing when I am at my best?

Following these steps, suggests Dr Linley, can help us break out of the pattern of negative, self-recriminatory thoughts and become a spotter of strengths in ourselves and others. It is a skill we can learn by simply practicing to spot strengths in whatever we are doing, wherever we are, with whomever. It is an orientation of mind: a mind prepared to look out for, and acknowledge a strength when it has been spotted. I guess that is why I like his delightful term, strengthspotting and can recommend trying it out.

Story 8

Finding Inner Strengths

Happiness-Enhancing Characteristics

Problems Addressed

Struggling with an old, long-established behavior
Trying to stop doing something
Struggling with an unhelpful coping strategy
Wanting to get rid of an inappropriate approach behavior
Lacking the skills or means to resolve an issue

Resources Developed

Discovering that we all have strengths
Discovering that our strengths can be accessed
Learning to enable greater levels of optimal functioning
Learning to identify and use strengths
Discovering things we are good at
Finding strengths that give a sense of fulfillment
Shifting thoughts, feelings, and actions toward more positive experiences

Outcomes Offered

Feeling greater personal strength
Finding a sense of fulfillment
Experiencing more positive feelings
Becoming more hopeful

Emma came to see me about an eating problem. She said, "I eat when I am bored, frustrated, anxious, and angry—for psychological reasons. It makes me happy." What she believed made her happy was quite specific: chocolate. With almost any emotional swing she would gorge a family size block of chocolate, a full packet or two of chocolate biscuits, or half a tin of Milo.

As I am sure you know, trying to stop any long established behavior can be difficult, especially if it is a behavior that we enjoy, that meets a psychological need, and that offers such strong rewards as the chocolate was doing for Emma. It provided instant pleasure when she was in distress, and she had empowered it with the ability to "make" her happy. Telling herself to stop doing something that served as an effective, even though unhelpful, coping strategy with such powerful rewards simply hadn't worked.

The message for me as her therapist was clear: if she hadn't been able to effectively tell herself to stop, there was probably little point in me repeating something that had already failed. I recalled the old adage that says, "If something ain't working, do something different."

On the positive side, Emma had a good awareness of her problem and her deficits in attempting to deal with it. What she didn't have just yet was the means to resolve it or the strengths that might enable her to get there. That being the case, the question I faced was *How might she and I build those strengths and means to reach a happier outcome? Would it be more helpful for her to focus on her strengths?*

Fortunately, strengths are natural propensities that each of us have. Emma and I first needed to discover hers. After graduating, she committed herself to developing an academic career before having children. She had been married for 12 years and was in her late thirties when she had their first child. She was now a full-time mother of her four-year-old daughter, Samantha, and a one-year-old son, Jason.

While we may not always be aware of our strengths, they are there and can be accessed. When we are using our strengths, we feel at our best, are doing the things that are good and healthy for us to do, and experience a sense of energy. If Emma wanted to enable greater levels of optimal functioning for herself, would it be helpful for her to learn to identify and use her strengths more? Would mobilizing her strengths help her better manage her emotions and eating patterns?

Seeking to explore these strengths, I simply asked Emma, "What are you good at?"

"Not much," she replied in the negative. "All I seem to do is change smelly diapers and think about what to feed the kids next." Her voice was flat and monotonal, her arms folded across her chest, her body hunched forward.

When we talk about our strengths, such behaviors usually change. Strength-oriented conversations evoke more positivity, energy, and engagement. We sound happier, more confident, and more relaxed. There is a passion in our voice, our conversation is free flowing, and we tend to explain things in more detail.

When Emma told me what she was *not* good at, I asked, "Then what do you see you have been good at in the past?"

"I think I was good at supervising research," she answered. "I loved to challenge students, to ask questions, to ensure that their research design was sound. I think I was also good at lecturing. My courses were commonly rated highly by students and I took off several teaching awards."

"What would you say you enjoy doing most?" I continued with my enquiries.

"Research and supervision have to be high on the list. I enjoy the intellectual challenge. But I think my greatest enjoyment came from singing. I belonged to the university choir and a quartet from the choir formed a small group. We used to sing for weddings, conference dinners, and those sorts of things."

"When do you think you have been at your best?"

"Definitely when I was singing. I used to get a bit nervous before but once I started to sing it was like every other worry and thought just floated away."

"That sounds like an important skill to have," I affirmed before asking, "How did you enable that to happen?"

"The four of us in the quartet were great friends, we had a lot of fun rehearsing and practicing and, I guess, I was totally focused into what we were doing." A smile had crept into the corners of her mouth, her speech sounded livelier and her mood lifted noticeably.

"And what are your aspirations for the future?"

"I am planning to go back teaching next year perhaps part time and it would be nice to start singing again. But I don't know if I'm going to have time now that I am a mom."

Emma had defined what she wanted to do. With just a few specifically targeted questions, she had found the things that she was missing in her life, the things that she was good at, and the things that gave her a sense of fulfillment. She had an idea of when she could start to put these into practice for herself but saw some hurdles in the way and, at this point, wasn't quite sure as to how she might actually achieve them.

For me, Emma demonstrated how the things that we say to ourselves and the questions we ask ourselves can determine the ways we think, the feelings we experience, and the behaviors we engage in. While she was focused on smelly diapers, negative feelings, and seemingly unmanageable behaviors of eating chocolate she thought negative, self-deprecating thoughts. She experienced the negative feelings she was thinking about and engaged in unwanted behaviors such as eating excessive amounts of chocolate. By stopping to explore questions about her strengths, Emma began to shift those thoughts, feelings, and actions toward more positive, hopeful, and practical experiences.

Sometimes, it may be helpful just to ask ourselves similar questions. What am I good at? What do I enjoy doing? What are my peak experiences in life? When do I feel at my best? How did I enable that to happen? What are my aspirations for the future? What can I do to make them happen again?

Story 9

When Life Sucks, Laugh Out Loud

Happiness-Enhancing Characteristics

Problems Addressed

When life sucks
Anger
Feeling out of control

Lack of energy
Seeing the need for change
Tearfulness
Guilt
Poor self-image

Resources Developed

Spotting strengths in others
Spotting strengths in oneself

Outcomes Offered

Becoming aware of a loving nature
Rediscovering playful times
Finding the ability to laugh out loud
Being aware of strengths, qualities, positive attributes

"Life fucking sucks," I read in the letter that Emma handed me in our second session. "Anger is everywhere. The rage has got to go. I hate this, I am out of control and our kids are copping it. I don't have the energy or feel that I care (but I do very much). Samantha is being yelled at, screamed at, pushed, shoved, poked. No wonder she doesn't know how to handle herself when she gets frustrated. What is going to become of our family? I have to change or I am going to have to leave for the sake of the kids. Samantha needs her space and it's only going to get worse as she gets older. I can't keep it all together. Our poor darling Samantha. Please let this stop!!"

As I put the letter down, Emma tearfully said that her anger toward Samantha flew against all her principles, and conflicted with the image that she had of herself as a mother. So difficult was this subject to initiate verbally that she had put it into the hand-written letter.

What was Emma to do? Did she try to control these reactions that she felt to be so uncontrollable—something that hadn't worked for her so far—or did she try to build greater feelings of strength and control? It didn't take a psychologist to see that Emma felt stressed, frustrated, angry, and guilty. Her self-image had taken a battering. This was not how she saw herself, or how she wanted to be.

However, how do you help someone whose self-image is so shattered or who has a long history of self-effacement or self-denigration to spot, acknowledge, and use their own strengths? How could she learn the ongoing skills to live a calmer, more relaxed, and happier life for herself and in relation to her daughter?

If someone's self-image is as low as Emma's to ask them what they are good at or what their strengths are is likely to meet with negative responses: *Me? Nothing. I'm a hopeless mum. I can't control my temper, etc.*

Often it is easier to learn to spot strengths in others before we learn to spot them in ourselves. This we can do by listening for the strengths, abilities, or qualities in others, asking people about their strengths, and/or watching for telltale signs of a strength such as the greater enthusiasm and energy that occurs when people are discussing them.

"What do you think you might notice if you start to look out for the strengths you see in Samantha?" I asked. "Perhaps you might like to jot down just three qualities you see in her each day."

At first the request took her by surprise, as she had been so focused on the negative, problematic aspects of Samantha's behavior. Because what we focus on is often what we see, Emma started to shift her attention and began to see a different child. She began to speak of things like her daughter's independence and determination as positive qualities. She became more aware of Samantha's playfulness, creative engagement, and laughter. Samantha, as any child is likely to do, responded to the positive attention with more positive behaviors, and the mother–daughter relationship quickly began to improve.

After asking Emma to then spot strengths in her husband and her son, it was an easier transition for her to begin to spot them in herself. Wanting to help her do this specifically in regards to her maternal strengths, I asked Emma, "When do you feel you are best as a mother? When are the times that you feel really good in your mothering role, the times that you feel that the real you is shining through?"

"That's not too often at the moment" she answered.

"I wasn't asking how often they occurred," I responded, "but rather what those times and feelings are like when you do have them."

"I guess they are the loving kind," she said. "The times when the day hasn't gone too bad, and I lay beside her to read her a story and feel her falling asleep in my arms."

"Are there other such times when you feel really good about your role as a mom?" I enquired.

"The playful times. The times when we are just fooling around and she does those funny things that have me laughing out loud."

By looking for the strengths, qualities, positive aspects of her family and herself, Emma was able to make the transition from thinking that life sucks to being aware of what it felt like to laugh out loud.

Story 10

Using and Developing Strengths

Happiness-Enhancing Characteristics

Problems Addressed

> Struggling with a problem behavior
> Struggling with unwanted emotions
> Looking for how to implement strengths

Resources Developed

> Learning to recognize strengths
> Defining the ways and means to implement strengths
> Starting to use strengths productively
> Finding practical steps to engage strengths

Outcomes Offered

> Feeling better and happier
> Feeling more in control
> Relating happier and more relaxed with family
> Relating happier and more relaxed with self
> Engaging strengths to enhance happiness

"What's next?" Emma asked me. "I have discovered some of the strengths in my family and myself but where do I go from here? How do I use them?"

Emma had initially told me about a problem of gorging on chocolate when she felt bored, frustrated, anxious, or angry and later mentioned how she had given up on many of the things that brought her pleasure and enjoyment to devote herself to the role of motherhood but her self-sacrifice and devotion seemed only to have resulted in a tense, angry, and unhappy relationship with her young daughter.

Emma was able to spot many strengths in herself as a person, a teacher, a singer, and a mother. Now that she had discovered these qualities, how could she use and develop them for the ongoing benefits of herself, her daughter, and their relationship? She had successfully defined *what* her strengths were. The questions facing her now were *how* to use them, and *when* she could do so.

This enabling process revolved around questions like, *How can you enable and develop these loving and playful strengths in your role as a mother? How can you create more of the intellectual challenge you are good at and miss? How can you recapture that mindful engagement you have when singing?*

When she said she was most looking forward to getting back to work and singing, I asked, "Then *how* and *when* do you see you might start to resume those things?" While it is good to have the desire to do the things we want, it is also important to define the ways and means we can implement them or make them happen.

"I would feel guilty about putting the kids into childcare. I would feel that I failed as a mom," she said.

"But aren't you feeling guilty and a failure at the moment?" I asked, confronting her gently. "What would be the difference?"

Within a couple of weeks, Emma had enrolled her daughter and son in a day care facility for two half days a week, arranged to resume some part-time PhD supervision, and rejoined the singing group to which she had previously belonged. Her husband offered to look after the children while she went to evening rehearsals. As she again started to use her strengths, she started to feel better and happier in herself. This, in turn, seemed to have her relating with her children in a happier and more relaxed manner.

I found Emma an inspiration, not only in the ways she was able to identify her strengths but also in the ways she could start to use and engage in those strengths to enhance her happiness as well as that of her children and family.

Story 11

What's Right with Him?

Happiness-Enhancing Characteristics

Problems Addressed

> Seeing only the problem, symptom or dysfunction
> Seeing what is wrong with a person or self
> Holding false beliefs about oneself

Resources Developed

> Learning to ask what is right with a person or self
> Discovering your own strengths
> Discovering your abilities or resources
> Learning to use your strengths to overcome current problems
> Finding strengths in what others see as a problem

Outcomes Offered

> Enjoying the use of your strengths
> Enjoying a more fulfilling, productive, and rewarding life
> Experiencing meaning and purpose
> Earning and enjoying self-respect

One of psychiatrist Dr Milton Erickson's most famous cases was a long-term mental hospital patient who was deluded in believing he was Jesus Christ.

For me the story illustrates how what a lot of people may see as a problem, a symptom, or a dysfunction may actually be a positive resource. It also illustrates how Dr Erickson as a therapist was less interested in the common clinical question, *What is wrong with this person?* and more interested in questions such as, *What is right with you? What are your strengths? What abilities or resources do you have? How might you use your strengths, abilities, and resources to overcome this set of current problems?*

Contrary to the way many other therapists were viewing mental health at the time and unfortunately still do, Erickson seemed to ask himself, *Can a significant problem also be a significant strength? If, for example, a person feels intensely depressed is it not possible for them to also feel intensely happy?*

Long before the advent of modern psychiatric medication, Dr Erickson worked in a mental hospital where he met this long-term patient who believed he was Jesus Christ. The man spent most of his days sitting on a bench, waving his hands as he "blessed" the people walking by. Initially Erickson joined him on the bench, sitting next to him, saying nothing, just being with him. Eventually, Erickson began a conversation with the man and remarked, "I understand you have experience as a carpenter."

This put the man in a bind to which he had to agree. If he was Jesus, of course, he had that experience of being a carpenter. If he didn't have that experience, then he could not have been Jesus and his delusion had to change.

Giving him some sandpaper and pieces of wood, Erickson encouraged the man to begin sanding wood. Finding a strength in what everyone else had seen as a problem, the man began his first steps toward a more positive and productive life. Gradually, he developed his woodworking skills in the hospital's facilities. In time he was constructing shelves and bookcases for his ward. As the quality of his work improved, doctors and nurses began requesting bookcases and paying him for his work.

Was he cured? No. Unfortunately, he still had significant problems.

Was he leading a more fulfilling, productive, and rewarding life for discovering an ability or strength he had? The answer is a definite yes. His days were filled with meaning and purpose. He had become more than just another patient in the hospital. He was useful and added value to his world. He had earned the respect of those around him and, in doing so, earned self-respect. His life was significantly improved because someone had looked beyond his problems to find his strengths. Someone had paused to ask not what was wrong with him but what was right with him. This question helped him, first, to discover a personal strength and, second, to make use of the strength to improve his well-being.

If I was in the position of choosing a therapist for myself, I would definitely want someone like Dr Erickson to help me explore what was right with me.

Story 12

Finding Hidden Strengths

Happiness-Enhancing Characteristics

Problems Addressed

Feeling plain or unattractive
Having low self-esteem
Having low self-worth

STRENGTH-SPOTTING

Resources Developed

> Having curiosity
> Being a good observer
> Attending to detail
> Being highly focused
> Being patient
> Looking for positive attributes
> Being open to discovering beauty

Outcomes Offered

> Knowing your own current beauty, strengths, and qualities
> Seeing your future, desired beauty, strengths, and qualities
> Developing your future core beauty and qualities

My sister is a teacher who recently related to me a story she tells her students. It is not an unusual story but what I find interesting is the way she uses the story to help her students put the message into practice.

She tells them the story of a young girl—but it could just as well be about a young boy—who one day noticed a small, plain-looking caterpillar crawling across the ledge of her bedroom window. She watched as it nestled itself in the sheltered corner of the ledge, began to spin a chrysalis and gradually buried itself in the chrysalis—a very plain, gray lump that anyone walking by would hardly have noticed. However, our little girl kept observing. When she woke in the morning, she rushed to the window to look at the caterpillar's little hidey house. When she got home from school, it was straight to the window sill cocoon. She was so curious she could barely take her eyes off it.

Knowing that tells us some of our little girl's strengths, doesn't it? She had a strong sense of curiosity, she was a good observer, she could attend to detail, she could be highly focused, and she was patient. In the end, these qualities that she exercised reaped their reward.

One day as she sat by the window sill watching the chrysalis, something happened, something that not many of us get to see. Was she imagining a slight movement at one end of the chrysalis? No, it became more noticeable. The chrysalis began to break open and a creature began to wriggle its way out. A small head, followed by a thin body but it was nothing like the caterpillar that had hidden itself away. Shaky, delicate, fragile, it slowly unpeeled six thin wobbly legs and began to stretch out two crinkled, wet, and unextended wings on each side of its body. Then the butterfly hung upside-down. The little girl didn't know this was because it had to pump blood into the wings to inflate and dry them before it could fly. She just saw how beautiful it was.

She didn't know that the brilliant colors were to help it hide and blend in with its environment, or help it attract a mate, or send a warning out to predators, or make it look bigger with the 'eyespots' on its wings, or help it soak up the warmth of the sun. No, it just looked very beautiful.

Having told this story, my sister asks her students, "What beauty are you hiding within you?" She asks them to talk about and write down their current beauty, strengths, and qualities that, like the caterpillar, may not always be that visible to others.

When the caterpillar hid itself away in the chrysalis, the little girl had no idea that such a spectacular creature might emerge. In a young child, it may be hard to look into the future and see the devoted, loving parent, the dedicated teacher, the sports hero, the medical-breakthrough scientist, or the compassionate friend that they will one day become. So my sister asks, "What beauty do you *want* to see emerge in you as you grow up?" She usually invites her students to participate in a dress-up day in which they can come dressed-up as the sort of person they might want to be in the future. If you were to do that, how would you imagine yourself dressing up, looking, acting, thinking, and feeling? What do you see as your core beauty or qualities that you yet want to develop?

Butterfly stories have long been used to metaphorically illustrate the emergence of potential inner beauty. I think what my sister does highlights how a beautiful example can *and* needs to be applied if true beauty is to really emerge.

STRENGTH-SPOTTING

3   On Being Empowered

Happiness is when what you think, what you say, and what you do are in harmony.

Mohandas K. Gandhi

Introduction

Hopelessness, helplessness, and powerlessness have long been known to be associated with unhappiness, low self-esteem, and depression. Not surprisingly, the converse is also true. Hopefulness and empowerment are linked to a fulfilling, purposeful, and happy life.

Researchers have long demonstrated that we can *learn* to be helpless from how we were parented, from our life experiences, from our mindset, and from our own self-talk. To me this is good news because if it is possible for us to learn helplessness and powerlessness, then is it not equally possible for us to learn hopefulness and empowerment? If so, how can we learn new feelings of hopefulness and empowerment?

Researchers in the field of happiness, well-being, and positive psychology often ask people, "What *makes* you happy?" While this may be a useful research question, it is not a useful question to ask in counseling or therapy. Why do I say this? Simply put, it is disempowering for at least two reasons.

First, to say it *makes* me happy when my spouse is loving toward me, when the sun is shining, when my boss gives me a bonus, etc., means that I am relying upon someone or something else to provide me with happiness. I externalize it and make myself powerless. What happens if my spouse is having a bad day and is not particularly loving at that time? What happens if the weather turns inclement or my boss is unfairly critical about a job I've put extra effort into? If we rely on factors that are outside of our control for our happiness and well-being, we are likely to feel disempowered when they don't meet our expectations—and therefore unhappy rather than happy.

Second, thinking something or someone *makes* us happy empowers that object or person to control our feelings and our well-being. In reality nothing *makes* us happy. Happiness comes from within rather than without. We create happiness through our own state of mind. If I was to add emphasis to Gandhi's words that I chose to open this chapter I would want to say, "Happiness is when what *you* think, what *you* say, and what *you* do are in harmony."

The following stories seek to provide examples of how to value and appreciate oneself; how to expand early learnings and abilities; how to develop empowering self-talk and self-concepts; how to grow from trauma; how to accept oneself; and how to gain, enjoy, and use personal resources.

Story 13

Self-Comparisons

Happiness-Enhancing Characteristics

Problems Addressed

Making self-comparisons
Self-doubts
Feeling inferior
Lack of confidence
Insecurity
Feeling frightened

Resources Developed

Developing patience
Appreciating one's own beauty
Appreciating one's own qualities and characteristics

Outcomes Offered

Value and appreciate oneself

There is an old story of a samurai warrior, though it could equally be about a teacher, a businessman, a parent, an athlete, or anyone really. The warrior took pride in his job, he sought to do well, and others looked up to him. He felt confident and good about himself until another, young warrior joined the platoon. This younger warrior was driven and competent. The older warrior started to make comparisons. He saw what he had been, began to experience self-doubts, and felt inferior. With such doubts, his confidence diminished and, with it, his performance. Not knowing what else to do, he went to seek the advice of a well-known Zen master. Sitting with others in the presence of this serene and self-contained master he felt even more inferior. In turn he got to ask his question.

"Why am I feeling inferior?" he asked the master. "Why has my confidence gone? I have always been a brave, strong, and competent warrior. I have faced death many times without lacking confidence or feeling fear. I have never felt like this before. Why am I now so uncertain, insecure, and frightened?"

"Can you please wait?" the master replied kindly. "When everyone else has gone, I will answer your questions."

The warrior waited and waited. People flowed in and out all day, visiting the master, seeking his advice and leaving. Why did the warrior have to wait? He found himself growing impatient for an answer but still he waited. As evening approached, the flow of people diminished and the warrior eventually found himself alone in the room with the master. "I have waited as you asked," he said. "Everyone has gone. Can you now please answer my question?"

"Let's step outside," replied the master.

The master pointed to two trees growing side by side in his garden. "See those trees," he said. "Each is different in its own way. Each has its own beauty, its own characteristics. However, you will notice that one tree is a little taller than the other. I have lived here with these trees for many years. I have watched them and meditated on them daily and in all that time I have never seen any problem or conflict between the trees. I have never heard one tree say that it is superior or inferior, or ask, 'Why do I feel inferior beside you?' Why do you think that is?"

"It's obvious," replied the warrior. "Trees don't compare themselves to other trees. They just don't do it."

The master looked the warrior in the eyes, and said, "Then why ask me? You already know the answer."

Story 14

Utilizing Limited Resources

Happiness-Enhancing Characteristics

Problems Addressed

>Self-doubts
>Awareness of limited abilities
>Self-recrimination
>Feeling useless

Resources Developed

>Building on limited resources
>Utilizing early learning experiences
>Expanding the finite
>Discovering future potential

Outcomes Offered

>Expanded early learnings
>Expanded abilities
>Awareness of potential

It can be easy for us to doubt ourselves at times or to give ourselves a hard time over what we may see as our limited abilities. Maybe we think we are not as good as someone else at something, and then we start to slip into all sorts of self-recrimination. *Why would anyone want to fall in love with me? Who would want to employ me? I'm a hopeless mother. I'm useless at . . .* whatever.

It is true that we can't necessarily do everything well. We are all limited in our resources. Our abilities are finite, and sometimes I wonder if it is what we have or how we use it that determines if we are riddled with self-doubts or buoyed with self-confidence.

I don't know if you recall how you learnt the alphabet as a child. Did you sing along with the Sesame Street song? Did you repeat it again and again and again until it became familiar? Or did you learn it by associations, like A is for apple, B is for ball, C is for cat?

What everyone knows is that the English language has just 26 letters in it. To me it seems like a relatively small number of letters, a pretty limited resource, on which to build a whole language. From those few letters we build words, we construct the words into sentences, and the sentences into stories, conversations, letters, novels, text books, emails, songs, drama, and many other forms.

How many words do we create from those few letters? Nobody seems to know. People who study these things say that it is impossible to count the number of words in a language, because it's so hard to decide what actually counts as a word in the first place, and because language is constantly evolving as words come and go. There are Shakespearean words, for example, that have long fallen out of use and new computer words that weren't in our language just a few years ago. Suggestions are that we have, at the very least, a quarter of a million distinct English words, without counting inflections (such as where *dog* becomes *dogs*), and words from technical and regional vocabularies.

In a 4–5 minute speech we would use around 600–700 words. Assuming we speak for a couple of hours a day, we probably express about 15,000 to 17,000 words. That builds up to around 115,000 words a week or more than 6 million a year. And then we haven't even taken into account the words we read and hear.

How many sentences can we create from the words we created from those 26 letters? I don't know that anyone has ever counted or guessed at the number of sentences we use but by compiling those sentences we can create conversations, plays, and novels. A novel may range from 7,000 words to 120,000 or more, and, in one year, the USA alone publishes close to half a million novels, and this doesn't include text books, journals, magazines, newspapers, or other publications. Then there is Britain, Canada, Australia, and other English-language countries that also publish novels. How many words, how many sentences, how many novels or works of literature can we potentially create from our humble 26 letters in any one year?

The creative ways we now use those letters of the alphabet may never have been within the realm of conception when, as a young child, you were learning to sing along with the Sesame Street song. Yet now you are probably, unconsciously, using those letters to contribute to the estimated 7 billion text messages sent and read every 30 hours just in the USA.

From those 26 little letters we can create so much. They build words and sentences that inform us, educate us, communicate emotions, entertain us, and make life both easier and, at times, more complex. We use them every day without thinking about them and, because English is the international language, they are the basis on which a whole planet communicates. They make our life possible. But I bet, like me, you have no idea how many words you have created in your own vocabulary from those few letters, or how many words or sentences or paragraphs you have spoken in your life. So why do I cite all these facts and statistics? It really comes down to just one question: Do we put ourselves down by saying, "I am hopeless. I only know 26 letters," or do we acknowledge that we have the skills to take a very finite resource and turn it into an infinite ability?

Story 15

What's in a Name?

Happiness-Enhancing Characteristics

Problems Addressed

    Negative self-talk
    Disempowering language
    Disempowering self-concepts

Resources Developed

    Becoming aware of self-talk
    Discriminating negative and positive language
    Discriminating disempowering and empowering language
    Choosing helpful self-talk

Outcomes Offered

    Positive self-talk
    Empowering language
    Empowering self-concepts

"What's in a name?" asked Shakespeare in his famous play, Romeo and Juliet.

Names, and words, can and do have meaning. They communicate images and ideas to us. Say or think "Mum" and those three little letters conjure up a whole image of what your mother may look like, what her nature or personality is like, and how the two of you relate. Because we think in words, words shape our thinking and our experiences. If you think of the world as a scary and frightening place, that is the way you are likely to experience it, and your experience will in turn shape the thoughts and words you have about it. Think of the world as wonderful, beautiful, and enjoyable and you are likely to experience it as wonderful, beautiful, and enjoyable.

Let me offer you another example. In recent years, I have been privileged to work overseas as a volunteer clinical psychologist in what the world calls 'developing' countries. But even using the word 'developing' gives me cause to hesitate. While they may not be as 'developed' as Western countries economically or technologically, they may be more developed culturally, communally, and spiritually. In fact, some of the poorer economic countries in the world rate high, or well developed, on happiness scales.

In two countries I have had contact with agencies that assist women who have been abused, suffered at the hands of alcoholic, aggressive husbands, or needed shelter for themselves and their children. These two agencies work with a similar group of people, they are similar in their constitutions, and provide similar services. However, they have a difference and—as I am sure would have interested Shakespeare—that is in their names. I want to be clear that I don't say this to be critical of their names but rather to simply reflect my observations and the way their names may be perceived by others, particularly those seeking their services.

In one country, the agency is called the National Council Against Violence or NCAV. It is a large, well-respected organization providing a very helpful service to many people. I am not sure how it sounds to you but, when I reflect on its name, to me 'National Council' has a very formal, perhaps almost authoritarian sound. It has a 'big brother' tone to it, as though someone else—someone or something big and authoritarian—is looking after you. While that may have a sense of protection and security to it, especially if you are coming from a place of abuse, anxiety, and insecurity, it does not communicate an empowering message. Women who have been abused have often been dominated by someone more powerful and more authoritarian. May an agency whose name reflects similar attributes not be keeping a person in a similar place of feeling disempowered? Let me hasten to say that though the name may suggest that, the services provided by NCAV certainly do not. It is a caring, concerned, and compassionate service, wanting to help each of the women who seek its assistance to empower herself toward a happier future. My concern is not in the service but more about how the name may be viewed.

The name also speaks of what it is 'Against' rather than what it is for. It says that it is in a battle or fight and, I wonder, does this not also reflect the undesired process an abused person is already in? Has their situation not been one of a conflict, fight, or battle? Is it helpful for an organization to purport to follow a similar process?

Then we come to the word 'Violence.' By stating the problem, the name also highlights the problem. This is what it draws attention to. While it may be useful, and even essential, to bring awareness to such problems in the community, surely awareness is but the first step toward finding a solution or outcome. Again I find myself wondering, if I was in the position of being an

EMPOWERMENT

abused person would it be more helpful for me to focus on the violence or the potential of peace and happiness beyond the violence? Would it be better to be focused on the problems that have been, or the outcome I would prefer to achieve?

Compare this name to the sister organization in the second country that shares a similar purpose and goals. There the agency is known by the anagram, RENEW. Renew immediately conveys a positive expectation. It speaks of making good, restoring, refreshing, and replenishing. The name of this agency immediately communicates a message of hope and positivity. It seems to acknowledge that things may have been bad in the past but at the same time opens the potential for things to be different in the present and future. It breaks away from old patterns of power, authority, and dominance. It is not caught in sad stories of past problems but looks forward to new stories of hope, potential, and empowerment.

This message is even more strongly emphasized when one looks at the words that make up the anagram RENEW. They are: Restore, Educate, Nurture, Empower Women. What a positive, hopeful message! They don't speak of what the organization is fighting against but of very empowering concepts it wants to achieve for each of the people who seek its services.

Maybe I am being somewhat pedantic in the emphasis I am placing on a few words but I do happen to agree with Shakespeare that there is something in a name. Throughout my career I have seen the power of words that people use and the potent influence of language in shaping their experience. Consequently, I think it does us well to examine our words, our language, and how we use them. What are we saying to ourselves? How does that influence the ways we see ourselves and our world? If it is not helpful, how can we change it?

I wonder if you were feeling battered, abused, or disempowered and came to two offices side-by-side. On one door the sign read National Council Against Violence. On the other door it read Restore, Educate, Nurture, Empower Women. Based just on the name, which would you think to be the more helpful for you? Which door would you choose to walk through?

Similarly, I wonder about the language we use to describe ourselves and our world. Are the words we employ about ourselves and our world negative or positive? Like the names of the agencies I have mentioned, are they disempowering or empowering? Which words would you prefer to have describe you?

Story 16

What Are You?

Happiness-Enhancing Characteristics

Problems Addressed

Encountering life's difficult challenges
Facing potentially traumatic situations

Getting into hot water
Facing troubled times

Resources Developed

Finding someone to listen patiently and empathically
Looking at the processes and principles
Exploring different processes of change
Learning skills to deal with this current set of circumstances
Learning skills to deal better with future life challenges

Outcomes Offered

Life is not without challenges
We can learn from life's challenges
We can grow from trauma
We have choices about our direction of growth

A young woman had been going through some troubling times in her life. The things that challenge us, the things that traumatize us, the things that bowl us off our feet for a while, can come in many different and varied ways. Sometimes they come as relationship problems; the falling out with a best friend, a difference of opinion with a lover, or pressures imposed on us by a boss. They may be slow, gradual, and build up—like those irritating, niggling things that continually pester us, annoy us, and nag at us. They may be something big and traumatic such as being seriously injured in a car accident or losing a home, families, or friends in a natural disaster, like a typhoon, tsunami, or wild fire. I am not sure exactly what it was for the young woman I mentioned but she sure felt the need to talk and sought out someone she could trust. It may have been a friend, a partner, a priest, a therapist but for her it was her mum.

Her mum listened patiently and, to the young woman's disappointment, did not offer any wise words of advice or recommend any particular paths of action. Instead of attending to the specifics of the current situation, the mother looked beyond, wanting to help her daughter not only overcome this set of circumstances but be better able to deal with those challenging life events that inevitably face all of us from time to time. So instead of responding verbally, she opened a cupboard door and pulled out three similar sized pots that she sat on the stove. She quietly added equal amounts of water to each pot. In the first she put a potato, in the second she placed an egg and in the third she emptied some ground coffee beans.

"What are you doing?" asked the now curious daughter.

"Wait and you will see," replied the patient mother.

Frustrated that her mother was not directly replying to her very real questions, the daughter nonetheless waited, perhaps not all that patiently.

Eventually, the mother removed the potato from the boiling water and asked, "What has happened?"

"The potato has become softer," replied the daughter.

EMPOWERMENT

"Yes," said her mother before lifting the egg from the water. "What has happened to the egg?"

"It has become harder," said the daughter wondering where this was leading.

"Good," said the mother, draining the water off the ground coffee beans into two mugs. Showing the coffee grinds, she asked, "What do you see has happened here?"

The daughter looked a little puzzled and said, "The ground coffee is probably a little softer but much the same."

Taking the two mugs, she sat down at the table with her daughter and explained, "When we, as people, get into hot water, face troubled times, experience challenges we tend to respond differently."

"When I put the potato into the water it was hard, solid, and well defined in its appearance and shape. When faced with the challenge of the boiling water, it became softer, less firm, and weaker. If I took a potato masher to it, I could squash it and, you might think, totally destroy its former shape and character. However, the process is transforming. The potato has *changed* into something totally different. From something tough and inedible it has transformed into something soft and delicious."

"On the other hand, the egg, which was soft and fluid inside, when faced with the same challenge became firmer, more solid, and tougher. You could peel its shell off now and it would still maintain its shape. It would still be identifiable as what is was, but firmer and harder. While it has changed in different ways from the potato, the challenge has also enabled it to become more palatable."

Then, as she sipped on her coffee, she asked her daughter, "What do you see has happened to the coffee beans?"

"As I said," replied the puzzled daughter, "they don't appear to have altered."

"Right," agreed the mother. "Like the potato and egg, they faced the same challenge but they altered very little in themselves. In fact, instead of appearing to change within themselves, they actually altered their environment. They changed the things around them for the better. They made the water turn into this coffee that we can now sip and enjoy."

The mother had been around long enough to know that life was not without its challenges, that there would be times when we would all, metaphorically, end up in hot water. Such times would, by their very nature, be transforming. We may not be able to alter the challenges but we do have some choices about how we emerge from those challenges. And those choices we make can be either disempowering or empowering. We can learn from them, not only how to deal with the current challenges but how to be better equipped for other challenges we will inevitably face in the future.

From the look in her daughter's eye the mother knew she didn't need to ask the next questions. She didn't need to ask, "Do you see yourself as being like the potato, the egg, or the coffee? Which of the three would you prefer to be? How can you handle this, and future challenges, in ways that enable you to make the most helpful choices for your happiness?"

Story 17

Finding Strength in Flaws

Happiness-Enhancing Characteristics

Problems Addressed

    Seeing one's imperfections
    Feeling inadequate, ashamed, and hopeless
    Making negative self-comparisons
    Not living up to one's potential
    Feeling a sense of failure
    Feeling powerless

Resources Developed

    Acknowledging our perceived 'deficits'
    Learning to use our perceived 'deficits'
    Transforming perceived negatives to positives
    Finding empowerment

Outcomes Offered

    Accepting oneself
    Valuing oneself
    Becoming a source of beauty and joy
    Becoming empowered by 'imperfections'

EMPOWERMENT

Once there was a woman whose daily chores included having to walk from her village to a river to gather water. It was hard work hauling the two large, laden pots at the ends of a pole stretched across her shoulders up the hill to her home. One of her pots was perfect and always carried a full measure of water home while the other had a crack in it. By the time the woman got home, the cracked pot had leaked so much that it was only half full.

Even when she could afford to buy a new one, the woman kept hauling the cracked pot all the way uphill to her home knowing it would only be half full when she arrived. Even the pots were curious why she didn't discard the cracked one and replace it with a new pot.

Of course, her perfect pot felt proud of its achievements, and why shouldn't it? It did what it did very well. What more could one ask of it?

On the other hand, the cracked pot felt inadequate, ashamed, and hopeless. It compared itself to the perfect pot, and felt miserable. It was not doing what it should be, not living up to its potential. Its sense of bitter failure was reinforced each day as the water it felt powerless to contain trickled out along the side of path.

One day as the woman set the pot down beside the river to fill it, the pot asked the water bearer, "Why do you continue to carry me? I can't do the same job as the other pot. I feel ashamed of myself, ashamed of this ugly, useless crack that leaks water all the way home."

The woman replied to the pot, "Have you noticed how I always carry you on the same side? Have you noticed how flowers grow all the way from the river back to the house? And have you noticed how they only grow on your side of the path and not on the other pot's side?"

The pot confessed it hadn't.

"Well," continued the woman, "because I knew about your crack, I have made use of it. Sometime back, I planted flower seeds on your side of the path. As we walk back every day, you have been kindly watering them for me. Being a poor family we don't have much in life but for the last few years I have been able to pick those beautiful flowers to decorate the house and bring joy to my family . . . and all because of you.

"While the other pot," she added, "supplies us with our essential water, you supply our humble lives with water, beauty, and joy."

Story 18

Using Your Resources

Happiness-Enhancing Characteristics

Problems Addressed

> Having limited resources
> Having different resources

Resources Developed

> Recognizing using own resources
> Learning to use finite resources
> Thoughtfully planning
> Constructively developing your resources
> Learning to pleasurably enjoy the outcomes

Outcomes Offered

> Gaining and enjoying pleasure from resource utilization

As I sat on the carpet with my grandsons, Oscar aged six and Taran aged two, I upended the bucket of Lego blocks on the floor. The interlocking blocks are all oblong and in just a few basic colours. Though I have never taken the time to count them, there is a finite number in the bucket. The resources I had given them were limited. I was curious. What were my grandsons going to do with those limited resources?

I suppose they may have done nothing at all with what they had been given. Just because we have something doesn't necessarily mean we will use it, or even use it well. Fortunately, they did. Maybe it had something to do with the fact that they had the resources available, something to do with the fact that someone was willing to sit with them, offering time and support, or—more importantly, whether they acknowledged it or not—that they had resources within themselves.

Taran, the two-year-old, saw the resources and made quite simple use of them. He began stacking one on top of the other, not yet aware that to construct a tower you really need a sound base or foundation from which to ascend. He placed the blocks randomly, not always even or balanced, and it wasn't long before they fell, crashing to the floor and scattering across the lounge room. He burst out laughing. Quickly he learnt to recognize what had happened and use those resources for his own amusement. He began to stack them up again only this time, before the tower had reached its own critical crash point, he gave it a push. As it fell with a bang to the floor and once more scattered across the lounge room, he again burst out laughing.

Six-year-old Oscar's approach was different. He saw the resources he had before him but sat studying them for a while prior to commencing his construction. First, he formed the blocks in a line, the bulbous lump of a cockpit at the front and a tailfin at the back. Then he shaped a pair of wings and a tail plane that he attached. Holding the Lego plane in his hand, he ran it along an imaginary runway on the carpet, taking off and flying it around the room before landing back on the carpet.

While Taran recognized the resources available and used them in a basic but fun way, Oscar's approach was more developed. He saw what resources he had available to him, thought about how he might constructively use them, formed a plan in his mind, put his plan into practice by constructing the plane, and then proceeded to employ it for his pleasure and enjoyment.

Taran continued to build tower after tower that crashed to his mischievous giggles. Differently, a totally engrossed Oscar pulled his plane apart and reconstructed the blocks into a train that he then puffed around an imaginary track.

I was intrigued how, when given an identical resource, ability, or potential opportunity, it can be approached so differently. Do you do nothing with that resource, ability, or potential opportunity at all? Do you recognize and use it, simply? Do you develop it, recognizing the resource, thoughtfully planning how to use it, constructively developing your plan, and pleasurably enjoying the outcome? As I watched them I realized there are many ways we can approach a resource and many things we can perhaps do with the same finite resources we have. I also realized how, in those different ways, they could both gain and enjoy pleasure from utilizing their resources. I guess that's the sort of thing that happens when they have a psychologist for a granddad.

EMPOWERMENT

4 On Being Accepting

My happiness grows in direct proportion to my acceptance, and in inverse proportion to my expectations.

Michael J. Fox, actor

Introduction

Acceptance is a core ingredient for a life of well-being. Fighting against what cannot be changed only leads to frustration, stress, anxiety, and unhappiness. Unfortunately, the more that we struggle to control things, the more we fight against the odds, or the more we engage in a tug of war with them, the more it often prolongs and intensifies an unwanted experience. Try to fight your anxiety about getting in an airplane, speaking in public, or whatever, and what happens? You are likely to feel more stressed and anxious.

Paradoxically, if we give up the fight against unwanted emotions, research is showing that acceptance can lead to a dissipation of emotional intensity and duration thus putting us in a better position to make choices about how to manage both the situation and our experience of it. Acceptance is not a soft option or copout but rather a process of change in itself. If someone has been fighting a long, no-win battle against anxiety, depression, anger, substance abuse, or any other issue, to shift to a more accepting position is to begin a process of change.

Battling against, trying to change, or control certain emotions and behaviors—particularly when they have a long-term, established history—may not work. The battle is likely to further exacerbate feelings of stress and distress and, therefore, heighten the problems even further. If a person has not so far been able to make that change, then acceptance of those emotions and behaviors may be the first step in a new process for making things different in the future. To discover that you can sit with the intensity of your anxiety or your depression and nothing disastrous happens, can often undermine the fear that people have about some catastrophic disaster being imminent.

When overcome by feelings, thoughts, or behaviors that we feel powerless to control, we are likely to feel disempowered. By accepting those feelings, thoughts, or behaviors—by learning that we can sit with them and not be overwhelmed by them—can put the ball back in our court and thus facilitate a new sense of empowerment.

The following stories speak about the acceptance of life's inherent sadness and joys, about when to give up the fight, when to step back, and when to go with the flow. They talk about the temporary, impermanent nature of emotions, about acceptance at both intellectual and experiential levels, and about learning to make wise, practical choices for enhancing acceptance . . . and, hence, well-being.

Story 19

Accepting Death and Dying

Happiness-Enhancing Characteristics

Problems Addressed

    Facing sorrow
    Facing loss
    Facing grief

Resources Developed

    Accepting the natural course of life
    Accepting life's inherent sadness and joys

Outcomes Offered

    Ability to cope
    Ability to be happy

A woman once went to see a wise man to ask his advice. The woman's father was getting old and needed care. The family was considering placing him in a nursing home. Not surprisingly he didn't want to leave the home where he had lived for many years, loved his now departed wife, and raised his family. It was his home, his sense of place, but, in the eyes of his family, he could no longer cope. What if he forgot to switch the gas off, or slipped and fell when no-one was there to help? As he was getting old and frail, they feared that death was on the not too distant horizon. How would the family cope with this? How would they manage the loss of someone who had always been there for them, had loved them so much, and given so much for them?

"Please," the woman asked the wise man, "give us your advice on what we need to do. What will happen in the future? How can we cherish positive memories of our father for the family's future generations? How can our family be happy now and in the years ahead with the prospect of death on our doorstep?"

The wise man turned to his desk, pulled a piece of paper to him and wrote. He studied his words, as if to be sure he had them exactly right. Then handed them to the woman. She read:

"Father dies,
child dies,
grandchild dies."

"What is this?" the woman exploded in anger. "I asked you to give us something helpful in our time of need, something to help our family cope and be happy. All you have given me is about death and misery. Why write something as depressing as this?"

The wise man answered quietly, "Think of it this way. If you were to die before your father that would bring unbearable grief to your family. If your child was to die before you, that also would bring unimaginable sorrow. If your family, generation after generation, passes away in the order I have described, and you are able to accept that this is the natural course of life—with its inherent sadness and joys—then you will be able to cope and be happy."

Story 20

Going With the Flow

Happiness-Enhancing Characteristics

Problems Addressed

Feeling battered and pounded
Battling against external forces
Trying to preserve inner peacefulness
Feeling out of your depth
Battling against the flow or tide
Feeling panicky

Resources Developed

Learning to go with the flow
Learning to relax
Learning to give up the fight
Learning to relinquish the battles you can't win

Outcomes Offered

Acceptance
Enjoying, effortlessly and absorbedly
Being free to enjoy the journey

Some years ago I vacationed on the Cocos Islands in the Indian Ocean. The islands fascinated me in many ways. They are a ring of low, coconut treed tips of a large underwater volcano, rising just a few yards above sea level. From the outside the islands are pounded by wild turbulent seas while the inner lagoon maintains a fairly constant tranquility. And that intrigued me as an interesting metaphor. How do you maintain an inner tranquility when all around is pounding at you? If you have a low level of self-esteem—or, like the islands, a metaphorically low profile—how can you hold out against the forces that are trying to wear you down? How can you build the barriers that will enable you to preserve an inner peacefulness?

On Direction Island I found another metaphor. Everyone had told me that I had to visit 'D.I.' as it is known locally. There, they said, is a channel between the islands that is rich in colorful coral and brilliantly beautiful fish, making it the atoll's supreme spot for snorkeling. Pulling on my snorkeling gear I eagerly dived into the channel. Talk about plunging in the deep end. Suddenly I found myself not only out of my depth but swimming against the flow. The tidal current was carrying me out to the turbulent sea rather than into the scenic channel. I began to feel panicky and started to battle against the tide. What if I should be swept out to sea and into the breaking waves? I might not be able to get back and could drown.

I began to swim toward the shore but was being swept out even further and faster. I swam harder, working my arms and legs harder, and feeling even more panicky but the flow was against me. The tide was more powerful than my strokes. I tried to catch my breath for a moment, to pause in my struggle, and think. The channel was narrow and so the current should be too. Maybe instead of either getting carried away by it or struggling fruitlessly against it, there was another choice. Perhaps I could go with it, swimming out to the side as I did and thus break away from the narrow current. Soon I emerged from the fast current and was able to make use of the in-flowing waves, riding them toward the shore.

Having made it back to the beach, I stretched out on my towel, soaked up the gentle warmth of the sun, and allowed myself to relax and recuperate. After a while, I gathered my gear and started toward the boat to take me back across the lagoon. Passing an island resident, he asked, "Did you enjoy the channel?"

"Oh, I didn't get there," I said, trying to sound casual and avoid the unnecessary details but, from what he said next, I guessed that he had known my mistake.

The comment he made stuck in my mind. I followed his advice, walked up to the opposite end of the channel, pulled on my snorkeling gear again and hesitantly slipped into the water. From this end, the current carried me effortlessly through the channel. Floating face down on the surface, I watched an abundance of beautifully colored and shaped corals drifting beneath me with tropical fish playfully darting about. At the end where I had previously entered, I now exited. *It helps*, I recall thinking, *to know which way is the more helpful or pleasant to travel.*

I walked back along the beach, re-entered the channel where the local resident had advised and again drifted with the flow. It was effortless and absorbedly enjoyable. I filled the rest of my afternoon, drifting in pure pleasure, and was left with a richly rewarding lifetime memory.

And what, you may be wondering, was the comment the local resident made? He said, "There's no need to fight against the current, especially if it is a battle you can't win. Let yourself go with the flow. That way you are free to enjoy the journey."

Story 21

A Train of Anxious Thoughts

Happiness-Enhancing Characteristics

Problems Addressed

> Intense anxiety
> Worrisome thoughts
> Physical symptoms of anxiety
> Social withdrawal
> Sleeplessness

Resources Developed

> Realizing there are choices
> Learning to step back
> Learning that emotions can and *will* go
> Discovering that emotions are impermanent and temporary

Outcomes Offered

> Awareness that emotions come *and* go
> Acceptance of emotional impermanence
> Skills to observe, acknowledge, accept, step back from, and let emotions pass
> Skills to paradoxically take control by letting go

I once saw a client who told me about an incident that changed his life. The reason he visited me is that he had been experiencing intense anxiety. He could see that it usually started in his thoughts: when he began to worry about life's stresses, his body responded. His stomach felt like a coffee percolator on constant boil, his head felt heavy and he couldn't get to sleep.

The incident he described was toward the end of our sessions together. It was just a common day-to-day event that most people would not even take notice of but the meaning he gave to it was a turning point on his path to freedom. He was standing on the station platform as he had done every working day for years, waiting for the morning commuter train. He was watching for it, waiting for it, and anticipating it when he felt his anxiety begin to rise. It was then he made the association.

"This is like my anxiety," he thought. "The more I look for it, anticipate, or expect it, the more it is likely to arise."

As the train came into view, he said that—like the anxiety—it was just a small spot on the overall scene that he was viewing, a little dot in the big picture. But the more he focused on it, the larger it loomed and the closer it came. Soon it was charging into his awareness, its noise overwhelming, and its vibrations shaking his body.

As it pulled into the station, he told me, "I realized in a way I have never realized before that I had a choice. Did I step on that train, a train of anxious thoughts, and get carried away with it as I had done previously? Or did I step back, let the train pass, and let those thoughts pass with it?"

He made a courageous choice. Physically and metaphorically, he stepped back and let the train he had been catching at this same time every day for the last I-don't-know-how-many years pass.

As he watched the train pull out of the station, he said he again realized how it paralleled his anxiety. "If you don't step on board," he said, "if you don't invest in it, you don't get carried away with it. You can stand back and let it pass. In fact, it felt good to know that, like the train, my anxiety may loom into awareness at times, pull into the station, perhaps stay a while, and then it *could* and *would* go. It would not remain permanently, forever."

"As the train left," he observed, "it began to diminish in size, disappearing out of my view and consciousness. But also the sound, the vibrations, and the feel of it rapidly faded as I let it pass."

Yes, I thought, how right he was. Feelings—good and bad, helpful and unhelpful, wanted and unwanted—come *and* go. They are not permanent, they are not fixed or forever. If like that man, we can observe them, acknowledge them, accept their presence, step back from them, and let them pass, we take control. As I heard him say triumphantly, "*I* let it pass."

Story 22

This Too Will Pass

Happiness-Enhancing Characteristics

Problems Addressed

Difficult times in life
Feeling dismissed
Not feeling understood

Encountering change
When things are not as you want or expect

Resources Developed

Learning to discriminate between emotions and actions
Learning to accept emotions
Learning that emotions are temporary
Learning to make choices about managing emotions
Learning to manage when life is not what I want or expect it to be
Learning from experience

Outcomes Offered

Acceptance
Experience is the best teacher
This is the way it is
This too will pass

I have to admit there have been times when I have been going through a tough period and caring, well-meaning friends have quoted, "This too will pass." Rather than helping it has left me feeling like telling them where to go. Not that I would. After all, isn't one of life's important lessons learning to discriminate between having an emotion and acting that emotion out?

Nonetheless, when life has been at a difficult point and friends have glibly said, "Oh, this too will pass," my emotions have welled up. I *know* my friends are right. Life has taught me that experiences and circumstances do—and will—change, alter, and pass. However, equating the logic and the emotions at the time can be two different things. Their comments feel like they have dismissed the intensity of my feelings, not understood where I am really at, or think the uttering of a few words will somehow right everything that feels so terribly wrong at the time.

At one such time in my life I set out for a walk along my favorite beach. Walking can be a contemplative experience, and the value of the contemplation is often determined by the content on which we focus. Contemplating problems can be problematic. Contemplating the experiences of the moment can be distracting at the least and enriching at the best. Contemplating our desired outcomes or desired future can be empowering for change. Contemplating acceptance can lead to acceptance.

As I walked, I noticed how the beach had changed. Last week it still had its summer appearance. The sands were pristinely clean, golden and squeaky. They sloped in a gentle, even gradient to the water's edge where water swished gently onto the shore. The ocean was calm, clear, and enticing. It had felt peaceful and soul-soothing to walk along it. It had been this way for months and months. It was how my recent experience had taught me it would be and how I had come to expect it would continue. Then things suddenly changed.

This week, the weather and seas changed. The sands now looked grey, dull, and lacking luster. They felt cold and soggy underfoot. The waves had cut into the gentle gradient creating a sharp edge with a one- or two-foot drop. Smelly banks of sea weed had washed up on the shore. The waters washed around them causing eddies and cutaways. The waves rose in grayish, muddy walls to hurl themselves at the beach, dumping the dirty sea weed, weather-worn wood, old plastic bait bags, empty drink cans, broken bits of plastic, and tangled masses of fishing line. It seemed like it had been building up this rubbish for ages, awaiting this very moment to hurl it my way. No longer did I find the sea enticing me. Even walking was different. The previous peaceful, soul-soothing strolls had now turned into a challenging hike, up and down over humps of weed, across washed up logs, in and out of sand gullies, always watchful for the wave that seemed out to get me as soon as my attention wandered. At one point, the waves had cut into the dunes creating a sand cliff some 10 to 12 feet high, seeming to also create a metaphor for my own current challenges. No matter how tall the cliff stood, the waters, like negative thoughts, were eroding it at its very base and threatening to cause it to collapse on itself.

The experience was different, not what I had set out expecting or wanting. It had changed from last week and would continue to change over the next days and weeks of the season. I could not alter what was happening. I had no power over it. But I did have a choice over *how I* thought about it and *what* I now did.

Did I avoid what no longer met my expectation or thoughts of how it should be? Did I face it, force myself to front the new challenges and deal with the changes that were beyond my control? Or did I accept it, knowing that life never is exactly the way I would always want or like it to be? *Face it, George*, I thought to myself. *This is the way it is.* Temporary, as changes tend to be, the summer beach had passed. In turn, the winter beach too will pass and a new summer beach will return. Then I realized. I had not been told but rather I had experienced what people mean when they say, *This too will pass.*

Story 23

Paddling Against the Tide

Happiness-Enhancing Characteristics

Problems Addressed

When life is tough
When life is damn tough
When things just doesn't make sense
Self-doubts
Helplessness and hopelessness

Resources Developed

Accepting there is no point in battling against the flow
Accepting there are things we can't control

Learning to go with the flow
Discovering somethings can be scary *and* exhilarating
Facing new, unexpected challenges
Noticing and appreciating beauty
Discovering there are times to put in the effort and times to relax
Learning when to go with the flow and when to steer your own course

Outcomes Offered

Acceptance
Empowerment
Enhanced confidence

Sometimes life is tough. Sometimes it is damn tough. Sometimes it just doesn't make sense. Sometimes we question and doubt ourselves: *Why is this happening to me? What have I done to deserve this? Why me?*

That's how Sarah-Jayne told me it was for her. She was feeling pretty help-less and hopeless, and knew she needed to do something to change directions, to find something new and stimulating for her. As her adult children were into kayaking, she decided to join a club and learn to kayak herself.

It was not long after that she told me that she was planning a camping and kayaking weekend with her sons and their families. As I am sure we have all discovered at various stages of our life that some of our most important learnings come through our experiences, I asked Sarah-Jayne to observe her experiences over the weekend to see what happened that might be relevant or helpful in what she was working on in therapy.

When I next saw her, she told an interesting story. On the first day, her two fit and kayak-seasoned sons decided to give themselves the challenge of paddling *up* a small rapid. Now, anyone familiar with kayaking will know you usually paddle down a rapid, going with the flow. Sarah-Jayne decided to join her sons on the challenge. Bending forward, digging their paddles deep and testing their strength, they held their own against the rapidly flowing white water but every time Sarah-Jayne got into the stream she was swept backwards downriver. After several attempts, she turned her boat and let the waters carry her downstream toward a bank where she stopped to rest for a while. She said, speaking I am sure about more than a kayaking experience, "I discovered there was no point in battling against the flow. I had to accept that sometimes there are things I can't control, things that are stronger than me or exceed my ability to handle them."

"Having discovered that," I asked, "what did you do then?"

"I realized that if you're getting nowhere fighting against the current, there is only one choice left: you need to go with the flow. My sons followed as sup-port buddies but the waters were still turbulent even though they had started me off on gentle rapids. To me the white water seemed to boil wildly around me. 'Paddle,' they called. 'Go with the flow but keep your speed up so that you are in control. You can't control the flow or speed of the water but you can control how you handle it. You can steer and choose the directions you want to go.'"

"I shouted *Wow* as I came out of that first rapid," she said with a triumphant look on her face. "It was so damn scary but so damn exhilarating to know I could get myself through safely."

After the rapids, the river widened and slowed. And she began to slow with it, slowing her paddling and letting the flow of the river carry her while she simply made a few correcting strokes here and there to stay on course. As the river opened into a large pool the wind whipped up, blowing straight into her face and threatening to blow her backwards. Again she had to lean forward, dig her paddles deep and test her muscles. She said, "Just when I thought the going was getting easier, I suddenly found myself facing another unexpected challenge." And that too spoke to her about her life experiences.

Coming out of the pool, she once more relaxed into going with the flow. As she later commented to me, "In those quiet times, I realized I didn't have to be so focused on my paddling. Drifting with the current, I began to appreciate the magnificent trees that edged the river, notice the birds that stood on the banks fixedly watching the water for a possible feed, and hear the variety of birdsongs on the air."

"When I woke the next morning I knew there would be much of the same ahead. I had given up trying to battle against the flow but I knew that even going with it would bring challenging times and quiet times. It would demand I paddle hard at times and sit back to quietly enjoy at others. There would be times to put in the effort and times to relax. There would be times when I would need to choose to go with the flow and times when I would have to steer my own course."

Then she added a final comment, "That's rivers, and that's life."

Story 24

Acceptance, Choices . . . and Laughter

Happiness-Enhancing Characteristics

Problems Addressed

When encountering an unexpected catastrophe
When disaster strikes
When life is not what it *should* be

Resources Developed

Realizing stories don't all end happily for ever after
Finding alternate solutions
Realizing life is not what it should be

ACCEPTANCE

Discovering acceptance at an intellectual level
Discovering acceptance at an experiential level
Learning to make wise and practical choices

Outcomes Offered

Acceptance
Skills in making choices
Laughter

I am often delighted to receive emails from colleagues who have attended my training workshops or read my books. Following workshops on the use of metaphors and stories in therapy, I am commonly surprised to receive therapeutic stories from colleagues that they have written or used with their own clients. This is one such story that I expressed in my own words.

My colleague said she was preparing a PowerPoint colloquium at university as part of her assessment requirements when the computer's hard drive crashed just after she had the CD-ROM drive replaced. She said that as an adult with years of computer experience and a reasonable IQ, she should have known better than to leave her computer repair to the week before such an important presentation. Perhaps, she thought, I can save my presentation onto my new CD-ROM, if only I can get it repaired. The hapless computer technician, who she described as a strapping young lad with a surprisingly soft voice, looked puzzled when he realized that she intended to try to save her work on a read-only drive. Suddenly, she said an understanding flooded through the reptilian parts of her brain that she used for the retention of computer information: she had mistaken the capabilities of a CD-ROM for a CD burner, and had just paid out for a part that was not going to save her work after all! Nonetheless, she informed the technician, she still needed to save her PowerPoint presentation.

"No problem," he said, with the assuredness of both the young and the knowledgeable. "You just need a flash drive."

Yet another expense, and another delay, when she was already under pressure. But the horizon was looking clearer and brighter. *My worries will be over*, she assured herself. *I will be able to make a back up copy of my PowerPoint presentation, transport it to university, and deliver it in time for the date of my colloquium.*

Now, I am sure you have read enough stories and had enough life experiences to know stories don't always end happily ever after. Disaster can strike, and did. While shutting down the computer just hours after the technician, the computer baulked, and assumed a passive resistance pose worthy of Mahatma Ghandi. She described being forced to hold the power button until its life force turned off in an almost audible electronic scream of protest. *Nothing good can come of this*, she told herself . . . and, unfortunately, she was right. The next morning, to her surprise, disgust, and fear, it wouldn't even go though its routine disk scanning procedure!

Hysterical, she rang the technician who couldn't come for another day. When he finally arrived, he pressed a few buttons, turned around to her, and said the thing you never really want to hear from any kind of professional, "I've never seen this before!"

During the following days she returned to what writers had long used before her: good old pen and paper. While feeling deeply comforted in the knowledge that at least this was reliable, she continued preparing for her colloquium on metaphors and therapeutic stories, based on a the workshop she had attended with me, my book, *101 Healing Stories*, and a literature review of the area.

It was sitting back on the lounge room couch instead of in her computer chair, she came across one of my stories on acceptance, *Life is not what it should be. It is what it is.* She related how the story tells of the author's own trials and tribulations while organizing a conference. At the end of the tale, after many setbacks and frustrations, the conference went ahead, but not before the author saw a handwritten sign outside a shop that read, "Life is not what it should be, it is what it is."

My colleague said she grasped the moral of the story immediately on an intellectual level, and could certainly relate to it after having completed a fourth-year thesis and now with her current presentation trauma. However, the story failed to make an impact on her emotionally. It didn't make her feel any better, she stated. *Good for you, George*, she murmured to herself. *This* shouldn't *be happening to me!* Nonetheless she decided to include this story in her presentation anyway. And now I, appreciatively, have the chance to include hers in mine.

And, you may wonder, what was the outcome for her? After hundreds of dollars had left her wallet, she finally got the computer back. The cause of its ill health was a Trojan horse virus that mercilessly attacked its hard drive despite having several anti-virus programs. She was disheartened to learn that, like any prophylactic, they are not totally reliable.

Her relief, however, was short-lived when the phone rang. After weeks of trying to set up a practicum for the duration of her university vacation with a community organization, the manager called back and asked, for the third time, when she would like to start the practicum. As the university semester was to commence the following week, and she needed access to clients in order to write up a case study, she replied, "Right now!" Then the manager announced she was about to go on leave and couldn't offer a placement until she returned—in another six weeks! This was too late for my colleague to complete the case study, and there were no other possibilities available at such short notice. Bewildered, frustrated she hung up the telephone.

Then, she said, she again remembered the story: *Life is not what it should be. It is what it is.* More than just grasping the moral of the story on an intellectual level, she could now understand and experience it. In her own words she concluded, "If life is not what I expect it should be, if it is what it is, if there

ACCEPTANCE

are things out side of my area of control, like the computer and the practicum, my only wise and practical choices are to accept them for what they are. Instead of crying in defeat, I laughed. This time I realized that I could either chuckle at the recent events in my life that had not gone to plan, despite my best attempts, or I could make myself miserable. I choose to laugh."

5   On Being Mindful

> Your mindfulness will only be as robust as the capacity of your mind to be calm and stable.
>
> Jon Kabat-Zinn

Introduction

The simple act of closing your eyes and focusing your attention brings about an amazing change in brain, body, and mind. This act, commonly known as mindfulness, has grabbed a lot of attention in the psychological literature, been subjected to more research than ever in its history, and found its way into everyday therapeutic practice. Despite the recent scientific interest, mindfulness has a millennia-old and varied history across most religions, faiths, cultures, and healing disciplines. While there is a deep similarity in the physical, mental, emotional, and spiritual processes of mindfulness, practice can vary from a few seconds of mindful focus—such as on chewing an item of food—to a life-time meditation retreat in a Himalayan cave. With an estimated 80,000 possible meditation practices, clearly there is no one sole way of meditating or mindfulness practice (Yapko, 2011, p. 3).

Commonly mindfulness is used to: (1) achieve relaxation, (2) attain spiritual awareness, and (3) bring about personal change. Recent research, linked to the development of technologies in the neuroscience areas, has enabled us to see what is happening in the brain while people engage in mindful practices. Not surprisingly, this research, along with outcome studies, is confirming what meditation practitioners have been telling us for a long time: Taking time to focus your attention has a variety of psychological benefits in the reduction of depression and depression relapse rates, the diminishing of stress and anxiety, the treatment of borderline personality disorder, and the therapy for various substance abuses. At the physical level, it has been shown to enhance immune system functioning, to facilitate dermatological healing, assist with chronic illness, help cope with cancer, and better manage pain. Spiritually and emotionally—as both Buddhist practitioners and neuroscience researchers tell us—it can, indeed, be a path to happiness.

Given these benefits, how do you develop this helpful skill and walk the mindful path to happiness? Perhaps the most effective way is to sit with a master practitioner to learn the simple skills for achieving this focused state of mind. Another is learning from the experiences of others, such as related in the following stories where you will discover the values of sitting, observing, waiting, and experiencing. You will learn about how to let the mind clear, how to engage mindfully in activities you may not have expected, how to connect mindfully with nature, how to engage in a loving kindness meditation, and how to use your meditation practically.

Story 25

If You Sit and Wait

Happiness-Enhancing Characteristics

Problems Addressed

> A troubled past
> Holding high expectations
> Disappointment when expectations are not fulfilled
> Thinking versus experiencing

Resources Developed

> Learning to sit and wait
> Taking time to observe
> Taking time to pause and enjoy
> Experiencing beauty
> Being alert to metaphors

Outcomes Offered

> The value of observing and experiencing
> The value of sitting tranquilly
> Acceptance of unfulfilled expectations

"If you sit and wait long enough something will come to you," said Trapper Rick. And that is exactly what we were doing: sitting on the bank of the Kakweiken River somewhere up an inlet in the maze of deeply indented coastline of northern British Columbia, Canada—waiting, hopefully, to sight a grizzly bear.

Trapper Rick had a somewhat dilapidated A-framed cabin tucked away on the riverbank right above a set of waterfalls with uninterrupted and unsurpassed views down a spectacular valley. When we arrived, he stood still for a few minutes, quietly surveying the scene as if taking it in for the first time and then, almost as if speaking to himself, said, "It's an honor to live here."

His deep love of these woods and the critters that live here with him was apparent.

Rick had a rough-lived, deeply furrowed, and darkly tanned face. He had known the wild side of civilization as well as he knew the wilds of the woods. He wore a spotted bandanna around his head and a grey beard with a moustache, tinged nicotine ginger. A naughty, cheeky twinkle in his eye defined him as a lovable rogue. His speech flowed with an endless stream of engaging stories. Trapper was a title he wore as proudly as a medical graduate calls himself Doctor.

This was the character I found myself sitting beside on a moss covered rock on the banks of the Kakweiken River when he said, "If you sit and wait long enough something will come to you." I thought he was talking about grizzly bears. I was there with an expectation. I wanted to see a bear in the river, scooping out salmon to fatten itself for the winter hibernation. We sat and waited, and waited, and waited, without sight of a bear.

Despite, or because of, my disappointment, I began to observe the stream opposite as it wove its way into the main river. Obstacles had fallen in its path, unexpected storms had felled trees across its bed, and winter floods had rolled boulders into its course. For each obstacle it adapted, finding a new route over, around, or under in its journey onward towards the river. I found myself wondering what metaphors it told, and then wondering whether I should be *thinking* or simply *experiencing* the beauty of this pretty little waterway twisting through the green forest, between mossy banks and over smooth, glossy rocks. Did I sit back and simply enjoy the soothing rhythm of the babbling waters? Did I pause to appreciate the clear fragrance of the mountain stream mingled with the aroma of fir trees and damp soil?

As my gaze drifted down to my feet, I became aware of variously shaped and colored pebbles on which they rested. I began to think that they represented a metaphor for Rick's life and, indeed, for many of our lives. Starting out rough and rugged, they were shaped and smoothed by their experiences of life tumbling along with the river. Some of their early faults and scars were still visible and I couldn't help wondering how different they might have appeared before their encounter with the river. Then thoughts faded as I simply experienced the beauty of their colors, their shapes, and their patterns, and the sound of the river gurgling around them.

Somewhere I lost track of time. To this day I have no idea of how long we sat on the riverbank simply observing and experiencing.

We never did see a grizzly bear at that spot. Not even a deer, or an elk, or a bald eagle. But I had to agree with Trapper Rick. It may not be what I had expected or hoped for. It may not have even been the sighting of something external but rather something internal: a memory, a thought, an idea, an experience . . . or simply a sense of tranquility. Yes, if you sit and wait long enough *something* will come to you.

Story 26

Letting the Waters Clear

Happiness-Enhancing Characteristics

Problems Addressed

Worry
Rumination
Depressive thinking
Lack of control
Powerlessness
Helplessness

Resources Developed

Learning from experience
Learning to wonder rather than worry
Noticing the pleasant, non-worrisome sensations
Learning to sit and observe
Learning and practicing mindfulness

Outcomes Offered

Mental calmness and clarity
Appreciation of time in quiet observation and mindfulness

A young man once went to see a wise man to seek his advice. The man was plagued with worries that endlessly raced around in his head, churned over and over, and felt totally out of his control. Psychologists might call it rumination, like a cow endlessly chewing its cud. Buddhists might call it the monkey mind, like a troop of ceaselessly chattering monkeys. I don't know what his worries were about. They could have been about work, about relationships, about finances, about his children, or about anything in fact. No matter how we might label his thoughts or what their content may be, the man was caught in a process over which he felt powerless and helpless.

This did not escape the wise man's attention as he listened quietly to the younger man's story. He knew it was not helpful for him to be constantly going over and over these old, unresolved matters. It was not resolving the problem. In fact, it was making things worse. Now the young man had two problems. First, the seemingly unchangeable problems he was facing and, second, his worries about them. *Knowledge alone*, thought the wise man, *is not going to change his worrisome processes. He may learn better from experience.*

The wise man rose, walked into his modest kitchen, collected a large glass jar, and said, "Come, follow me."

The worrier was curious and, as he followed the wise man, he noted that his curiosity had overridden his worries. While he was *wondering* what the wise man was doing, he was not *worrying* so much.

They followed a narrow forest path where the young man began to notice the tall, straight, barky trunks of the trees, hear the sounds of birds and smell the sweet forest fragrances. Soon they reached the banks of a river where waters raced over rocks in a series of rapids.

"What do you notice?" asked the wise man.

"The river is muddy and dirty," said the young worrier. "It is endlessly racing by, churning over and over." It felt like he was describing his own thoughts.

"Do you think you can control the turbulent waters?" enquired the wise man.

"Maybe if you built a huge dam," said the man, "but if you mean me, personally, I would have to admit I couldn't."

The wise man handed the younger his glass jar and said, "Here fill this jar with some water from the river."

When he had, the wise man asked, "Do you have control of the water in the jar?"

The man replied, "I scooped it out of the river, I hold it in my hands so I guess I control it . . . but only this small bit."

The wise man smiled, nodded sagely, and began to walk back to the house with his companion following. When they arrived he asked the man to set the jar on a shelf, then sit cross legged on the floor and look at the jar.

"What do you notice?" he asked.

"The water is muddy and murky."

"Good, keep sitting and quietly watching it for a while."

Nothing appeared to be happening but the man did as suggested, keeping his attention on the water. However, something was happening so imperceptibly that he hardly noticed. Now that the water was still the mud began to settle, the water gradually growing clearer. Almost as imperceptibly, as he kept his focus on the still water, his mind too began to grow calmer and clearer. I am not sure if he was aware of how his breathing also became calmer, his body felt more relaxed, or time had passed almost without him noticing. Was it two minutes or 12 minutes or 20 minutes that he sat there? Regardless, the mud had now settled to the bottom of the jar, the water was so clean it looked drinkable, and his inner being felt similarly clear, clean, and calm.

"What are you going to do now?" asked the wise man when he saw the worried man had observed the changes that came through sitting quietly and mindfully attending to something.

"Perhaps I need to take a walk by the river when feeling worried or troubled," replied the man peacefully, "collect a jar of water that I can set on a shelf at home and spend time quietly observing it."

"Ah," commented the wise man. "However, it is not just the water that has cleared but also your own mind. When and how can you practice just quietly sitting and letting your mind clear like the water, even without a jar of muddy water?"

When the previously worried man smiled and nodded quietly, affirmatively, the wise man realized his student appreciated that the water was merely an illustrative metaphor. True change had come through his own process of sitting quietly and allowing his focused mind to calm.

"Is there anything else I can say or offer?" asked the wise man.

"No, thank you," came the smiling reply as the man tranquilly left the wise man, and walked into the rest of his life with a new-found peace.

Story 27

Mindfulness in a Rice Paddy

Happiness-Enhancing Characteristics

Problems Addressed

Disappointment
Ruminations
Wanting to relax
Being distracted from goals
Holding negative thoughts
Being ambivalent
Facing new challenges

Resources Developed

Taking mindful action
Allowing thoughts to wash away
Finding mind-absorbing experiences
Enjoying joyful company
Being focused on the task at hand
Experiencing time distortion

Outcomes Offered

Mindful engagement in daily activities

Recently, while working as a volunteer clinical psychologist in Bhutan, I found myself overwhelmed with disappointment. I had put months of planning into trekking a remote high altitude trail, gained government permission to visit the usually restricted region, been driving my body into fitness for months, and had worked at acclimating to the altitude. However, at the last moment, unseasonal weather blocked the trail in deep snow, closing the door on my once in a lifetime chance.

Riddled with mixed emotions of despair and frustration, I decided to spend some time meditating at a favorite spot on the banks of a local river. The path to the river drops steeply off the road edge, descends through a forest of blue pine trees before flattening out and traversing the narrow embankments between flooded rice fields. It makes its way across a bridge, swings sharply to the left through a potato paddock, then again drops to large, seat-sized boulders at my mediation spot on the edge of the lively river where, previously I have found, all thoughts are quickly washed away in the mind-absorbing sound of its rushing waters. But I never made it.

On the way, five women stood in a line, calf-deep in muddy water, across the breadth of a rice paddy the size of an Olympic swimming pool. Arched over at right angles, they were planting 10cm-long rice sprouts. Their colorful pink, purple, gold, and blue skirts and tops, reflecting in the brown mirror-like water of the paddy, would make a lovely photo, so I requested their permission to snap it. They laughed and giggled. Then, when I lowered the camera, one shouted, "Try, try," gesturing for me to join them in the mud.

Isn't it interesting how our mind often finds all the negatives? At least mine can. Joining them would mean taking off my boots and socks, getting my feet wet and muddy, putting wet, muddy feet back into my socks and boots. What would I do with my new camera? If I put it on the narrow embankment, could it fall or be knocked off and ruined forever in the muddy waters? And wasn't I meant to be meditating by the river, anyway?

I paused for a moment, thinking. If my socks got wet and muddy I could wash them out back at the hotel. I could find a reasonably safe spot for the camera. I could give the planting a few minutes, then go on to meditate. And, heck, I had never planted rice in my life before.

Soon I was unlacing my boots, peeling off my socks, rolling up my trousers and sleeves, and joining the women in the mud. The pleasantly warm temperature of the water caressed my calves. The sensuous texture of slippery mud squished between my toes and around my feet. I felt the soft suppleness of the rice seedlings (that one woman passed to me) in the palm of my hand.

She took me under her wing, gesturing with her hand across the field, "Straight, straight." "One, one," she chastised me when her watchful eye caught me unwittingly burying two seedlings together. I had to concentrate, carefully ensuring that I selected just one seedling at a time, pushing it sufficiently into the uneven muddy bottom to ensure it stayed—not buried too deeply that it drowned beneath the water nor too shallow that it floated out. I also had to focus on maintaining a straight line, linking up with the women on either side of me, and spacing the seedlings at the same distance apart as my fellow workers.

Thus focused, I worked away in the joyful company of these chatty, giggling women backing my way down the field until my heels hit the embankment at the far end. Our job was done in what felt like just a few minutes—and I was not aware of a single disappointing, frustrating thought of the trek entering my mind. Only then did I notice my fingers were cold from constant immersion in the water, my fingernails and toenails were black with mud, and the sun had dropped below the mountain peaks. When I checked, an hour and a half had slipped by while I was so mindfully engaged in planting rice.

I pulled socks over my wet, muddy feet, slipped on my boots, and picked up my camera. "Kadriche La," I said in the local language. "Thank you," they chorused back in English. "Log jay gay" I added. "Bye, bye," they echoed with waving hands and moved onto the next field.

And that was how I set out to meditate at a favorite spot on the banks of a local river, let go of my disappointed thoughts . . . and ended up mindfully planting rice.

Story 28

Nature-Guided Mindfulness

Happiness-Enhancing Characteristics

Problems Addressed

Desire to practice mindfulness

Resources Developed

Choosing a natural environment in which to meditate
Focusing awareness on visual sensations
Focusing awareness on sound sensations
Focusing awareness on smell sensations
Focusing awareness on taste sensations
Focusing awareness on tactile sensations

Outcomes Offered

Calmness of thought
Peacefulness of feeling
Sense of serenity
Feeling of well-being

There are many things we learn in our childhood that we are not consciously aware we have learnt. One of those unwitting childhood discoveries for me was that, if feeling upset or distressed, a walk along the beach or through the woods would quickly change my emotions. Only years later did I develop a professional interest in how such contact with nature can enhance our feelings of well-being. I heard both colleagues and clients telling me about how time in nature could help them relax or lift their mood. What was happening here, I wondered and so set about to study it. After years of research I found that there was very clear evidence that being in contact with nature has distinct physical, psychological, social, and spiritual benefits. So I wrote a book about it entitled, *Nature-Guided Therapy.*

Of the many ways that nature benefits our well-being, one is through nature-guided mindfulness. Recently while conducting a training workshop for colleagues on this topic, my sponsors had thoughtfully chosen a venue in the midst of a nature reserve that was home to a river, wetlands, a variety of vegetation, and many species of native birds. To demonstrate an exercise in nature-guided mindfulness for them, we sat outside on a grassy embankment and I simply guided the group through the awareness of each of their senses. You may want to close your eyes and envision it as I describe what we did.

"First," I began, "you may want to tune into your sense of sight, focusing your gaze up in the sky, looking at the color, and variations of the color in the sky. Be aware of the clouds, their shapes, their colors, their movement, the gradual alteration in shape."

"Gradually allow your eyes to drift down into the trees, looking at their shapes, observing their colors, seeing the movement of the leaves in the breeze. Slowly lower your gaze through the branches down the trunks and on to the shape and variations in color of the bushes below the trees. Let your gaze slowly drift down at a pace that is comfortable and relaxing for you."

"Then allow yourself to look at the wetlands, the reflections of the bushes, trees, clouds, and sky. Be aware of the slight ripple on the surface and the movement in the reflections. As you bring your gaze to the near embankment, allow yourself to observe the shapes and colors of the grasses, the twigs, and the leaves on the ground near your feet. Maybe rest with your eyes closed to let yourself more fully experience your other senses."

"Can you notice the soothing, soporific sounds around you like the gentle rustle of the leaves in the breeze, occasional song of a bird, or croak of the frogs? Aware of the volume of those sounds, their tone, their pitch, their undulations."

"Then let yourself tune into your sense of smell. What are the fragrances, the aromas, the subtle smells that fall on your nostrils?"

"You may be curious to wonder if there are any taste sensations in the air or on your tongue."

"And what are the tactile sensations you experience on your two square meters of skin? Can you feel the warmth of the sun, the cool of the breeze, the firmness or softness of the ground where you sit, or temperature?

"You may want to allow yourself a little time to simply enjoy those sensory experiences. What are you noticing the most? Can you be more aware of one sense than another, or of the combination of all? When you are feeling comfortable in those sensations, then gradually step yourself back through them. First, observing your tactile sensations, then any taste sensations that may be present, followed by an awareness of any smells or fragrances. Then taking your time to observe, at your own pace, what sound sensations you might again be aware of before slowly opening your eyes and gradually lifting your gaze up from the grasses, leaves, and twigs at your feet to the reflections in the water, the bushes and trees beyond, and finally back up to the clouds and the sky."

As I guided my colleagues through this exercise over 15 to 20 minutes, I was reminded that it is our senses that put us in contact with nature. By quietly taking time to mindfully observe our senses of nature, we are likely to experience a calming of thought, a peacefulness of feeling, a sense of serenity, and a feeling of well-being.

Story 29

Loving Kindness Meditation

Happiness-Enhancing Characteristics

Problems Addressed

Desire to learn meditation

Resources Developed

Assuming a meditation position
Focusing attention on breathing
Focusing on compassionate feelings
Extending loving kindness to

(a) yourself
(b) friends
(c) family
(d) those who challenge you, and
(e) all living beings

Outcomes Offered

Compassionate feelings
Quality relationships
Peace of mind
Enhanced happiness

When I first began to learn meditation, my teacher instructed me in a mindfulness exercise entitled loving kindness meditation. Back then I did not dream that this ancient Eastern practice of mindfulness would one day be validated in Western science, but this is exactly what has happened. Researchers say this particular mindful practice has a powerful influence in ensuring our peace of mind and level of happiness.

After my teacher had invited me to sit comfortably, hands gently rested on my lap, and my back in an upright position, he asked that I fix my gaze low on the floor immediately in front of me. As I describe what he taught me you may find it helpful to sit comfortably and find a spot to fix your gaze, too.

"Begin by focusing your attention on your breathing," he said. "Simply allow yourself to observe that flow of air, the easy rise and fall of your chest with each breath you take, without trying to control it or regulate it. Maybe you can be aware of the flow of the air through your nostrils, a little cooler as you inhale and a little warmer as you exhale. Continue to observe it for a few moments, letting your breathing and your mind begin to experience a sense of quiet and calm."

"As you feel your breathing is becoming relaxed, so you may want to focus on the region of your heart, thinking about your heart feeling warm, filled with tenderness and compassion. And as you do, imagine someone or something to whom you feel a deep sense of love and caring: a loved pet, a young baby, or another person toward whom you feel unconditional love. Letting your love, care, and kindness exude toward that being."

"Then imagine extending those feelings of loving kindness to yourself. Imagine yourself receiving and experiencing those feelings of loving kindness."

I have since learnt that there are many different ways of practicing a loving kindness meditation, with different teachers doing it in different ways. Some people are able to effectively imagine extending and experiencing the sensations of loving kindness. Some people find it easier to repeat to themselves, in a mantra-like way, words such as, "May (the name of person) have loving kindness. May they know love, peace, strength, and happiness in their life." Other people may think about three or five things that they could like, love, and care about in themselves or the other person. Some say you should focus solely on others and not on one's self. Whatever helpfully accesses your feelings of loving kindness is what is important.

My teacher continued, "Once you experience those feelings of loving kindness yourself, then imagine extending them to your dear friends, surrounding them with feelings of love and compassion, seeing them content, peaceful, and happy."

"Having allowed yourself time to do this, then extend those feelings on to your family, those you get on well with, as well as those you find challenging. From your family, extend your feelings of loving kindness to other people who may challenge you, by whom you have felt hurt, or who have been hostile to you in some way. Then spread those compassionate, caring feelings out to all of your connections, all the people you know and encounter in life."

"Finally, spread your feelings of care, compassion, and kindness to all living beings, to all people and creatures on the earth. Then, when you are ready gradually opening your eyes and bringing those feelings of loving kindness back in to your day-to-day life," my teacher concluded.

Having gently led us through the meditation, he encouraged us to practice this mindfulness exercise in our daily lives, recommending that we find a quiet place where we could comfortably sit by ourselves, turn off the phone, and allow 10 to 20 undisturbed minutes for focusing our thoughts on extending loving kindness to ourselves and others.

Having experienced it, I could under stand why generations of meditation scholars and masters have practiced this particular mindfulness technique. I could also understand why scientists have more recently concluded that it is a powerful tool for enhancing compassionate feelings, quality relationships, peace of mind . . . and happiness.

Story 30

Being Mindful and Practical

Happiness-Enhancing Characteristics

Problems Addressed

Physical discomfort
Emotional discomfort

Resources Developed

Learning to sit mindfully and focus attention
Learning to observe and let go
Practicing brief and single-focused mindfulness
Surrendering to discomfort
Learning to be practical
Collaborating mindfulness with practical steps

Outcomes Offered

Enhanced comfort
A variety of mindfulness practices
A wise approach to using mindfulness practices

Once a student of mindfulness proudly told her meditation master that she had successfully used mindfulness to help her deal with a physical pain. The master gently asked, "*How* did you do that?"

"As you have taught me," she replied. "I sat in a meditational pose, focused attention on my breathing, aware of the flow of air through my nostrils as I inhaled and exhaled. I observed my thoughts as they come and go without hanging onto them: observe and let go."

"I have gradually built my practice up from minutes to hours. I practice other things you taught like mindfully focusing on my senses and awareness of life's small tasks like eating or brushing my teeth. I take brief moments to mindfully focus on my body when paused at traffic lights or uninterested in TV commercials. I have become mindfully engaged in day-to-day activities like washing dishes or taking a walk."

"By doing these things, previously I had only been able to let go of worrisome thoughts, but now I have been able to use them to help deal with pain as well."

The master listened, then responded with a story from his own experience. "I had a serious case of shingles some years back," he said. "Like you I was determined to deal with the pain through mindfulness practice—and try not to be upset by it as it was causing me intense agony. For the first few hours I managed simply to observe the pain, but though I could observe it, the pain still existed. Slowly and surely it continued to wear me out."

"Eventually, it wore me down so much that I just lay on my bed in pain for many long hours, and wept. Immediately after surrendering to the pain in this way I felt much better—for a while. However, the relief was short-lived and the pain again returned in its full intensity."

"When that hadn't worked as fully as I hoped, I went to a physician. I sought out someone who was a master on shingles and pain. I followed his advice, I took his medication . . . and when I felt better I was again able to helpfully practice my mindfulness."

I don't know about you but to me this story speaks several important messages: Sometimes meditation and mindfulness can be helpful in easing our discomfort, be it emotional or physical. Sometimes—but not always—it is possible to observe the discomfort and let it go. Sometimes it may be a matter of surrendering to it. And sometimes it is important to be practical, acknowledge that our problems are bigger than our skills, and seek the assistance of someone competent in the field. Then we can practice our mindfulness collaboratively with the practical steps.

6 On Being a Reframer

There is nothing either good or bad, but thinking makes it so.
William Shakespeare, Hamlet Prince of Denmark

Introduction

Have you noticed how two people can see the same situation very differently? Recently I read the story of an Amazonian explorer and his native guide. When the explorer began cursing the boot-entrapping clay they were trekking through, the stick he tripped over, and the threatening sounds of wild animals, the guide said, "What you see as annoying clay, we see as a potential bowl. What you see as a useless stick about to trip you up, we see as a useful arrow to obtain food. What you hear as a predatory animal in the jungle, we hear as the sound of a fresh meal."

The tale illustrates that there is no single way to perceive an object or event. It may be positive, as things were to the native guide, or it may be negative, as things were to the unfamiliar explorer. And, because there is no one way to see or think about an event or experience, the story also highlights that we have a choice about whether we see something in a positive or negative frame.

Reframing is the process of changing the way you look at something—from positive to negative or negative to positive. Changing your perception of an event, a person, or an experience also changes your experience of it. Reframing can turn a stressful, traumatic event into a useful learning experience. If your day doesn't go as planned, you can frame it as the most disastrous day of your life or a small hiccup in an overall wonderful life. Shifting, or reframing, our attitudes and perceptions from negative to positive can help relieve significant amounts of stress, lift feelings of depression, facilitate growth from trauma and create a happier, more optimistic life.

The stories here address the reframing of ideas through the acquisition and utilization of new information. They look at adopting practical and wise attitudes, at seeing both the positive *and* the negative, and at discovering the ability to change. They show the step-by-step processes for adopting healthier, more helpful, and happier frames of mind. Changing the way you look at life can truly change life itself.

Story 31

Changing Perceptions

Happiness-Enhancing Characteristics

Problems Addressed

Holding false ideas
Forming inappropriate opinions
Basing ideas on limited information

Resources Developed

Learning to reflect on one's own observations
Learning to adapt ideas to new information
Discovering ideas can and do change
Learning how thoughts determine feelings and actions

Outcomes Offered

Thoughts can change
Ideas can be reframed
The importance of being well informed

A row of bushes that divided my property from my neighbor's had gradually overgrown our boundaries. One morning my neighbor took to them with his chainsaw. The roar of the saw cut into the stillness of the morning. The smell of fuel filled the air.

I was working in my front garden when the chainsaw throttled back and my neighbor called out, "Good morning, George." He turned around to a guy who was helping him. "Rolf have you met George? Poke your head through the hole in the bushes and say hello."

"Hi Rolf. Pleased to meet you," I called out to the figure obscured behind the bushes. He did not bend down to look through the bushes and grunted a brief, "Hi."

I hadn't previously met Rolf but already I was forming an opinion. *Rude guy*, I thought to myself.

Later Rolf moved into my driveway to gather the branches and twigs that had fallen over the fence. He walked slowly, apparently devoid of energy, and carried a heavy wooden pole that he used to hook and raise the twigs without having to bend over. *Lazy guy*, I thought and wondered why my neighbor had bothered to have someone so sluggish assist him.

When Rolf encountered a twig he couldn't lift with the wooden pole, he tried to flick it over the fence without bending down to pick it up. After several efforts, he braced the pole firmly on the ground in front of him, slowly sliding down the pole, keeping his back straight and bending from his knees. Suddenly it dawned on me: Rolf had a major back problem, difficulties in moving, and probably significant pain. *Poor guy*, I thought to myself, now feeling sorry for him.

Rolf persisted. Slowly, methodically, at his own pace, he used the pole, or slid down it, to pick up each branch and twig that had fallen on the wrong side of our fence. He didn't stop until all were gathered and then he slowly made his way back along the driveway, over my neighbor's front lawn, and through the gate to where my neighbor was still wielding the chainsaw. *Brave guy*, I thought, now admiring his tenacity. He obviously had major problems but he wasn't lying in bed bemoaning his misfortune. He was up and doing things, choosing to live with his pain rather that give up on living because of it.

As he again disappeared behind the bushes, I began to reflect on my own observations. What had happened to my thinking? How had I gone from thinking of him as a rude and lazy person to seeing him as one who was brave and tenacious?

Rolf had not changed from the person who couldn't bend over to greet me through the bushes. It was my opinion of him that had. How had this happened? With each new piece of information, I created a new story . . . and, in turn, changed my experience. I went from seeing him negatively to admiring his tenacity. As the Greek philosophers taught us, it is *not* what a person, event, or experience is but how we *perceive* that person, event, or experience that determines how we feel about it and how we relate to it. Thank you, Rolf, for helping me to rediscover: Change your story, change your life.

Story 32

What Is the Best Choice?

Happiness-Enhancing Characteristics

Problems Addressed

> Suffering of a loved one
> Suffering caused by external factors
> Suffering that could have been avoided
> Anger, rage, and the desire for retribution

Resources Developed

> Accepting what cannot be altered
> Choosing to work with rather than fight against
> Learning to research and explore possibilities
> Turning potential grief and anger to productive kindness and compassion
> Reframing attitudes in more helpful directions

Learning not to get caught up in negative emotions
Learning not to respond impulsively or reactively
Looking to the future
Being proactive

Outcomes Offered

Acceptance
Reframed ideas
Thoughtful rather than emotional decisions
Reliance on logic and reason to drive actions
A future-focused orientation

Any loving parent wants the best for their child. How would you feel if your three-year-old daughter seemed to be suffering a typical bout of chicken pox but suddenly had multiple organ failure and cardiac arrest? Imagine then, if you can, that unbeknown to you at the time, she is suffering from well-known complications of chicken pox: Toxic Shock Syndrome and the rapid flesh-eating bacterium Necrotising Fasciitis that is speedily destroying her body and putting her life in danger. Try to imagine that the doctors have failed to recognize these symptoms, failed to correctly diagnose the illness, and, as a result, your daughter is left with major disfiguring and disabling problems—for life. Imagine that you later learn your daughter's extensive suffering could have been avoided if the hospital and physicians had recognized the problem. This is exactly what happened to three-year-old Isabel and her parents, Charlotte and Jason.

How would you feel and react? As a parent, anger is the first word that comes to my mind. The desire to protect our offspring is strongly hardwired through evolution and biology. Parents want and need to look after their kids if our species is to go on surviving. Threaten the young of any species and the parent is likely to attack. Anger, rage, and the desire for retribution empower us with the energy to protect our young. It would not have been a surprise to anyone—doctors and hospital included—if Isabel's parents had sued, seeking to make the doctors accountable for their actions, perhaps even rationalizing that it may prevent them making similar mistakes in the future.

They didn't. Acknowledging that Isabel would have a difficult life ahead because of her continuing deformities and need for extensive plastic surgery, they decided that money alone was not going solve the problems and that the trends in suing were only likely to put potentially good doctors off studying medicine.

So what did they do? Unable to alter what had happened to Isabel, they decided the best thing they could do to prevent these problems occurring for other children, was to help doctors reduce errors in diagnosis and improve patient care. Instead of fighting against doctors, they chose to work with them. In honor of their daughter and all patients whose lives have been impacted by missed or delayed diagnosis, they created a charity called Isabel Healthcare to

REFRAMING

help clinicians around the world do the best job possible for their patients. Working with the pediatrician who helped save Isabel's life, they spent two years researching an improved diagnostic tool. With its greater speed and accuracy, it is now used by many top-rated hospitals in the United States and in over 100 countries worldwide.

This story of Isabel's parents intrigued me. How does a person shift from attitudes of potential grief and anger to productive kindness and compassion? How did Isabel's parents make that big leap from suing doctors to supporting them? What can we learn from what they did? How too can we reframe our attitudes in more helpful directions?

The first step by Isabel's parents was what they did *not* do. They did *not* get caught up in their negative emotions. They did *not* respond impulsively or reactively to what would have been very natural parental feelings. It can be easy when we feel strongly or passionately about something to act on such emotions but it may not always be the wisest course of action.

Second, tough as it was, they accepted what had happened to Isabel and them. Unfortunately, the clock cannot be turned back. What had happened could not be changed. Isabel would have continuing lifelong problems and suing wasn't going to alter that.

Third, they looked to the future. Accepting that Isabel's circumstance would not change, they asked what could be done to prevent similar things happening to others, and were proactive in doing it.

Finally, they relied on logic and reason to determine their actions. What was better? Was it better to join the throng of legal suits against doctors and thus risk putting people off studying medicine as a career as well as increasing medical indemnity insurance premiums and the overall cost of health services? Or was it better to support, work with them, increase the effectiveness of their skills, and improve the overall quality of health services? Logic obviously dictates the latter is the most beneficial to the most people.

What about Isabel? How is she? Well, it seems her parents' wise and considered course of action has paid off. Isabel is now described as being a healthy and beautiful teenager. And other children worldwide are being saved from going through the same suffering.

Story 33

Can Do, Can't Do

Happiness-Enhancing Characteristics

Problems Addressed

Conflicting ideas
Facing different and opposing attitudes

Disappointment, unhappiness, and depression
Helplessness and powerlessness

Resources Developed

Learning to see both the positive and negative
Learning to assess the positive and negative
Assessing which is the most helpful
Discovering the ability to choose

Outcomes Offered

Assessment of positives and negatives
Assessment of helpfulness
The ability to choose
Empowerment through choices

Are you as fascinated as me by catching snippets of others people's conversions at times?

The other day as I was out for a walk, I passed a couple of cyclists heading in the opposite direction. They were a mature-age couple and I wondered later if this same conversation had taken place many times in the past.

"We do," he said, in that raised voice that cyclists tend to use, as he spoke to his partner following in his wake.

"No, we don't," she called back.

"Well, we can do," he replied.

"No, we can't," she said as they cycled on and were gone before I could be privy to the rest of the conversation.

It sounded like a kid's game—can do, can't do: can do, can't do—and highlighted for me two different and diametrically opposed attitudes. One was positive, first affirming that we do and, second, acknowledging that even if we don't then we possibly can do. This attitude opens doors, it allows for possibilities, it can foresee future potentials even if they aren't currently present. The other was negative, closing doors, limiting possibilities, and denying future potentials.

Another thing I found interesting was that two people could hold two such different views about whatever the topic might have been. There was no absolute. Neither person was necessarily right or wrong. Their attitude was just a particular point of view that each had chosen to take.

If it is a choice then, I found myself thinking, *which attitude is the most useful or helpful to hold?*

Of course, it pays to realistically assess what is and isn't achievable. I may not, for example, be able to change the time the sun will rise tomorrow, the weather we have today, the behavior of another driver on the road, the decision by my boss to retrench me, or my lover's choice to leave. If I don't accept the reality of the things I cannot change, if I hold onto a false optimism, I am destined to disappointment, unhappiness, and maybe even depression.

The can-do-can't-do game is not one that is just played out between people as was happening for these two cyclists but it is one we can play out in our own heads as well: Those times when we are of two minds about something, when we are experiencing an internal tug-of-war, when we feel caught between the devil and the deep blue sea, or are rendered helpless and powerless by our internal indecisiveness. *Can I? Can't I? Will I? Won't I?* At such times it can be easy to get so caught in the struggle that we forget we have a choice.

If I have that choice, then it pays to ask, "Which attitude is the more useful for me to hold?" *Can do, can't do, can do, can't do.* "Which belief or attitude will serve me best?"

Story 34

Finding Creative Alternatives

Happiness-Enhancing Characteristics

Problems Addressed

Feeling trapped
Encountering terrifying situations
Lacking control
Sense of powerlessness
Fear
Self-limiting thoughts
Inhibited desire to be happy

Resources Developed

Questioning and challenging self-limiting thoughts
Considering alternative viewpoints or perspectives
Letting go of current negativity
Shifting attitudes toward the positive
Selecting or adopting more positive and useful images

Outcomes Offered

Suspension of self-limiting thoughts
Reframing of negative images
Selection and adoption of positive attitudes
Utilization of reframed images for more positive actions and emotions

"I want to see the sun," she said. "I want to *feel* the sun," she added with emphasis, "but it's like a mountain is in the way and blocking it out. It feels like I have a huge task ahead of me to dig away the mountain, to excavate it, to get it out of the way before the sun can shine on me and brighten my life again."

Some 25 years before Lisa was trapped in a terrifying situation over which she had no control. A number of subsequent and similar experiences seemed to validate this sense of powerlessness and fear in her mind. Despite several attempts at therapy, she still felt she was unable to dig away the mountain that so inhibited her desire to be happy.

As I listened to her graphic metaphor, I recalled an experience of my own that I thought may help her examine and revisit her own image. So I asked her to close her eyes and proceeded to describe it.

"When you said about the mountain being in the way of sun, it reminded me of a time recently when I was trying to photograph a sunset behind an island. In the cliffs at the end of the island was a cleft in the rocks and I thought how beautiful it would be to see the sun shining through the hole in the rocks, and how much more beautiful to photograph it shining through as well. The problem was that the island was in the way. The sun was not in a direct line for me to be able to photograph it shining through the cleft."

To change or reframe a self-limiting thought the first step is to question or challenge that thought. Was Lisa's current image of the problem a helpful one for her to hold? Was it the only possible way for her to resolve these issues?

"Unfortunately," I continued, "I could not move the island to allow the sun to shine through. Nor could I move the sun to align it with the hole in the rocks. I guess that sometimes in life there are things that are unmovable or unchangeable. Sometimes there is a past that cannot be undone or altered— no matter how much we may desire the contrary. So while I could not move the island or the sun I realized I could move myself."

Having questioned a current unhelpful thought or image, the next step to reframing it is to be open to considering other possible alternative views. How else could Lisa envisage getting on top of the problem? What other more helpful, more practical, more achievable ways were there for her to see and feel the sun without having to excavate a whole mountain?

"I started to walk up the beach. Gradually the sun appeared to move closer to the cleft but it was actually *me* making the movement. By shifting myself I was able to align the sun with the hole in the rock. The golden, warm light of the sunset shone through and I was able to capture the image on my camera. Even more importantly, I captured it in my mind in a way that I can now revisit it whenever I want."

Once we have explored other possible thoughts, images, and solutions we need to select or adopt one that is more positive and useful for us.

As I told Lisa the story of my experience I saw the corners of her mouth lifting in a smile. When she opened her eyes she said, "I felt like I could laugh. I felt so happy. Even before you started telling me about moving along the beach I realized that I could climb the mountain and not have to dig it away as I had previously been so frustratingly focused on doing. I realized I had to get on top of it, to climb to the summit, if I was to allow the light and the warmth of the sun to brighten up my life."

Story 35

A Terrible Gift

Happiness-Enhancing Characteristics

Problems Addressed

Suffering from a disability
Facing a life-threatening circumstance
Facing major life challenges

Resources Developed

Developing mind–body control
Learning the art of observation
Learning from personal experience
Sharing your learnings with others
Acknowledging the terribleness of reality
Accepting reality, what cannot be changed
Learning to move beyond the concept of "terrible"
Reframing ideas through practice and training

Outcomes Offered

Acknowledgement of reality
Acceptance of reality
Reframing of negatives to positives
Holding both negatives and positives together

Have you have ever heard of Dr Milton Erickson? He was a famous psychiatrist whose name is up there with the likes of Sigmund Freud. The reason I mention him now is because he suffered with polio, a condition that he described in a strangely paradoxical way as "a terrible gift." How could a polio sufferer describe his illness as a gift? How could a gift be described as terrible?

Erickson's life was challenging from the beginning. As a child he was both dyslexic and color blind. He contracted polio at the age of 17, saying later that, as he lay in bed, he overheard the three doctors tell his mother in the other room that her boy would be dead in the morning. He decided he wouldn't be . . . and he wasn't.

Nonetheless, he was bed-ridden, totally paralyzed, and speechless. Able to only move his eyeballs and hear, he utilized his only abilities to become an astute observer of people and his environment. He developed a strong awareness of the significance of non-verbal communications between people such as body language, tone of voice, and the way that non-verbal expressions can contradict verbal ones. He learnt that his sisters could say "no" when they meant "yes" or vice versa, or that they could offer another sister an apple yet hold it back.

He carefully observed how a baby sister began to crawl, knowing that, like her, he too would have to learn to stand up and walk again. Could he recall how his muscles previously stood and walked? Slowly, concentrating on these 'body memories,' he began to resume his speech and arm movements. Again utilizing his abilities he employed the growing strength in his arms to undertake a solo, thousand mile canoe trip. By the end, he was able to walk again with the aid of a cane.

Lacking the physical strength to follow in his father's footsteps as a farmer, Erickson devoted himself to study, became a medical student, was intrigued with psychiatry, obtained a degree in psychology, and went on to become one of the world's most famous psychiatrists.

In his fifties, post-polio syndrome resulted in severe pain, muscle weakness, and paralysis, confining him to a wheelchair. From his own personal experience of pain, he learnt important things about both pain and pain management that he was able to share with patients and students. Indeed, students flocked from all over the world to sit at the feet of this master of their profession and learn from his wisdom.

Milton Erickson died in March 1980, aged 78, leaving a lasting legacy to the fields of psychology, psychiatry, psychotherapy, and hypnotherapy. Would he have made such a contribution if he had not had polio? Erickson described his polio, paradoxically, as a terrible gift. While it might seem like a mixed message by using the word 'terrible,' he first *acknowledged* that it was a horrible, rotten, and undesired thing to happen to someone. If he could have wound back the clock of time, if he could have altered history, I am sure he would definitely have preferred a life without polio. The reality was that it was terrible. Who would wish polio, pain, suffering, illness, trauma, or disability on themselves? It was truly a terrible thing to have happen, especially to someone so early in life.

If he had stayed with that one word, seeing his polio solely as 'terrible,' what would have been the consequence? My guess is he would likely have felt depressed, disempowered, and not achieved the many things he did.

Seeing it as 'terrible' allowed him to not only *acknowledge* the reality but also *accept* it. This, unfortunately, was what life had dealt him. He could do nothing to change it. There was no point in fighting against something that would not alter, no point in being bitter or miserable. Non-acceptance of the terrible reality of his polio would result in immense despair. Then he would have the unchangeable fact of his polio *and* he would be horribly depressed to boot.

On the other hand, if he accepted the fact that he had polio *and* that it was a terrible, unchangeable fact, then he was free to get on with life.

However, this for me is where the really interesting bit happens. Erickson then *moved beyond* the concept of 'terrible' to describe his polio as a gift. How does someone do that? How do you shift from seeing the terribleness of a life-disabling problem to viewing it as a gift? I guess, first, there is something essentially practical about it: if you can't alter a disability, how can you use it to your benefit? Seeing a problem as a gift adds a positive to it, it opens up hope, and it contributes meaning.

I guess too, it was not just a sudden, mind-changing revelation for Erickson but rather something he worked at—perhaps even constantly having to remind himself, time and time again, that there were better, more helpful ways to view his personal challenge. Did he lie in bed at night reminding himself of the daily benefits the polio had afforded him? Did he reflect back on life valuing the fact that, because of the polio, he chose a career in medicine rather than farming? Did he think when working with a pain patient, "I have my own pain to thank for what I have learnt and can share?" I don't know exactly *how* he trained his mind to think of a potential negative in such positive terms. There are many ways we can practice thinking more of the thoughts we want.

However, it was as he lay paralyzed with polio that Erickson developed and honed his own abilities to observe, understand non-verbal communications, use mind-body healing processes, and manage pain. These in turn formed the basis for his ground-breaking approach to psychiatry that has helped ease the suffering of many, many others. I have often wondered in life's tough times how I can be more like Erickson. How can I truly acknowledge and accept how terrible something is, *and* also see it for the good it may hold as a precious gift?

Story 36

It May Not Be As Bad As You First Think

Happiness-Enhancing Characteristics

Problems Addressed

> Feeling embarrassed
> Feeling stupid
> Hopelessness and helplessness
> Self-beration

Resources Developed

> Reframing skills
> Looking beyond the first, and worst, imagined scenario
> Seeing things may not be as bad as you first thought

Outcomes Offered

> Holding a positive attitude
> Seeing beyond initial impressions
> Looking for the positive outcome

Isn't it interesting how, at times, you can learn something unexpected from an unexpected person in an unexpected place or circumstance? I was staying in a hotel in Reykjavik, the capital city of Iceland, when it happened. I lost the door card to my hotel room. Usually I am careful and routine with this. I always put the door card in my wallet along with my credit and other cards. However—jetlagged out of my mind after some 40 hours of transit from Australia—I lost it, and lost it well. It had to be in the room as I had let myself in with it. Nonetheless, multiple strip searches of my wallet, my pockets, my bags, and the room itself failed to find it. I felt embarrassed, stupid, hopeless, helpless. I would have to go to reception and confess to my stupidity. I berated myself. *How dumb can you be?*

To help put you in the picture of what happened next, I need to let you know that I have written eight books—four of these about the use of metaphors and storytelling as tools for communicating important life messages. Consequently, I like to think of myself as having at least a little knowledge on this topic. But the hotel receptionist, Unnur, was a true master. As we walked up the stairs, a new key card held in her hand, she told me a story within a story. "I had a dream recently," she began quite casually. "I was standing in front of a mirror. I put my hand to my head and a large clump of hair came away in my hand. I looked at my hand. It was full of hair and I felt so distressed. Was I going bald? Was I going to lose all my hair? In my distress, I looked back at the mirror. Only a small clump had come away. It didn't look so bad as I had first imagined. I brushed the rest of my hair across the patch. It looked much better, almost normal. Nobody would really notice it at all."

"My interpretation of the dream," she continued with the confidence of a professional dream analyst, "was that you might initially see something as bad but it may not be as bad as you first think."

"Then," she added, "I recently had a car accident. It was, without question, my fault. I had not looked properly and backed into a bollard damaging the car's fender and breaking a rear light. My first thought was, 'Damn! The car repairs will mean I can no longer afford the new dress I wanted for Christmas.' Then I thought, 'I have enough dresses any way. I don't really need to spend more on another.' I realized that no one had been hurt or killed, so that was good."

As Unnur pushed the key card into the lock and opened the door, she concluded, "Sometimes you might see something as bad but it may not be as bad as you first thought."

Yes, I thought as the door closed behind me. At first, I had felt embarrassed, stupid, hopeless, and helpless about losing the door card to my hotel room but if I had not lost it I would never have seen this master of metaphor plying her story-telling skills, been reminded of the value of holding a positive attitude, nor gained the story that you have just heard. Thanks to an unexpected story from an unexpected person in an unexpected place I was reminded of an important life message . . . and felt better. *Something you see as bad may not be as bad as you first thought. In fact, something positive may unexpectedly emerge from it.*

REFRAMING

7 On Changing Patterns of Behavior

> Behavior is the mirror in which everyone shows their image.
> Johann Wolfgang von Goethe, writer, artist, and politician

Introduction

Having established patterns of behavior can be helpful and functional. For example, having a morning routine of getting up at the same time, eating breakfast, taking a shower, and brushing your teeth in a certain order means you don't have to reinvent that pattern of behavior every day to ensure that you get to work on time. These patterns are usually established through repetitive rehearsal like learning to drive a car. At first you have to think carefully about where the pedals are and how you depress one while you release another. You have to concentrate on how smoothly or sharply you turn the steering wheel and how your feet can be operating the pedals while your hands are managing the wheel and indicators and, at the same time, keeping your eyes on the road. Through practice, these behavioral patterns become so ingrained that you may not even notice when you are doing them. Such patterns provide stability, safety, and efficiency in our lives. Once learnt, we don't have to stop and think through the process each and every time we use them.

Once our minds have learnt such patterns, they are less likely to make value judgments about which behaviors are helpful and which are not. Some behavioral patterns can be beneficial; others may be unhelpful or even potentially self-destructive. Patterns of smoking, drinking, drug use, overeating, or anorexia can have extremely harmful physical, psychological, social, and family consequences. Learned patterns of responding to stressful or difficult life circumstances with anxiety, depression, or anger can also be deleterious. Similarly, we can learn unhelpful patterns of behavior about relationships. Take a child whose father may have struck them in anger, perhaps many times. It may have been functional and self-protective for that young child to develop patterns of fear, withdrawal, and avoidance of the aggressive figure but to take those patterns into adult relationships with all authority figures or all males can have a negative impact on work, social, and intimate relationships.

If we keep following the same old, unwanted, or unhelpful patterns of behavior, we end up having the same old results. So how do you break or change those patterns? How do we create more helpful, happy behaviors?

These are the questions explored and explained through the stories of this section. The first talks about learning new patterns of behavior, the second examines breaking complex processes down to achievable components, and then there is a tale about learning to discriminate between helpful and unhelpful behaviors. The next story provides strategies for change, followed by an example of how to change behavior by using positive thoughts, emotions, and actions. Finally, I share with you a delightful story a friend shared with me about how he changed the patterns of behavior of fellow passengers on a bus trip.

Story 37

Learning Something New

Happiness-Enhancing Characteristics

Problems Addressed

> Changing patterns of behavior
> Creating new behaviors

Resources Developed

> Learning to do something new
> Changing patterns of behavior
> Learning can, and often does, take time
> Taking a step-by-step process
> Having patience and more practice
> Extending the learning

Outcomes Offered

> Learning and change are possible
> Improvement of self, circumstances, and behavior
> Take time, step-by-step and patience
> Enjoyment of the achievement

As I stood on the back verandah and stretched my arm out, three kookaburras flew down and landed on it, eying me and my hands closely.

"Wow! How did you get them to do that?" my visiting friend asked.

How did I, I wondered. *How do you learn to do something new? How do you change a pattern of behavior?* It was certainly not something that happened suddenly any more than asking your dog to sit for the first time ensures that he does, or teaching your children to use cutlery for the first time guarantees their readiness to be taken out to a five-star restaurant. Learning can, and often does, take time.

I can't even remember when it began but I do recall it was a step-by-step process. This Australian bird, the largest member of the kingfisher family, is known for its chuckling laughter that choruses through the forests at dusk and dawn. I think the kookaburras must have been hanging around in the trees while parrots came down to peck seeds from the bird feeder in the backyard. Kookaburras are not seed eaters but prefer insects like locusts and small reptiles like lizards. Wondering if they would eat meat, I placed some on a feeder tray but there it remained, untouched. Then, one day, the meat had gone. A few days later some more meat disappeared. Then I caught sight of a lone kookaburra who had made the discovery. At first, as soon as he saw me he took flight but over the weeks he allowed me to edge a little closer.

As well as taking time and being a step-by-step process, it was a game of patience for both of us. Soon the kookaburra began to anticipate the times I would put the meat out and was there before me. Patiently, inch by inch, I made my way closer to him, a process that took months. *Would he take it from my hand?* I wondered. I extended my hand out flat with the meat sitting on it but he flew off to a neighboring tree, watchfully eyeing me, and waited until I placed it on the tray and stepped back a little before again descending. I also have no recollection of how long it was before he stopped flying away at the sight of my extended hand and began to pluck the meat from it.

Once he had made this step, he knew he could safely do it again, and the more we did it, the more both of us became familiar with this new behavior— and the more we built a trusting relationship.

If he could eat from my hand, I then wondered, *might he land on my arm while he did so?* Again, step-by-step with time and patience and more practice, I put my arm between him and the hand that cupped the meat. At first, he refused to eat with my arm in between, then one day he tried to hop over my arm. For whatever reason, he eventually hopped onto my arm.

Now when I walk outside I extend my arm and, if he is around, he will immediately land on it—whether I am holding food or not.

After a while, he started to bring in his family. Each season new, squawking young kookaburras accompany him, hanging back in the trees while he gathers mince from my hand to take back to feed them. As they have grown, they have followed his behavior and started to land directly on my arm without the slow patient training that went into their patriarch.

I am careful to just allow them a small taste on intermittent days as I want them to forage naturally and not become dependent on me as their food source.

So when my friend asked, "How did you get them to do that? How did you change their behavior?" it triggered me to think about the process. How do you learn? How do you change or improve patterns of behavior? Like with the kookaburras, learning and change are both possible. We can all learn to improve ourselves, our circumstances, and our behavior. After some thought,

I was able to answer, "With time, a step-by-step process, patience, and continued practice."

Now I can have three or four kookaburras land on my arm at a time. They are willing to sit there patiently, usually longer than I am willing or able to hold up my arm. At times they will burst into a chorus of laughter. And I find myself laughing, too.

Story 38

Change Your Thoughts Change Your Behavior

Happiness-Enhancing Characteristics

Problems Addressed

Seeing tasks as too big, difficult, or challenging
Self-doubts
Doubts about abilities, skills, or tenacity

Resources Developed

Taking the first step
Learning to stop and assess progress
Recognizing boosts to confidence
Learning to focus attention
Taking confidence in achievements
Building on achievements
Learning to take it one step at a time

Outcomes Offered

Self-reassurance
A sense of achievement and accomplishment
Appreciation of intrinsic values
Enjoyment in the process

Change your thoughts change your behavior. How many times have I heard this in my training? How many times have I offered this seemingly sound advice to clients? And how many times have I had to rediscover it for myself?

Have you ever had the experience of looking at a task or challenge and thinking to yourself, *How will I ever be able to do it?* It seems too big, too much, too difficult, too challenging. You find yourself doubting your self, your abilities, your skills to learn, or your tenacity to get it done.

That's how I felt when my editor asked me to write a book of 101 stories that colleagues could use with their clients in therapy. At first I doubted myself. That might seem as strange to you as it does to me. I had already written seven books, including three on this particular subject. They have sold well, received good reviews, and gained much collegiate acclaim. All this you might think is good evidence for me to know I could do it. If I have done it before, surely I could do it again. But self-doubt does not always follow such sound logic or reason. I said no, declining her invitation.

Then one day as I watched a neighbor and his helper working in the garden, I found myself observing my own thoughts. They formed into a story in my head and a day or two later I jotted it down on my laptop. Was this the start of a book? I doubted it. I had recorded just one story. If it was to be a book I needed 100 more. It was still too formidable to consider.

However, taking the step of just writing one story began to focus my thoughts in that direction. I began to think back on stories I had previously used with clients. I began to note and record stories of life and experiences that I could potentially use with clients. This was something I normally did orally in my work as a therapist, but I didn't always record them.

A few months later, I had recorded 19. I was almost 20% on the way to writing the 101 stories I needed for a book, and that felt great. It was a boost to my confidence.

Then, like a sledge hammer it hit me: I still had 82 to go! Again the task loomed into overwhelming hugeness. I still had four-fifths to go or more than 80%. *Would I ever be able to do it?* I questioned in self-doubt.

Then I asked myself. *What do I focus my attention on? Do I look back on what I have achieved and allow myself the sense of confidence in my achievements? Or do I look ahead and scare myself about what I had yet to do? Do I use my past achievements as a foundation on which to build for the rest of the task? Or do I just focus on the current story I am writing and take it one step at a time?*

When I reached 50 stories, I paused to reflect again. I had now written half a book, but that meant I still had half to go. Was my proverbial glass half full or half empty? How did I see it? And did the way I see it influence the way I felt and what I did? If I had a choice, how could I choose what was helpful?

Time went by, stories accumulated. With 82 I was more than 80% there. Only 19 stories to go. Now the goal really seemed in sight. I felt like an athlete turning onto the final lap. I could see the finish line. *If you have come this far,* I reassured myself, *surely you have proven your ability to go the rest of the distance.*

There is a sense of achievement or accomplishment in getting to where you want to get, and we know that such feelings contribute to our happiness and well-being. Hopefully, too, there is a sense of intrinsic value or enjoyment in the process. Like the old proverb says: The enjoyment is often more in the journey than the arriving.

Well, as I am sure you have guessed, I got my 101 stories written. I tweaked them and tweaked them again. I got them to my publisher who put them into a book. Yes, I rediscovered: Change your thoughts and you change your behavior.

Story 39

Discriminating Behaviors

Happiness-Enhancing Characteristics

Problems Addressed

> When the going gets tough
> When feeling under threat
> When under pressure or stress
> Loneliness
> withdrawl
> Unthinking, habitual patterns of reacting

Resources Developed

> Learning to discriminate
> Learning to be calm
> Reassuring your mind
> Relaxing breathing and muscles
> Practicing new behaviors
> Coaching and encouraging others

Outcomes Offered

> Discrimination skills
> Choice about when to protect and when to relax
> Choice between helpful and unhelpful behaviors

Whenever the going got tough, whenever it felt under threat, whenever it sensed pressure or stress, the porcupine raised its long, fierce looking quills. They stuck up like a battalion of soldiers' spears, warning off any perceived threat. This had its advantages. It scared off animals that might otherwise want to make a meal of him but it also had its disadvantages. *Everyone* kept their distance, wary of his dangerous looking quills. From a distance, and with envy, he would watch the friendlier animals. They ate together, socialized together, and played together. They had family and friends to share life's day-to-day experiences and pleasures—all things he would love to have had in his own life. But instead the porcupine spent most of his time wandering the forest alone and lonely, a right prickly soul.

Whenever the going got tough, whenever it felt under threat, whenever it sensed pressure or stress, the turtle retreated into itself, pulling its head and legs into the sheltering protection of its shell. This had its advantages. It defended the turtle from animals that might otherwise want to make a meal of her but, as the porcupine had found with its quills, it also had its disadvantages. Everyone began to avoid the turtle who kept withdrawing into itself when anyone got close. From a distance, when she felt she could safely take a subtle peek out, she would watch the friendlier animals. They ate together, socialized together, and played together without having to constantly hide from each other. They had family and friends to share life's day-to-day experiences and pleasures—all things she would love to have had in her own life. Instead, the turtle, like the porcupine, spent most of her time wandering the forest alone and lonely, hiding its true self in a tough shell.

One day these two lone travelers met each other on a forest trail. The porcupine instantly thrust up his quills and the turtle instantly withdrew into her shell.

"Why do you do that?" asked the porcupine.

With its beady eyes peering out of a dark hole in it shell, the turtle asked, "Why do *you* do that?"

"Do what?" replied the porcupine.

"Raise those scary quills when you know I couldn't hurt you," said the turtle.

"It's what I've always done and always do," answered the porcupine realizing that it had become an unthinking habit, a habitual way of reacting whether the situation required it or not.

"I wish I was like you," said the turtle. "I wish I had quills to raise then I could keep my head and feet out and others would not see me as a recluse and want to avoid me."

"I wish I was like you," said the porcupine. "Then I wouldn't frighten others off and they wouldn't avoid me."

"Obviously your quills work," responded the turtle. "They keep enemies away. They keep you safe and alive. Maybe it is just a matter of learning to discriminate when they are helpful and when they are not. If I am not a threat to you now, can you let them down?"

"To do that I need to calm myself a little," said the porcupine. "Let me reassure my mind that you are safe, slow my breathing, and relax my muscles a bit." Slowly his quills sank back to the line of his body.

"Ah, that feels better," he added. "I feel so tense, agitated, and on edge when they are up. Now, what about you? How can you poke your head out again and begin to enjoy the things outside of that dark hole?"

The turtle, following the porcupine's example, tried to reassure her own mind that she was safe. She let her breathing and muscles relax a bit before slowly, carefully extending her head and legs.

"Hey, we did it," shouted the porcupine joyfully.

"Perhaps we just need to assess when times are helpful to raise quills or retreat into a shell and when they are not. And then practice," commented the turtle.

"Raise or relax?" said the porcupine like a mantra, practicing it as he did.

"Retreat or relax?" echoed the turtle, practicing as she spoke, too.

Together they wandered the forest trails as the closest of friends, coaching and encouraging each other to discriminate and practice what to do and when. They had learnt to choose the times to be protective—and the times to enjoy.

Story 40

Overcoming Fear

Happiness-Enhancing Characteristics

Problems Addressed

Fear
Symptoms of anxiety
Anxiety impacting on a relationship
Feelings of helplessness and powerlessness

Resources Developed

Using positive role models
Building preventative strategies
Learning to reality test
Appreciating the values of fear
Discriminating between real and imagined fears
Accepting the temporary nature of emotions
Learning to change emotions positively
Asking helpful questions

Outcomes Offered

Skills in fear management
Reassurance
Anxiety is a normal human emotion
Anxiety can be healthy and helpful
It is possible to build coping strategies
Calmness

Sam was afraid. It doesn't particularly matter what he was afraid of. He could have been afraid of public speaking, of heights, of being in crowded places, of urinating in public toilets, of meeting the opposite sex, of flying in planes, of driving on busy highways, or any of a great number of things. It doesn't matter what he was afraid of because the processes for developing a fear—and the processes for getting over it—are much the same no matter what the fear is about.

What did matter for Sam was that his fear was affecting his life, badly. When afraid he would experience butterflies in his stomach, his palms would become hot and sweaty, he felt flushed, his thinking became blurry and self-focused, and he just wanted to get out of the situation. His work and social life were being impacted as he felt he wasn't performing as well as he knew he could. His wife told him it was time he got over it. He couldn't put his finger on it, work it out, or understand what was going on. Sam felt increasingly helpless and powerless.

His therapist said, "I am amazed you have managed to cope with this intense fear for so long. How have you done that?"

"I don't know. I guess I have just done it," he answered.

"It is good to know that you can, at least in some circumstances and some times, even if not all the time," responded his therapist. "Perhaps it might be interesting to see how others do that. How does your wife get on top of fear? How do your work colleagues or friends deal with scary times? You might like to ask some people you know who cope well with stress how they do it."

One morning over breakfast, Sam asked his wife, "Are there times when you get frightened or scared?"

"I certainly get frightened about the kids at times," she said. "I worry if they may step out on the road without looking and get run over. And I worry about you at the moment. I am afraid for you and for us if things keep going on like this."

Sam didn't think her fears were on the same scale but still asked, "When you are afraid, what do you do?"

"I do what I can to prevent the feared thing from happening. As you know we teach the kids to look before crossing a road. We teach them to be careful. If I do all I can to prevent something, then I know there is less need to be frightened."

Not sure he had received the answer he was looking for, Sam asked a work colleague, "If you get frightened or fearful at times how do you handle it?"

"Who doesn't get anxious or scared from time to time?" came the reply. "For me the worst is having to talk in a formal meeting or conference. The fear keeps me on edge, keeps me alert, and is thus a good thing. It's a matter of learning to tell the difference between when you really need to be frightened and when you don't."

Sam hadn't thought that his fear might be useful or helpful to him, at least at some times and in some circumstances. Perhaps it was a matter of learning when to take notice of it and when not to.

Next he sought out a long-standing friend. "What do you do when you are frightened?"

"Fear is temporary, isn't it?" responded his friend. "I accept that it is there, then remind myself that it is normal and won't last forever. Fear is a common human feeling. If our ancestors didn't have a healthy fear of lions and tigers, we wouldn't be here talking about it. So I tell myself that the feeling will pass. Then I try to do something that feels nice, or is happier, or more relaxing— something that helps it to pass quicker. Usually I'm back to feeling pretty good pretty soon."

I wonder if Sam had asked even more people who manage their anxiety well what other answers or ideas he may have gleaned.

When Sam went to bed that night it was with lots of thoughts in his mind about the conversations he'd had during the day. What could he learn from the things his wife, his work colleague, and his friend did, from the people who cope well with stress? Was there something in what they said about prevention, acceptance, utilization of the fear, and discriminating when it is helpful and when not? How could he incorporate their approaches and attitudes into his own life?

If nothing else, Sam felt a reassurance that he was not alone, that fear was a normal human emotion, and, at times, might even be a healthy and helpful human experience. Acknowledging that others can and have built strategies to deal with fear effectively, he felt a new calmness in himself . . . and drifted into a peaceful sleep.

Story 41

Ask and You May Receive

Happiness-Enhancing Characteristics

Problems Addressed

> Indecision
> Self-doubt
> Lack of confidence
> Negative thinking
> Inaction

Resources Developed

> Using positive thinking
> Taking positive action
> Being self-confident
> Learning to change emotions positively
> Learning to just do it

Outcomes Offered

> Goal achievement
> Take courageous action
> Ask and you may receive

"How did you get the Dalai Lama to write a foreword for one of your books?" asked my good friend and colleague, Michael.

When Dr Helen Street and I were jointly writing *Standing Without Shoes* we discussed who we might like to invite to write a foreword. She suggested, "What about the Dalai Lama. You have had some privileged contact with him. Perhaps you can ask him. Nothing ventured, nothing gained."

Yes, it is true that I have been privileged to meet with him personally on several occasions. I participated with him in a symposium about Eastern and Western concepts of the mind. I shared afternoon tea with him before the symposium. I have had three audiences with him and attended several of his teachings. He is a master of Buddhist psychology and keenly interested in the science and practice of Western psychology. Core to his ideas and teaching is the concept that we all want to be happy and his life mission is to help show ways that we can be happier. As the book I was writing with Helen was about relieving depression and enhancing happiness, about showing ways for people to be happier, he seemed a logical choice for the foreword.

However, when I look back at my response to Helen's suggestion, I smile at myself. Isn't it interesting, at times, how we can stop ourselves doing something before we even start? That is exactly what I did. I found all the reasons why *not* to ask him.

"Oh, he is such a busy person," I told myself as much as Helen. "He would have no time to read and comment on our humble manuscript with his busy international itinerary. Anyway, why would he be interested in our small book by a couple of little known Aussie psychologists? And is it appropriate for us to give such a prominent world figure another task, or put him in a position of having to say yes or no?"

I guess we all know at some level that our thoughts and attitudes have the power to either limit us or expand us. They can grind us into inactivity (as they commonly do in depression) or inspire us to action (as they commonly do for people who are high achievers). Mine were certainly limiting me. I did nothing about writing to the Dalai Lama.

As the weeks ticked by, Helen and I discussed other potential people we could ask to write the foreword but none seemed to fit as well as the Dalai Lama. Still I hesitated, reluctant and full of reasons why I shouldn't.

Then one day I picked up a colleague's book and saw the Dalai Lama had written the foreword to his book. *Our book is equally as good*, I thought. Then the negative quickly set in again: *Perhaps he knows the Dalai Lama better than me. Perhaps. . . . Perhaps. . . .* And, my thoughts once more ground me into inactivity.

Nonetheless, Helen's words kept coming back to me: *Nothing ventured, nothing gained*. I believed we had written a book that would be helpful and practical for people wanting to enhance their well-being. Maybe it would reach more people and be more helpful with a foreword by the Dalai Lama. So, in a brave moment, thinking of that famous advertisement, *just do it*, I sent an email off to the Dalai Lama's secretary explaining what we were writing and asking if His Holiness may be interest in contributing a foreword. His secretary requested that we send a copy of the manuscript, which, of course, I did.

Immediately after, I departed for a month's teaching on a Greek island where there was no access to the internet. On arriving home, I found an envelope with the stamp of the Office of His Holiness the Dalai Lama on the back. Eagerly opening it, I pulled out two sheets of handmade paper, the Dalai Lama's logo at the top, the generous foreword followed, and his personal signature inscribed at the bottom. He had *just done it*!

"How did I get the Dalai Lama to write a forward for our book?" I replied to Michael. "I guess I asked."

"Cool story," he said sagely. "Ask and you may receive."

Story 42

Modeling the Behaviors You Want

Happiness-Enhancing Characteristics

Problems Addressed

Being distressed
Unacceptable patterns of behavior
Uncertainty about how to act

Resources Developed

Forming positive bonds on which to build change
Assisting others to adopt more desirable behaviors
Helping to guide or influence the behavior of others
Setting a role-model in our own behavior
Changing oneself to set an example for others to change

Outcomes Offered

Change is possible
Role-modeling can be an effective agent for change
Change yourself to set an example for others to change

A colleague and friend of mine in Bhutan, Pema Wangchuk, recently sent me a delightful and thoughtful story he wrote and has generously given me permission to retell it to you here. Pema has a passionate concern for the environment. I have also found him to be an astute observer of human behavior and a keen student of how to help change behavior for the better. In this story, he tells of journeying by bus from his home town of Mongar to attend a course in Bhutan's capital city of Thimphu.

"My seat was in the last row of the bus with four of us across the row. I always find it fun travelling in a bus, glancing out of the window at the beautiful environment, meeting the different characters of the passengers, and sharing snacks and drinks with nearby passengers as we communally do when journeying in Bhutan. Generously, the person sitting on my right side near the window offered the four of us snacks of chips and sweets as well as juice. While it was enjoyable sharing the snacks and juice, I found it distressing to watch the other two people sitting on my left throwing their used packaging and juice bottles out of the bus window."

"I felt like telling them to stop throwing their trash out into such beautiful, natural forests—but we all know what their answer would have been. Instead I kept my patience, putting my own snack packaging and juice bottle in my pocket."

Half way through the journey the bus stopped for a lunch break near a local hotel. As Pema walked from the bus, he dumped his trash in a dustbin near the hotel entrance. Following lunch he bought some snacks and fruit juices for the second half of their journey to Thimphu.

Pema picked up his story. "This time it was me who offered the snacks and the juices to my new-found, last-row friends which they accepted with a smile and thanks. After the person sitting on my left had finished, I hoped to set a good example by immediately offering to take his packaging and juice bottle . . . but he replied by saying that he would throw them out from the window."

"What was I to do? This was a crucial moment. I explained to him that it is not good to throw rubbish from the bus window. Offering an alternative, I said, 'Let me keep it in this plastic bag. I will throw it in the dustbin when we stop next.'"

"Not only did he give me the waste but he also gave me a smile. The other two seated in our backseat row heard and observed the interaction. As they finished their snacks, without question or comment, they put their waste in the plastic bag I had kept for that very purpose. I was so happy that I thanked them, appreciatively."

As I read Pema's story, I wondered what had worked to happily bring about such a change. How can we assist others to adopt healthier, happier, or more desirable actions? Is it in the things that we say, the things that we do, or perhaps a blend of both? Can we best help, guide, or influence the behavior of others by lecturing on what is appropriate or by setting a role-model in our own behavior?

Pema concluded, "In reflecting back on the events of the journey, I wondered if I had told them earlier not to throw the waste out of the window whether it would have created a problem between us, or triggered feelings of resentment and anger. To me, the story says that we need to change ourselves first if we are to set an example for others to change."

8   On Learning from Experience

Learning is experience. Everything else is just information.

Albert Einstein, scientist

Introduction

Actor Will Rogers, once said, "There are three kinds of men: Ones that learn by reading, a few who learn by observation, and the rest of them who have to pee on the electric fence and find out for themselves." This latter truly is the process of learning from experience.

Take the example of learning to drive a car. We may learn by studiously reading a driving instruction manual, we may learn by observing other people as they drive, but the majority of us learn from the experience of sitting in the driver's seat and doing it, hopefully, with an instructor beside us.

As many wise people throughout history have explained: experience is the best teacher. Let us pretend you are a young child back at school. The curriculum says you need to learn about the animals of the world. One teacher undertakes this task by showing you the pictures of the animals in a book and reading to you about them. Another teacher undertakes this task by organizing an excursion to the zoo. From which do you think you would learn the most? The experiential exercise of going to the zoo has you engaged in learning through observation and interaction. You are making discoveries of your own. You are gaining first-hand knowledge and having personal experiences of the animals rather than hearing about other people's experiences of the animals.

While most of us can readily recall examples of learning from our experiences, there are times when people don't appear to learn from life's experiences. A smoker may suffer a severe smoker's cough; a person using illicit drugs may have a number of bad trips; a person with an alcohol problem may have been fined for driving under the influence; a depressed person may be aware that getting depressed does not alter life's unfortunate circumstances—but such experiences have not resulted in a modification of the problem behaviors or emotions.

These stories offer examples of the processes of learning from experience. The initial metaphor speaks of learning to question assumptions and think through issues, calmly. There are tales about observing and making helpful choices, and about finding the people who can best guide us toward practical, experiential choices. In one, a father gives his son an important experiential learning around the concept that what you give is what you get. We all have metaphoric bridges to cross, possibly over troubled waters, as illustrated in the second last story. There is often much that we have to learn from kids, if we are willing to stop, listen, and observe. The last tale watches a child's experience of learning something new that took persistence, resilience to setbacks, a determination to keep practicing, and a step-by-step process before finally discovering the joy potentially inherent in experiential learning.

Story 43

Making Assumptions

Happiness-Enhancing Characteristics

Problems Addressed

Making assumptions
Believing in our assumptions
Taking actions based on our assumptions

Resources Developed

Learning to question assumptions
Examining the facts or evidence
Learning to stop and think through issues, calmly

Outcomes Offered

Question assumptions
Base actions on evidence rather than beliefs

It is easy for us to make assumptions about situations or people at times. However, our assumptions may not always be correct and can become a problem if we start to believe them and then begin to act on them. I once heard someone say that if you *assume* you are likely to make an *ass* out of *u* and *me*.

There is a story of a small rural village that was made up of just two parallel streets. One day a woman noticed the village elder rapidly walking out of the village with tears streaming down his eyes.

Why is he crying? she wondered and thought *Maybe someone on the next street has died.* Seeing a neighbor a short while later, she said, "I saw the elder walking out of the village crying. I think someone in the next street has died."

The neighbor told his neighbor, "Someone has died in the other street!"

Soon people up and down the length of the street were crying and grieving. Word spread to the other street with the result that the whole community became distressed, tearful, and fearful. Initially, nobody questioned it. The assumption the first person had made was believed by others and was being spread as though it were a fact.

Eventually, one of the wiser villagers asked, "Who has died? Where did the story came from?" But people were too confused and distressed to know or want to know. Someone said, "For all we know there is a deadly plague in the other street."

As you can guess, this assumption in turn was also picked up and carried through the village, spreading like wildfire. The residents of each street began to believe a plague had infected the other street, that people were dying by the score, and that soon it would be headed their way.

Now there were two *assumptions* (first, that a single person had died and, second, that a plague was raging in the other street) that had turned into *beliefs* (almost everyone had heard the stories and were treating them as fact) and were, in turn, to be converted into *actions*.

"We must escape," someone cried, "before the plague spreads into our street. That must have been why the elder left so hurriedly." People began to gather their families and essential requirements. In haste they started to flee the village that had been their lifelong home.

Again, one of the wiser villagers asked, "Who is it that has died? How do we *know* there is a plague in the other street? Where are your facts or evidence? Let's stop and think this through calmly."

But by now the people were too panicky to listen to such wise questions or pause to weigh up the facts.

"Should we burn the village behind us to kill the plague," someone called.

"Yes," shouted someone else, "We have to kill it before it kills us."

"How could we ever come back if our homes are riddled with plague anyway?" called another as people began to hurriedly gather flammable materials and set them alight.

With their homes blazing behind them the fleeing people encountered the elder who had rapidly walked out of the village with tears streaming down his eyes. He sat on a log under a tree, his eyes still red but now dry.

"Quick," they called. "Get up. Keep running. We need to escape the plague."

"What plague?" asked the surprised elder.

"The one that caused the death of the villager you were crying for when you hurriedly left the village," came the response.

"I was crying," acknowledged the even more surprised elder, "but I wasn't crying because anyone had died. I just needed to get into the forest air quickly to help clear my eyes. I had been peeling onions in preparation for dinner."

Story 44

Stone in My Shoe

Happiness-Enhancing Characteristics

Problems Addressed

> When the unwanted or unexpected happens
> Negative thinking
> Faced with a challenge
> Unforeseen problems
> Events outside of your control
> Self-rebuke
> Worrisome thoughts

Resources Developed

> Having a choice
> Managing pain
> Distracting attention
> Making logical and practical choices

Outcomes Offered

> Choice about actions
> Practical action
> Feelings of freedom and comfort
> Enjoy experiences

This morning I went for an early walk before coming into work. Forest fragrances filled the air. The crisp breeze encouraged a brisk walk—something I needed to do anyway if I was to get to work on time. Nonetheless, it started pleasantly as I soaked in the sights, sounds, smells, and sensations of nature. Then, when I least wanted or expected it, things changed. I felt a pain in my foot. A stone had found its way into one of my sneakers and now stabbed into my sole.

Isn't that life, I thought. Just when you have planned things out, decided what you want, arranged where you are going, and have a timeline to get there, something unexpected happens. Suddenly you are faced with a challenge you hadn't anticipated, encounter a problem you hadn't foreseen, or have the master plan turned upside down by something outside of your control.

While I couldn't change the fact that a particular stone had inconveniently lodged in my shoe, I did have a choice as to what I did about it. Given my tight schedule for the walk, did I just press on and get home as quickly as possible? If so, I also had a choice how I thought about it. Did I try to ignore it or did I worry about it while I kept on walking? As strange at this latter choice may seem, it is often what we do when we are faced with a problem that has occurred outside of our choice. Suddenly our lover leaves us, our boss tells us our job is terminated, or we have a major health problem and our mind goes round in circles worrying about why he or she left, revisiting what I might have said or done to prevent it, or having endless, repetitive, unhelpful conversations in our heads.

Did I curse myself for being in a rush, trying to fit a walk in when I was limited on time, picking a stony trail to walk along, or being generally incompetent at making good decisions? While it is easy for us to slip into self-rebuke at times, it doesn't necessarily help and may even compound our problems. Were I to take this course, I would end up with two problems instead of one. First, I would still have the pain of the stone in my shoe and, second, I would now feel bad about myself.

Did I try to manage the pain? After all it was the pain that was the problem I was experiencing. No longer was I aware of the forest fragrances, the crispness of the breeze, the blue of the sky, or the calls of the birds. My attention was solely on those few cells of my body where the stone impinged on it. Did I try to distract my attention, switch off the awareness of my foot, or focus back on the pleasures of the walk? I tried to bring my attention back to the bigger picture awareness of the pleasures around me as I kept on walking but my success was fleeting. The pain was real and, naturally, it kept demanding my attention.

I am sure you are already thinking *Why not just take off your shoe and remove the stone?* Of course, that is the logical and practical choice but not always the one we make when we are caught up in either the emotion or worrisome thoughts. I found myself thinking that I was time-limited and didn't have time to stop to remove it but realized to stop and remove the stone would occupy just a few seconds. Looking ahead I saw a rock beside the trail. I paused, lifted my foot onto the rock, untied my laces, removed my shoe and shook out the stone.

For a while I continued to feel where the stone had pressed into my sole but, having taken practical action, the awareness soon faded and I was again free to enjoy the experiences of nature around me as I strode out for home, freer, quicker, and more comfortable. And with a story I now have to share with you.

Story 45

Finding a Practical Solution

Happiness-Enhancing Characteristics

Problems Addressed

Facing a challenging problem
Seeking a solution

Resources Developed

> Finding the people helpful to you
> Finding practical solutions

Outcomes Offered

If you have a practical problem, find a practical solution

A man went to see a therapist complaining that he was suffering with insomnia and unable to sleep. The therapist took a long and detailed history, asking about the man's parents, childhood, siblings, education, work, relationships, and much, much more. As the hour drew toward its end, the therapist reluctantly acknowledged to the man, "I can find no history of past traumas, psychopathology, familial patterns, or other factors to account for your insomnia."

"Oh, that's easy," replied the man. "You see there is a terrible monster that lives under my bed and is waiting to jump out and kill me as soon as I go to sleep. So I don't go to sleep."

The therapist was pensive for a while, then said, "That is serious. You are obviously suffering from delusions. It will require a lot of therapy but I believe I can help cure you."

"How?" asked the man.

"Well," responded the therapist, "I will need to see you three times a week for at least the next two years. My fees are $200 per consultation but by the end of that time you should be OK or close to it."

The man said he would like to go home, think about it, and get back to the therapist. He never did.

Some months later, the therapist and man bumped into each other in a local shopping center.

"How are you doing?" asked the therapist.

"Great," said the man. "I have slept perfectly well every night since I saw you."

"How did you manage to do that?" the surprised therapist asked.

"After our session, I went to the pub," answered the man. "I told the barman about the terrible monster that lived under my bed and was waiting to jump out and kill me as soon as I got to sleep, and the lengthy, expensive therapy you recommended. He said he could fix it for $25 and he did."

Now the therapist was even more curious. "What did he do?" he asked.

The man replied, "He came around to my house and cut the legs off the bed."

Story 46

What You Give Is What You Get

Happiness-Enhancing Characteristics

Problems Addressed

> Putting others down
> Giving out anger

Resources Developed

> Learning put-downs invite put-downs in return
> Learning anger invites anger
> Learning to be happy, you need to give happiness
> Learning to be loved, you need to give love
> Learning kindness invites kind responses
> Learning to give what you want to get

Outcomes Offered

> What you give is what you get
> To be happy, give happiness
> To be loved, give love
> To get kindness, give kindness

I am sure you have heard the saying: What you give is what you get. I was reminded of it when I heard a story about a city-based father and son who went camping for the weekend. They chose a pleasant site on the banks of a babbling stream at the base of a towering cliff. The man encouraged his son to help erect the tent and, as he was driving the pegs in the ground with a hammer, the son slipped and hit his thumbnail with the hammer. "Owwwww!" he screamed. Hardly had he got it out than he heard a voice coming from the cliff. "Owwwww!" it screamed back.

Wondering who could be mimicking him, he called out, "Who are you?" The voice copied him again. "Who are you?" it called back.

"Stop being silly," he yelled at the voice in frustration. "Stop being silly," it yelled back.

Getting angry about whoever was mimicking him, he shouted, "You're a coward!" The voice shouted back, "You're a coward!"

Now, having been brought up in the city and never before camped in the country, the boy had never encountered an echo. Puzzled he looked to his father. "What's going on?"

"Listen to this, son," replied his father. He cupped his hands to his mouth and shouted toward the cliff, "I love you!" "I love you!" called back the voice.

Then the father called, "You are the best son ever!" and, of course, the voice answered, "You are the best son ever!"

The boy was curious but still couldn't work out what was going on. So his father explained. "It's called an echo. Your own voice bounces off the cliff. What you shout out is what you receive back. It's a bit like life. What you give to life is what life gives back to you."

"If you put others down, they are likely to put you down. If you give out anger, you are likely to get anger back."

"On the other hand, if you want to be happy, you need to give happiness to others. Give out loving and caring and you are likely to receive love and caring. If you want to get love, you need to give love. If you want more kindness, give more kindness."

"I love you, Dad," shouted the boy. "I love you, Dad," bounced back the echo.

"I love you, too, son," his Dad's voice replied quietly from beside him.

Story 47

Crossing Your Bridges

Happiness-Enhancing Characteristics

Problems Addressed

> Assuming life's paths will always be smooth
> Facing sudden, unexpected challenges
> Caught in a dilemma
> Uncertainty

Resources Developed

> Learning to face sudden, unexpected challenges
> Weighing up the pros and cons
> Acknowledging and accepting anxiety
> Looking ahead
> Making a commitment
> Learning to tread carefully and mindfully
> Moving on
> Reaching a point of no return
> Reaching a chosen goal

Outcomes Offered

> Weigh up the choices
> Make considered decisions
> Commit to your choices
> Cross your bridges as you come to them

Do you know the old Simon and Garfunkel song 'Bridge Over Troubled Water'? I was thinking of it as I crossed over a bridge while trekking in West Papua. Up to this point, I had been following a clear, defined path, singing quietly in my head, enjoying the pleasures of the journey through jungle with interspersed views of the New Guinea highlands. At such times, it is easy for us to assume that because our journey is currently following a smooth path that is the way it will continue to be.

Suddenly, I found it wasn't. The comfortable track ended abruptly at a deep, steep gorge where turbulent and murky waters roared and raced below. Somebody had felled a couple of small diameter trees across the gorge as a makeshift bridge. The logs were rough and uneven, branches still protruded from them—adding a greater degree of difficulty. The surface was slippery from damp and moss. In ways Simon and Garfunkel could never have imagined, this was indeed a bridge—of sorts—over very troubled waters, a long way below. A fall into those raging rapids would unquestionably be fatal.

As there was no way around it, I was faced with a question, "Do I go back or do I press on? Do I give up or do I face the challenge and forge ahead?"

To forge ahead had a downside: it meant crossing that bridge—with very real risks. Nonetheless to forge ahead also had an upside. It meant I could continue the journey, venture into places I had never been before, and, hopefully, have new, enjoyable discoveries.

To turn back also had its upside. By avoiding the bridge, I would avoid the potential risks and be safe. And it too had its downside. My very purpose for being here, for flying all the way to West Papua, for following this particular trek, would be ended. I would no longer be able to discover what joys and pleasures might lie over the bridge or around the next corner.

Both choices had their pros and cons. Both offered potential downsides and potential benefits. There was not a clear answer. I felt caught between the devil and the deep blue sea. In such a dilemma, what was I to do?

To cross the bridge, there were things I would put at risk such as a level of safety and security—perhaps even my life. However, having already walked several days to reach this point, I did not want to retread an old path any more than I wanted to give up on heading in the direction I had planned and anticipated for some time.

To move forward would not be without its apprehension or anxiety either. I knew I would be likely to have butterflies in my stomach, feel my palms grow sweaty, and experience a level of discomfort. Was it worth it for the unknowns and uncertainties on the other side? I had hope that it would be but, of course, I would not know until I got there and experienced it.

To make the first step would be a commitment. It would have me moving forward, stepping out into new experiences and new discoveries. Each hesitant step I would need to take carefully and mindfully, knowing that as I did I would reach a point of no return, a point where it would be difficult to turn around, a point where it would be as far to go back as to go forward.

To cross the bridge successfully, I would have to look ahead, watching my feet but also looking to my destination. Everyone knows, in such situations, the worst thing is to look down as that focuses attention on the dangers rather than the goal. *Where you look is where you are likely to go, so keep your eyes ahead*, I reminded myself.

I also realized that once I had crossed there would be no turning back. What was behind me would stay behind me. I could not go back. I could not alter the past. I could not change what had happened in the past. I would need to accept the choice I had made, and move on.

To cross my challenging bridge would not necessarily mean there were no further bridges or challenges to be met. It would not necessarily mean a smooth and clear path ahead. Nonetheless, to reach the other side meant

I could move on, be open to new possibilities, and discover more pleasures along the way.

What would I do if there were more challenges I hadn't yet expected, I wondered. Then I thought, *Just the same as I have done here. Weigh up the choices, make a decision, and commit to that choice. Yes, let's cross our bridges—even those over troubled waters—as we come to them*, I chuckled to myself.

And if you are wondering, yes, I did it!

Story 48

Discovering the Joy of Learning

Happiness-Enhancing Characteristics

Problems Addressed

A novice learner
Awareness of risks
A dilemma

Resources Developed

Learning something new for us to learn, observe, or discover
Finding a desire to learn
Developing a persistence to try
Developing a resilience to occasional setbacks
Finding the determination to keep practicing
Learning to take it step-by-step

Outcomes Offered

Excitement about achievement
Discoveries about self and abilities
New-found skills
Excitement, joy, and pleasure

On an interstate visit to my family, I offered to take my young grandson to the park. He responded keenly, asking if he could ride his new tricycle. At this point, he was still a novice learner, never having ventured further on his trike than his front lawn. As there was no footpath on the way to the park, we would have to travel along the side of the road, which, in the quiet suburban area, fortunately, did not have much traffic. In addition, it was slightly uphill to the park and so a little too steep for his young muscles to put sufficient pressure on the pedals. Conversely, on the way home it would be downhill with the possibility that the trike would pick up too much speed for him to control. I felt in a dilemma: should I take him or not?

I guess we are all constantly learners in life. And, isn't this part of life's excitement? There is always something new for us to learn, observe, or discover. So far my grandson had picked up the basics of when to put pressure on a pedal and when to take it off, of how to turn the handlebars and of how to keep balance. In learning, he had not always got these right. At times he hadn't put sufficient pressure on the pedals to move the trike and learnt he had to press harder. At times he had put pressure on the wrong way, started to move backwards, and learnt which way he had to pedal to move forward. At times he had turned the handlebars too acutely and toppled over with the trike, learning not to turn too sharply. At times he had fallen, cried with fear or hurt, but each time he got back up, reseated himself on the trike and tried again. He displayed those essential qualities we all need to exercise if we are going to learn: a desire to do it, a persistence in trying, an unwillingness to be put off by occasional setbacks, and a determination to practice and practice and practice again.

Given what he had already done, he was now asking my assistance to extend those skills beyond the paved areas around the house. How could I deny him such a desire to learn? How could I assist him to build his skills, even though I knew there risks involved?

When we are learning, we don't always get it right first time. Like the old saying says: If at first you don't succeed, try, try, and try again.

We may need to take it step-by-step. So with this in mind, I picked up their dog lead, looped it around the handlebars of the trike and took a little of the weight as I walked and he pedaled up the hill toward the park. My grandson pushed on the pedals, learning to apply a little more pressure on the ascent. When we got to the park, he was buzzing with excitement about his achievement: The first time he had ridden outside his own fence, the first time he had ridden to the park, the first time he had pedaled up a hill. Yet, it seemed to me, he had learnt something about more than just riding a tricycle. He had also learnt something new about himself and his abilities. He had discovered how learning to do something new can open up new options and possibilities.

After we played on the swings and slides for a while, it came time to return home. I wrapped the dog lead around the seat support this time to brace him against racing downhill too quickly. The descent was yet another new experience for him. Now he had to learn not to pedal as hard as he did going uphill, but to brace against the pedals so that the trike did not gather too much speed. Now he had to learn how to hold the handlebars very steady for the slightest turn at the increased speed could mean both he and the trike going for a tumble. The slight descent made the effort of pedaling so much easier that he was chuckling out loud with delight as his little legs spun around with the rapidly turning pedals on the downhill run. His new-found skills were giving him excitement, joy, and pleasure . . . and had me wondering whether we tend to forget such joy of learning as we grow older. Would it benefit us to pause at times, reflect on the joy of our own childhood learnings, and enquire of ourselves what new learnings may recapture such pleasure and excitement for us here in the present?

We had barely got through the gate before my young grandson leapt from his trike, helmet still on his head, and raced through the door shouting, "Mummy, mummy, I rode to the park and back all by myself!"

9 On Being Compassionate

No one is useless in this world who lightens the burden of it to anyone else.

Charles Dickens, writer

Introduction

Across cultures and time, it has long been known that our individual well-being is closely related to the well-being of those around us. Religions have taught that compassion and altruism are the foundations of a good and happy life. Jesus Christ told us to love our neighbors as we love ourselves. The Dalai Lama says that inner peace and happiness come from reducing self-centeredness and increasing compassion. These comments are not saying you should love and care for others to the total neglect of yourself any more than they are saying you should look out for 'number one' to the total neglect of others. Caring for others can indeed be self-caring and to effectively care for others you need to adequately look after you and your well-being. It is more a matter of loving you *and* loving others.

Such traditional teachings are being confirmed in the science of positive psychology as it explores what contributes to our happiness and well-being. From this we have confirmation that the very happiest of people have a network of good, close interpersonal relationships. Happy people are people people. They are interested in others, care for others, and stretch out their hand to offer help when it is needed. These are some of the sound bases on which good interpersonal relationships work. If you meditate on showing loving kindness to others your own happiness levels increase and if you actually engage in actions of helping others, some research has shown, your happiness is likely to increase more than those you are helping.

Genuine compassion is based on the recognition that others have the same right to happiness as you—including your enemies. You cannot harbor negative feelings toward others and expect them to be friendly to you. If you act harmfully toward others, you can expect they will act harmfully toward you. In contrast, and by simple logic, if you want your world to be friendly and caring then you must be friendly and caring toward others. Compassion naturally promotes such a positive atmosphere, it leads to positive relationships, and, in turn, facilitates feelings of peace, contentment, and well-being. Caring for others is, in turn, caring for you. And to be caring of others you need to be caring of yourself.

The stories of this chapter explore the research basis of how helping others can help the self, offer case examples of showing compassion, and examine the issue of when you may need to show tough love. They draw on the importance of benevolent intentions and how kindness leaves lasting impressions.

Story 49

Can I Help Myself by Helping Others?

Happiness-Enhancing Characteristics

Problems Addressed

Perceptions of being victimized
Having a major illness

Resources Developed

Finding unexpected benefits
Discovering that givers can be receivers
Perceiving you are helping others
Having a positive, enhancing role in others' lives

Outcomes Offered

Lowered levels of depression
Enhanced feelings of peacefulness
Knowledge that helping others can help the self

I am always fascinated by research in which researchers undertake an experiment expecting to find evidence to support their hypothesis and end up finding something quite different or unexpected. How often in work, recreation, relationships, or life—as well as research—do we set out with an idea of how things should turn out only to find that they don't? And finding the unexpected may turn out to be a bonus rather than a disappointment. If we are open to the possibilities, it can challenge us, change our perspective, and allow us to learning something new.

This is exactly what happened for a colleague, Dr Carolyn Schwartz, while undertaking postdoctoral research at Harvard Medical School. Working with people with multiple sclerosis (MS) she set out to explore which of two different programs or interventions would have the greatest benefits in enhancing the patients' health-related quality of life. The first one she called a coping skills group in which the people with MS were taught coping flexibility to manage their illness and thus, hopefully, improve their quality of life. This group was seen as the active intervention and Dr Swartz fully expected it would be the one to yield the most benefit to those who were participating.

In the second intervention, people with MS were simply offered telephone support by fellow MS sufferers. For this, five lay people with MS but no professional counseling background were trained in active listening skills so that they could empathically listen without giving directive support when the research participants phoned. They were not to divulge their own personal information, but rather to listen deeply, responding either with statements that rephrased the participants own words so that the participants felt heard and understood, or to ask questions that deepened the communication and allowed a further exploration of themes or feelings raised by the other person. Each of these active listeners had a case load of five to 15 people with multiple sclerosis who could call them for 15 minutes once a month for one year. All of the supporters or active listeners were women who had a broad range of disability from their MS. Some had no apparent symptoms while one was wheelchair-bound and had only one functional finger. In age they ranged from their early thirties to early sixties.

Dr Swartz looked on the active listening as a control group intervention, which in scientific jargon means the group you don't expect to change and, therefore, can use as a basis to measure the changes in the other group. And this turned out to be correct. The gain in the active listening group was not anticipated—or found to be—as great as the improvement in the coping skills group.

To ensure that the research guidelines were followed closely, Dr Swartz met with the active listening peer supporters as a group each month, collecting the same outcome data on these supporters as she did on the participants.

"Who knew what we'd find?" she later questioned. "As these five supporters seemed to blossom before my eyes, I turned my investigations from the supported to the supporters—and discovered that the givers were the ones who were receiving!"

Even though the supporters were doing no more than listening, they perceived that they were actually helping others, as perhaps they were. They also told Dr Swartz that the experience of being active listeners changed their perception of their own illnesses. Whereas previously they had thought of their own MS as something that had victimized them, now they saw it as a vehicle for having a positive and enhancing effect on others' lives. As a result, they felt less depressed by the restrictions imposed by their illness and more peaceful.

Dr Swartz adds an important qualification when she says, "Helping others is beneficial as long as it is balanced by a recognition of one's own capacity and needs." In caring for others, we also need to care for ourselves. If we are doing that then engaging in and acknowledging our acts of kindness is likely to have us becoming both kinder and happier.

Story 50

Find Somebody Worse Off Than You

Happiness-Enhancing Characteristics

Problems Addressed

> When dreams turn into nightmares
> Lack of control
> Depression
> Helplessness and hopelessness
> Suicidal thoughts

Resources Developed

> Extending help to others
> Becoming less worried about personal issues
> Developing a sense of purpose
> Building self-esteem through helping others
> Discovered that helping others can help the self

Outcomes Offered

> Compassion and caring emotions
> Self-improvement
> Greater happiness

"Find somebody who's worse off than you are, and see if you can help them," said Brian's psychologist.

"I just laughed," Brian later commented. "I said, 'Who could be worse off than I am?'"

Brian had a long-held dream to be a farmer and give his children a country lifestyle. So he and his wife purchased a small property to fulfill their dream of an agricultural life. After several good, happy years on the farm, the dream turned into a nightmare. As Brian had discovered, we may be able to—and, indeed, need to—aim to create our dreams. However, factors beyond our control may mean they don't always turn out the way we want. A long and devastating drought meant the farm could no longer support the family. Brian had to take additional employment away from home, rapidly falling from being a competent and capable husband and father to one who was tearful, depressed, and suicidal.

In retrospect, Brian commented that he didn't realize what was happening to him. "It was like somebody, something external, had taken over my life."

When depression hits it can seem like a vicious cycle. You don't feel like doing things, you feel less competent, and the less you do things the more you feel incapable and incompetent. Brian was no exception. He could no longer drive a car, a truck, or a tractor—and for a farmer that is bad news. His wife took over the running of the farm, the finances, and the family until eventually they walked off the land, leaving everything behind except for their furniture and dog.

Feeling helpless and hopeless, Brian saw suicide as his only way out. After a couple of serious attempts, he found himself in hospital. And it was there that his psychologist said something that changed his life and the lives of many others.

He was advised, "Find somebody who's worse off than you are, and see if you can help them."

That's when Brian laughed and asked who could be worse off than I him? At the age of 56 years he was bankrupt, no longer owned a home, had very few belongings, and, literally, described himself as a pauper.

"You'll find someone," came the reply. His therapist's idea was like a planted seed that continued to grow in Brian's awareness. After volunteering at a city charity, his psychologist began to notice a change. Brian was less worried about his personal issues and was awakening each day with a sense of purpose and self-esteem.

While Brian's voluntary work had been in the city, his heart was still with the rural people who, like him, were doing it tough. Wanting to help the people he cared about most, he started his own charity that he called Aussie Helpers and raised funds by regular Friday night raffles at a country hotel. Soon his charity had enough funds to start up a thrift shop, then a second, and eventually a vehicle to deliver boxes of groceries and personal hygiene items to farmers in drought-stricken areas.

Seeing that farmers' needed labor but could not afford laborers, Brian recruited three volunteers from a homeless shelter in the city. While the farmers benefited from the assistance, so did the volunteers. Like Brian they discovered that helping others can help oneself.

Brian's wife now describes him as a changed man. From a major depression he is now showing compassion and caring emotions that she says she had never seen in all the years of their marriage. In his own words, Brian says that though he lives in a rented house and basically has no material possessions, his marriage is "better than it ever has been, and I've never been happier in my life."

Not everyone is a Brian but every time I hear his story I find myself wondering *What is it he discovered that was so valuable to him? How might that discovery be helpful for me and others? How can helping others also be of benefit to me?*

Story 51

It's My Job

Happiness-Enhancing Characteristics

Problems Addressed

Selfishness
Looking out for 'number one'

Self-sacrifice
Depression

Resources Developed

Thinking and praying for others' health and happiness
Extending thoughts of genuine loving kindness
Looking for the moments to practice
Being self-regarding or self-caring
Engaging in acts of compassion

Outcomes Offered

A better world
Compassionate attitudes
Compassionate actions
Enhanced well-being

"It's my job," she said almost dismissively. And it was not the first time I had heard her say it even though I had only met her rather recently. She had been a nun for the past 17 years, sought to study her chosen path in some of her religion's best renowned institutions, and spent three years in a silent retreat. She had an enquiring mind, a serenity of presence, and a very genuine, caring smile. In fact, you may say her life is devoted to caring.

The first time I heard her say, "It's my job," was after I had told her about a close family member who had been diagnosed with cancer and was facing a long process of grueling treatment. "What is her name?" she asked. "I will pray for her."

"Thank you," I replied, "that's kind."

"That's OK. It's my job," she answered with a smile.

The second time was when another family member had been admitted to hospital in an emergency situation. Again, she quietly enquired, "What is his name? I will pray for him."

Again I thanked her and again she smilingly replied, "It is my job."

I began to think, whether one believes in the power of prayer or not, there must be something special in the act of devoting one's life to thinking about and praying for the health and happiness of others. To extend thoughts of genuine loving kindness to fellow humans, would you not need to feel loving kindness yourself, first? Would it not, as a sort of by-product, also benefit your well-being?

It seems all too easy for us to think of ourselves as the center of the universe, to get caught up in our own little world, our own thoughts and emotions. In our Western culture, we have had many books telling us we should look out for 'number one' as if I am the only one among the seven billion people on this planet who really matters. Such books and philosophies hold an assumption that I am the first and the most important being, while everyone else is lower down the scale and, therefore, of lesser importance.

In times of despair we cry out, "Why me?" as if the universe has especially targeted me as such an important person to heap all its refuse on. In better times we seek *my* pleasure, *my* financial gain, and *my* goals with perhaps scant regard for the feelings, needs, or well-being of others. Yet it hasn't always worked for us. Western countries where the culture of self is so high are also the countries with the highest and most rapidly escalating rates of depression.

Would the world be a better place if more of us saw it as our job, our responsibility, or our purpose in life to be more mindful of others, to think beyond ourselves, and extend wishes of well-being to others?

I asked my nun friend, "How can an ordinary, average person do that? How can we be more mindful of others without taking on the vows of a nun or monk, or without spending three years of our lives in a silent retreat? How can we show more loving kindness on a day-to-day basis?"

"First," she replied, "be mindful of or prayerful for others. This is a state of mind, a way of thinking. It is about genuinely wishing for the health and happiness of *everyone*. Not just your loved ones, family, or friends, but everyone. You need to *think* compassionately even for the people who may have mistreated you, been cruel to you, or said hurtful things. This is a tough one but if you are honestly caring for them, they are less likely to be mean or cruel to you."

"It is easy for me as a nun," she continued. "I have the time to sit and pray for long hours but busy parents or working people may not have that time. Look for the moments that you do have: waiting at a traffic light, during a TV commercial break, just before slipping off to sleep at night. Take those times to think of, to pray for, or be mindful of extending loving, caring thoughts to those you love as well as those who may have given you a hard time."

"Second," she added, "compassion, for me, is not about being either selfish or totally self-sacrificing. Selfishness is where someone looks out solely for their own needs regardless of how this impacts on others. But this isn't logical. We need others, and we need good relationships with others, to be happy. In contrast, someone who is totally self-sacrificing gives to others with neglect of the self. This isn't good either. How can you go on caring for others if you don't care for you? I think psychologists talk of it as caring for the carer."

"Fortunately, there is a middle path, one I think of as self-regarding or self-caring. It is about caring for others in a way that is still caring for you."

"Then, third, being truly compassionate involves *doing*, it involves engaging, as they say, in acts of random kindness. You don't have to devote your life to being a nun or a Mother Teresa. It is the little things. Helping an elderly lady carry her groceries home; giving priority to the man with a walking stick; allowing the waiting car on a side street to join the line of traffic; smiling warmly at the stressed or bored shop assistant; offering to do some volunteer work with the needy. These all make the world a better place for others and us."

Unlike my nun friend, we may not all be able to make compassion our job but, if she is an example, it would seem that by wishing well-being on others we are also likely to enhance our own well-being.

Story 52

When Compassion Needs Tough Love

Happiness-Enhancing Characteristics

Problems Addressed

Father–son relationships
Drug abuse
Severe mental illness
Violence
Suicidal behavior

Resources Developed

Taking caring actions
Making tough choices
Having genuine love and care
Being cruel to be kind
Making the hard calls
Practicing tough love
Doing what you caringly believe is right

Outcomes Offered

Love, caring, and compassion
Tough love

Bill was facing an extremely difficult decision, and felt powerless about what to do. Whatever he did was going to be wrong in one way or another. "Is this what they call tough love?" he asked. "Are there times you have to be cruel to be kind?"

Bill's adolescent son had got into drugs. Both Bill and his son's teachers had seen the signs evidenced in the son's truanting from school, becoming secretive, sleeping away with undisclosed 'friends,' behaving irrationally, and becoming highly emotionally volatile. Efforts to discuss it and offer suggestions of seeking help by Bill only lead to belligerent outbursts.

The downhill slide into drugs and the associate problems had escalated by the son's late teens. He only seemed to come home to beg for or demand money—and get abusive if it was denied. As he wasn't washing, brushing his teeth, or eating anything apart from cheap instant noodles, his health was also on a downhill slide. He no long attended school, didn't have a job, and lived on a pension that instantly disappeared every 'pay day.' He suffered a fractured jaw, a foot broken, and had a tooth punched out. *Were they paybacks for drug debts?* Bill wondered.

Bill found text messages on his son's phone that suggested drugs being offered to him and his son offering payments in goods he didn't have. Was he stealing to get his supplies? Should Bill report it to the police? But then would his son be penalized or imprisoned? "It is a dilemma no parent should have to face," he said.

Like any loving parent, Bill wanted the best for his son: a happy, healthy, productive life. "Dealing with drug addiction," he said, "wasn't on my parental job description." Slashed wrists, hospital admissions, assaults on the hospital staff, arrests, more personal injuries, Hepatitis C—all became part of the growing tragic picture.

However, in those brief times when his son was clean, Bill still saw glimpses of the bright and capable young man his son had been, and that he wanted to believe he could be again. It tore at his heart to see what his son had become. But the big question was what to do about it? And for that there was no clear answer.

The son refused to see a physician, a psychologist, or counselor, or go to one of the rehabilitation centers Bill had researched. Offers, like moving to a different state to make a fresh start, met with violent, abusive reactions from which his son just stormed out with threats of suicide or homicide . . . and disappeared for days or weeks. Bill was left worrying—through sleepless nights—whether his son was lying dead somewhere.

"I would hate to be inside the boy's head and going through what he was experiencing," empathized Bill but also admitted that he feared for his own life and that of the rest of the family when his son was irrationally abusive. He started to hide knives and dangerous objects from his son. Out of desperation, he phoned the local psychiatric services who recommended the son be committed to hospital, forcibly if he wouldn't go voluntarily.

This left Bill with just two choices. He could do nothing, avoid triggering his son's anger, and watch him continue on a path of self-destruction or he could have him forcibly detained and begin some treatment. He knew his son would resist. *Would he be held down against his will and injected with a tranquilizer? Would he be Tasered as Bill had seen mentally ill persons treated on TV?* Neither choice was right. Neither was what a father should have to be making. There was nothing about this in any manual of fatherhood he had ever read.

However, if he really loved and cared for his son, as he did so deeply, he realized that sometimes you have to be cruel to be kind. Love, caring, and compassion alone are not always the best or most helpful option. Sometimes it is about tough love, about making the hard calls for the very fact that you do love and care.

As I tell you this, Bill's son is in hospital. Both Bill and I hope it will prove to be a turning point for him.

I don't know if it was any help to Bill but I shared with him something that got me through some of the challenging times of my parenthood. It was a comment a colleague of mine once made: "No matter what you do as a parent you are likely to be wrong. So, if you are going to be wrong, you might as well be wrong doing what you believe is right."

Story 53

Kindness Is Not Forgotten

Happiness-Enhancing Characteristics

Problems Addressed

Negative speech
Negative actions

Resources Developed

Becoming aware of the positivity ratio
Learning to avoid negative speech
Learning to develop positive speech
Learning to avoid negative actions
Learning to develop positive actions
Being aware of the selectivity of memory
Helping people to feel good

Outcomes Offered

Help people to feel good

It came in an email from a colleague. It was one of those statements at the very end, like a signature quote. The sort of thing you don't often get to, or the sort of thing you skim over without really noticing. But the three brief sentences of this one caught my attention for they seemed to speak a truth.

People Will Forget What You Said, It Began

I don't know if you have ever thought how many of the words we speak are lost forever. In fact, it can be pretty scary. Most of the things we say go unrecorded in our own mind let alone the minds of others. Sometimes I wonder, *How many words have I spoken in my life . . . and how many of those words will be remembered?* My guess is the percentage rate is infinitesimally low.

If people do remember what you said it seems to be the negative things they remember rather than the positives. Researchers call this a positivity ratio. Studies show that, in the work place, for every negative comment you make to someone you have say at least three positive things to balance the scales. In marriages or close relationships, the stakes are higher. There it is a five to one ratio. In other words, offer one down-putting comment to your spouse or partner and you have to come up with five strong positives if you are to get the relationship back on an even footing.

Given those statistics, it seems to me that we might as well be positive in our comments right from the beginning—or we could be faced with a lot of catching up to do. So while it may not be accurate that people *always* forget what you said, it seems that forgetting or remembering is something we do selectively.

People will forget what you did. So continued the statement at the bottom of my email

Here again, I thought there was some truth. Many of the things that we do, the gestures of kindness, the acts of goodness, the everyday caring like cooking, cleaning, maintaining, and doing for each other, can often go unnoticed. However, do one bad thing and it can be strongly remembered. Have you not met families who have fallen apart for one seemingly small thing someone once did? Or people who say, "I can never forgive him or her for what they did?" Or seen relationships break up over seemingly trivial matters?

We have all heard it said that actions speak louder than words. Our actions are often noticed and mentally recorded, especially if—like our words—they, too, are negative. All your good work, your years of devotion to your job, the extra hours you have spent in the office can be readily forgotten by the boss if you mess up on one particular task. Similarly, all your acts of love, generosity, or caring can be quickly forgotten if you do one unkind thing to a lover. Here again our positivity ratio comes to play. So, in general, people will forget much of what you did but what they forget and what they remember can be quite selective.

It was, however, the third and final sentence of the statement at the bottom of my email that really caught my attention. Herein, I thought was a sound truth:

> *People will forget what you said*
> *People will forget what you did*
> *But people will never forget how you made them feel.*

Story 54

With One Small Gesture

Happiness-Enhancing Characteristics

Problems Addressed

Sadness
Suicidal thoughts
Loneliness

Resources Developed

Feeling compassionately for others
Thinking positively of others

Offering friendship
Offering hope
Offering kindness
Discovering the impact of our words and actions

Outcomes Offered

Compassion
Friendship

Have you ever wondered how your words or actions impact on others? Have you ever wondered how a simple act of yours might influence the life of another? Or how a small gesture that cost you nothing can be seen as priceless by someone else?

Recently someone sent me a story that told just such a tale. The unknown author, who I will call Jack, began by saying that one day, when he was a freshman in high school, he saw Kyle, a new kid in his class, walking home from school, his arms full of books.

"What a nerd," thought Jack. "Why would anyone bring home all his books on a Friday?" Jack, on the other hand, had a busy weekend planned including a football game with his friends the next day, a party that night, and a bike ride on Sunday. He shrugged his shoulders and walked on.

Then he saw a bunch of kids running toward Kyle, knock his books out of his arms, trip him up, and start taunting him. Kyle's glasses went flying, and landed in some tall grass about 10 feet away. As he looked up, Jack saw a terrible sadness in Kyle's eyes. And his heart went out to him.

As he ran toward them, the other kids scattered. Kyle was crawling around looking for his glasses, tears in his eyes. Jack found the glasses and handed them to him. "Those guys are jerks. Are you OK?"

Kyle looked up and said, "Yes. Thanks!" with a smile that expressed genuine gratitude. Jack helped him pick up his books and, as they chatted, it turned out that he lived near Jack. They talked all the way home, with Jack helping to carry some of his books.

Jack soon found himself asking Kyle if he wanted to play football with him and his friends on Saturday. In fact, they hung out all weekend and soon became good friends.

Come Monday morning, Kyle was staggering back to school with his huge stack of books again. Jack joked, "You're gonna really build some serious muscles with this pile of books everyday!"

Kyle just laughed and handed Jack half the books.

Over their remaining school years, Kyle and Jack became and remained best friends. Kyle had matured into a handsome young guy who, while still a keen student, no longer looked so nerdy, even in his glasses. He was popular with the girls, and planned to study medicine.

When it came to their graduation, Kyle was valedictorian for their class. As he started his speech, he cleared his throat, and began. "Graduation is a time to thank those who helped you make it through those tough years, your parents, your teachers, your siblings, maybe a coach . . . but mostly your friends. I am here to tell all of you that being a friend to someone is the best gift you can give him or her. I am going to tell you a story."

To Jack's surprise, Kyle told everyone—parents, teachers, and fellow students—about the first day they met. Unknown to Jack, Kyle had planned to kill himself over that weekend. He talked of how he had cleaned out his locker so his mom wouldn't have to do it later, and so was carrying all his books home. He looked straight into Jack's eyes and gave me a little smile. "Thankfully, I was saved. My friend—without even knowing it—saved me from doing the unspeakable. He offered friendship when I needed it most. He offered hope when I had none. His kindness gave me life."

When I hear stories like this, I wonder, "How do our words or actions impact on others? How might a simple act of ours influence the life of another? How can a small gesture that costs us nothing apart from a little time or effort be seen as priceless by someone else?"

The unknown author of this story concluded: Never underestimate the power of your actions. With one small, kind gesture you can change another person's life.

BEING COMPASSIONATE

10 On Caring for One's Self

Loving oneself is crucial. If we do not love ourselves, how can we love others?

Dalai Lama

Introduction

Self-care can be a touchy subject. Looking after yourself is often seen by society as being selfish or overly self-indulgent. Perhaps it may help to differentiate between what is selfish and what is self-caring. Being selfish is about looking out for the self regardless of what effect it has on others. For example, selfishness would be about me making money or gains for myself out of someone else's gullibility, desperation, or substance abuse. It is about me taking care of my needs—emotional, financial, and sexual—without regard for how it affects other people or their well-being.

Self-caring on the other hand refers to taking good care of yourself in ways that not only makes your life more fulfilling but also extends to others. There is a truth in the old saying that no man is an island. We are social beings. We are—as systemic approaches to therapy have made us aware—interconnected, interrelated, and interdependent. We live in relationships with a spouse, families, work colleagues, friends, and our broader community. To be self-caring we need to care for others as well as for the self.

Nonetheless, much of the Western research into happiness has focused on the individual and individual well-being. As a result we have a good body of research and theories about what contributes to personal happiness and self-caring. Seligman (2011) postulates this in the PERMA model that states personal happiness is grounded in Pleasure, Engagement, Relationships, Meaning, and Achievement. If we are to care for ourselves, these are the five core areas we need to focus on and develop.

The stories in this chapter address questions like *How do you care for yourself? How can you build effective coping strategies? How do you cast off problems or issues and be free? How do restore your energy when running on fumes? How do you keep an even keel when the waters of life become turbulent? And how do you experience and manage risks safely?*

Story 55

Finding Ways to Self-Care

Happiness-Enhancing Characteristics

Problems Addressed

How do you cope?
How do you separate yourself from stresses?
How do you look after yourself?

Resources Developed

Recognizing the need to be self-caring
Learning to be totally engaged
Learning to let go of worries
Distancing self in thoughts and feelings
Looking forward
Having a positive attitude
Discovering your own personal, self-nurturing activities

Outcomes Offered

Self-caring
Self-nurturing
Good coping skills

Students have often asked me, "How do you cope seeing eight to 10 clients a day? How do you not take on all your clients' worries? Are you not a wreck at the end of the day?"

Their questions are real. How do you separate yourself from work, concerns about other people, or other issues in life? How do you look after yourself, how do you protect and care for yourself? The questions of my students and supervisees have forced me to ask myself, *How do I look after me?*

In reflection, I think there are several ways I do this. First, there is the need to recognize that I need to be self-caring, that I need to find ways to look after me, that I need to care for myself if I am to care for others. Failing to recognize and act on this need, to find time and ways for me, would quickly have me adding to the statistics on burn-out. On the other hand, recognizing and acting on this need to self-care puts me in an empowered position to look after both me and my clients.

Second, when I am at work, I want to be there, totally engaged, with that particular person in my office. I want to join them in their experience, help them explore ways through their problems, and celebrate their successes. I want to be focused and engaged in what is happening in that current experience. You might call it compartmentalizing: being in the room with that person, being present in the current experience, being in the moment, and respectfully closing the door when the shared time is finished.

Third, I realize it is not helpful for me, or the next person I see, if I am still carrying the worries of the last person I saw. If that were the case, I wouldn't be focused or present in the moment. The worries of the day would build up accumulatively—like a kid stacking Lego blocks so high that they eventually have to crash. If I personally took on all the stories I hear—of grief, trauma, abuse, despair, stress, suicide, powerlessness, and helplessness—by the end of the day I think I would be looking for a short rope and a tall building.

A fourth factor in my self-caring is the 30 minute drive home from work. This allows me not only a physical space from my office but also allows me to distance myself in thoughts and feelings. As I drive, I can begin to leave behind thoughts about what happened during the working day and start to think about the things I can look forward to on arriving home.

Fifth, there is an attitudinal factor. If my attitude is a problem-focused one, if I let myself get caught up in all the issues, challenges, or difficulties my clients are experiencing or the problems of my work place, then I am likely to feel bad. If, on the other hand, I am looking for solutions and outcomes, if I hold hope and have goals toward which I am working, I feel better, happier, and more content with my work. If nothing else, having a positive attitude is a practical position to adopt.

Finally, in addition to that, a little bit of self-caring can go a long way. I believe it is important to have, cherish, and maintain self-nurturing factors in your life, outside of work. For me they are things like sharing time with family and friends, having engaging activities, spending time in nature, finding new pleasurable challenges . . . but for each of us they may, of course, be different. I am not sure it matters what they are so much as the fact that we each spend time in our own personal self-nurturing activities.

So I am grateful when students ask me questions like, "How do you cope with your working day? How do you not take on all your clients' worries? Are you not a wreck at the end of the day?" It forces me to ask myself, *What are the things that I do? What is helpful in enabling me to cope? If I know the things that work, how can I ensure I do more of them? And what else is there to discover that might also help in my ongoing self-caring?*

Story 56

Finding Ways to Cope, Effectively

Happiness-Enhancing Characteristics

Problems Addressed

How do you cope?
How do you separate yourself from stresses?
How do you look after yourself?

Resources Developed

> Learning what not to do
> Giving up on the struggle or fight
> Learning what to do
> Creating and participating in self-nurturing activities
> Finding your own specific means to self-nurture

Outcomes Offered

> Self-caring
> Self-nurturing
> Good coping skills

Because students often ask me, "How do you cope with work? How do you not take on all the worries people share with you during the day? How do you ensure you are not a wreck at the end of the day?" it has helped me not only to examine what I do but also made me curious about how other colleagues care for themselves. So I have asked them: "What do you do to cope? How do you switch off at the end of the day? How do you care for you?"

If I had been hoping for a succinct and concise formula that I could take on board myself and share with you, I would have to confess I would be disappointed. The replies I have received have been many and varied: "I look forward to spending time with my family." "I enjoy playing sport." "I get involved in my hobby." "I help out with a charity." "I plan and anticipate my next holiday."

Though these specific answers varied from person to person and there has been no one-size-fits-all response, there are some things common in the process of what people do. First, what they *don't* do seems to be important. They don't *struggle* to cope, manage, or survive. They don't fight *against* the stresses they may be facing. They don't focus on the *problems*. They don't make mountains out of molehills.

Second, what they *do* do seems equally as important. They *create* and *participate in* self-nurturing activities that are pleasurable, engaging, and add meaning or purpose to their lives.

How do you actually make that shift? I have wondered. *How do you move your head out of a worrying space into a space of enjoyment and pleasure?* One day a colleague unintentionally showed me what she did. She works in an agency dealing with people who face the tough side of life. Her clients are people who have been abused or are abusers. They are people caught up in the tragic cycles of drug use and alcoholism, family violence, and even criminal activities. Every day she sees, is involved in, and deals with life at its very raw end. She is a caring and compassionate person who loves her work and dearly wants for those in her care to be experiencing a better quality of life. She gives of herself professionally and emotionally. When I asked her what she does in terms of self-caring, she gave me the same answers as many other colleagues. "I love

SELF-CARING

and enjoy my time with family. I look forward to weekends in the garden and with friends."

How she made that transition, I didn't discover until she invited me to dinner with her family one evening after work. We travelled to her home together. As we stepped through the front door she turned to face a dresser and, slowly, ritualistically placed her briefcase with all its work files on the dresser. She then moved, as if she was taking off a jacket that she wasn't wearing and hung this imaginary object on a coat hook. She looked at herself in the mirror, raised a hand to her forehead and drew it down her face taking on a sad look with a frown and down-at-the-the-corners mouth. Like you do when creating a clown face for a child, she then raised her hand, lifting it into a happy face with an upturned smile and bright, sparkling eyes. Only then did she call out, "I am home."

Her son and daughter bounced through to greet her. Her husband greeted her with a kiss. Work was left behind. Family time was about to begin.

Over dinner I asked her about her ritual. She said that her briefcase represented work and that she wanted to mindfully, deliberately set it aside, not carrying it further into her home than she needed. In taking off the pretend jacket she was symbolically removing the problems of the day, leaving them by the door, to pick up, along with the briefcase, on her way back to work in the morning. Moving her hand over her face was to wipe away the emotions of the day and put on a happier face, the expression and feeling she wanted to have at home. When she had done those things, then she could truly announce she was home, and feel free to get on with enjoying her family and her own life.

I guess each of us, like my colleague, need to find those specific ways or rituals that best suit us and our needs for self-caring. Slowly I have, and continue to, find ways for me. And wonder what ways you may find for you.

Story 57

Casting Off

Happiness-Enhancing Characteristics

Problems Addressed

> Need for freedom
> Tied to the familiar and secure
> A competitive, rule-driven, time-oriented life

Resources Developed

> Casting off the old
> Unhitching from the unnecessarily familiar and secure
> Letting go of what is holding you back
> Discovering freedom.

Discovering freedoms come with responsibilities
Learning to be free safely
Experiencing enjoyment
Going with the flow
Building acceptance

Outcomes Offered

Freedom
Enjoyment
Contentment

I have a friend who is a keen sailor. I have heard him say many times that the most exciting part of going sailing is casting off. It's an interesting term isn't it? And not one that applies solely to boating. We talk about casting off old clothes or unwanted goods. We talk about casting off old habits and even unhealthy relationships. I think there is a sense of something like that for him, too.

His working life is regular and time-ordered, arising at the same time each working day, following the same roads to work, stopping at the same traffic lights along the way, and doing the same tasks when he gets to work. That is a solid, secure, and routine part of his life just as the wharf to which his boat is tied is a solid and secure object. Casting off, I think, is symbolic for him. It is about more than just unhitching a rope that has you tied to a familiar and secure object.

Being tethered to the wharf has a purpose. It keeps his boat safe when storms arrive, when waters become turbulent and when ill winds blow. But being tethered does not allow the boat—or the sailor—to fulfill its own purpose. The very reason for a sailboat's existence is to sail, to be free, to enjoy when conditions are friendly, and to let go of what might be holding it back.

My friend, being a good sailor, always keeps a close eye on the weather. He knows the times when it is good for his boat, and indeed himself, to be secure and the times to be free.

For him, casting off or letting go from the wharf is a ritual just as much as we have rituals for others times of letting go. We have funerals for when people pass away, weddings for when we let go of singlehood to become a couple, retirement parties for when we finish working. My friend has his rituals, too. He checks the flag at the top of the mast to see that it indicates a fair wind, he ensures the motor is ticking over smoothly in idle, and he looks out for other boat traffic. He releases all but the last, necessary rope, coils the unwanted ones on the deck, slips the final one free, and nudges the boat's bow toward the sea. As he positions the boat for the wind to fill the sails and switches off the noise of the motor, a smile lights his face. He lifts his hands briefly from the helm and shouts to the sky and sea, "Freedom."

Nonetheless, he knows that all freedoms come with responsibilities. His sail boat is packed with safety gear, 'just in case.' He picks up the radio, logs in, keeps a radio watch, and will regularly report his position. "If you are going to be free," he once said to me, "you need to be free safely." Freedom is not just a reckless abandon of rules and responsibilities but, at its very core, an act or process of self-caring.

My friend is not a competitive racer. He has told me he is competitive, rule-driven, and time-oriented enough during the working week without doing the same thing in his recreational time. He sits in streams of congested traffic commuting each working day and sees no point of being congested in a flotilla of racing boats at the weekend. When he sails, he is not out to win but just to experience and enjoy.

Onboard, he tends to go with the flow, but not completely. He looks at where the wind and waves want to take him and where he wants to go, finding a comfortable balance between the forces without and those within. Then, having cast off what he wants to leave behind, he sits back, helm in his hand, smile broadening on his face, and looks the picture of contentment.

Story 58

Running on Fumes

Happiness-Enhancing Characteristics

Problems Addressed

> Lack of reserves
> Fatigue
> Burnout

Resources Developed

> Learning to explore the choices
> Learning to top up your reserves
> Planning to go the distance
> Using your reserves more wisely
> Making time for yourself
> Finding pleasure in the journey

Outcomes Offered

> Wise utilization of reserves
> Self-nurturing

"I'm running on fumes," he said. "You know what I mean?"

To that point, I had not heard the expression before but I knew instantly and graphically what he meant. His metaphor created a very clear image of where things were for him. His tank was empty, he had run out of fuel, he had nothing more to give, and the fumes weren't going to last much longer. He was in a desperate position of needing to refuel, and refuel in a hurry.

"How are things different when your tank is full?" I asked.

"It is like you were setting out on a long country drive," he answered. "You would be a fool not to top up your tank before you go. If you have the reserves to take you the distance you want to go, you can feel confident and secure. You can get on with enjoying the drive, free of worries about whether you are going to make it or not. But, if you start out without the necessary reserves, with your tank low on fuel, your mind is so constantly worried about how far it is to the next gas station, and whether you will make it that you can't sit back and enjoy the ride."

"It sounds to me," I commented, "that, if you are running on fumes, you started out on your journey without sufficient reserves in the tank."

His face twisted in an uncomfortable looking smile. "You can't do that" he said. "Everyone knows you don't start out on empty or without sufficient fuel."

"Then what do you need to do?" I explored.

"I suppose there are several choices," he replied thoughtfully. "The obvious one is if you are running low you need to top up your reserves. In fact, you may need to keep topping up, doing it several times over, if you are traveling a long distance. You can't expect your car to go on forever without refueling. It's a constant process. You need both fuel and continuing maintenance if you want your vehicle to work well for you."

"Another choice would be to look at the distance you plan to travel. Have you bitten off more than you can chew? Are you expecting you can do more than your reserves will allow you to do?"

"And a third thing might be to adjust your speed to use your fuel more wisely and get a better level of fuel consumption. Are you driving too hard? Are you driving too fast? Can you slow down and take it easier? Can you use you reserves better?"

"Maybe it is not a matter of one or the other," I reflected, "but perhaps a bit of all three: topping up your tank, adjusting how far or hard you are driving, *and* using your reserves more wisely. Starting with the first, what can you do to top up your tank?"

"Are we talking about a car here or me personally?" he asked.

I just shrugged my shoulders and let him continue in which ever direction he wanted.

"Perhaps it is all of the above," he said. "First, I need to make time for me, to get back into some of the things I used to enjoy but have neglected as work has become busier and busier. I need to start to appreciate life's little pleasures again."

"Second, I need to examine if I am driving myself to hard and fast . . . and that doesn't really need a lot of examination to find a conclusion. I need to look at whether I am taking on more than I reasonably can or should.

"Third, to use my reserves more wisely, I need to pace myself better in doing those things. To extend our analogy, I need to focus less on getting to a destination and more on the pleasure of journeying."

SELF-CARING

He thought for a moment or two, then added, "One thing's for sure, I am tired of running on fumes. It's time to top up."

Story 59

Keeping an Even Keel

Happiness-Enhancing Characteristics

Problems Addressed

> When buffeted about
> When inclement conditions prevail
> When tipped off balance

Resources Developed

> Using the resources you have available
> Finding a compromise
> Caring for the core part of you
> Enjoying the beauty of things
> Maintaining an even keel
> Enjoying the journey

Outcomes Offered

> Enjoyment of beauty
> Maintaining an even keel
> Enjoyment of the journey

I don't know if you enjoy watching sailboats out in a river, lake, or sea on a pleasantly warm summer's day as much as I do. Having been a sailor but no longer owning a sailboat for several reasons, I must confess to feeling a twinge of envy when I watch them, a desire to be out there sailing with them. To see their white, wind-filled sails and colorful spinnakers drifting across the blue of the sky and water, for me, holds a peacefulness and tranquility. To know that they are moving with nature and that, if on board, you would be hearing no more than the gentle swish of the water against the hull, feels like magic. As I was enjoying such a scene recently, I became aware that the beauty most of us see in a sailboat is only part of the picture.

What we observe usually is only the sleek hull, the tall mast, and the crisp sails above the water line. To a sailor, however, they are not primarily objects of beauty as much as objects of function. Ask any sailor about the hull of his vessel and he is likely to tell you, "It provides the boat with the buoyancy to keep afloat and serves as a base support for the mast, stays, and sails that give you your power and direction."

Ask him about the mast and he may reply, "It is the support and strength to hold up the sails. It is there to secure them in place even when forces outside try to buffet and tear at them. Sailboat designers know it has to be built strong and positioned precisely on the boat to gain greatest effectiveness and efficiency for the sails. Then the sailor needs to know how to use it for the best advantage. The mast is the sails' central core of strength."

He may continue, "The sails are not there just for beauty either, but also to serve a very real function. They are the boat's silent, fuel-efficient motor. They are what work in close collaboration with the wind and sailor's skill to provide power and mobility."

Most of us are aware that we need power and energy to move forward. And every sailor knows that, though you may not be able to alter the direction of the wind, you can always adjust your sails. In fact, it doesn't take long for even the most novice sailor to learn that a sailboat's course may not always be a straight line from A to B. Sometimes to get where you want to go you have to tack back and forth, using the resources you have available, finding a compromise, and making your way with patience.

However, how do you keep upright when the seas are turbulent and the winds are buffeting you about? There is a part of a sailboat that is not visible to the eyes of the casual observer and this is the keel. Like that inner part of us, that solid core of our being that we may not always show to rest of the world, the keel is an essential, if not most important, part of any sailboat. Sails might be dirty or worn, large or small, white or colored. Hulls can hold cabins or be simple pontoons. They can be clean or soiled, cared for or neglected, but without a functioning keel a sailboat simply could not work. As every sailor worth his salt knows, a keel has its positives and negatives. It is a compromise one has to make, a payoff for the benefits it provides. It adds weight to the boat and creates drag, therefore reducing speed. In these ways, it can be seen as a bit of a burden. Nonetheless, your keel is what keeps you upright. At times when the going gets tough, when inclement conditions prevail and you find yourself tipped off balance, it is your keel that stops you from turning completely over and sinking.

Just because your keel is out of sight doesn't mean it should be out of mind. Being hidden beneath the sea most of the time, it can become fouled. Barnacles attach themselves to it, sea grasses can use it as a base on which to grow, and like dust gathers in a house so slime can coat a keel. Your keel needs to be cared for. It pays to pause at times and check it, to clean it, to paint it, and to keep it performing well for you. If your keel is working well for you, then you are free to enjoy the beauty of other things—like the sails, hull, and mast. If you care for that core part, you are less likely to heel over . . . and more likely to maintain an even keel . . . and enjoy the journey.

Story 60

Managing Risks, Safely

Happiness-Enhancing Characteristics

Problems Addressed

Limited enjoyment
Limited fulfillment
Challenging or risky situations

Resources Developed

Learning the joys of risk-taking
Learning the rules of safe risk-taking
Learning to explore safely
Journeying with company
Learning to be prepared
Equipping yourself for the journey ahead

Outcomes Offered

Enjoyment and fulfillment
Safe risk-taking
Minimized dangers
Maximized safety
Self-care

Stories have developed throughout many cultures, over many centuries, to teach us many important lessons about life. One Slavic story I particularly like is about a strange, supernatural creature called the *lisovyk* that a colleague, Dr Julie-Anne Sykley, shared with me. Most people have discovered that life can be enriched by taking risks at times. People who limit the amount of risks they take also limit their range of experiences and consequently limit potential enjoyment and fulfillment. On the other hand, the more we risk, the greater our range of experiences and the more we are likely to enjoy a rich and fulfilling life. If we are to take risks, however, how can we do that safely? How can we experience challenging or risky situations, and survive them? What are the risk-taking rules we need to heed if we are to gain and not suffer?

Well, this is where the spooky Slavic sprite, the *lisovyk*, has something to say to us. Every forest in the Ukraine is controlled by a *lisovyk* and its natural riches and resources are at his disposal. He can manifest himself in many forms from a shabby old man to a giant with horns, a tall tree, a tiny blade of grass, or even a fearsome animal. If you were to seek him out you might find him dwelling in the most desolate of places like a hut that has been deserted for the winter or an isolated, uninhabited cave where he could be singing and whistling eerily to himself. While he is lord and master of all the forest animals, the wolves are said to be his most loyal helpers.

However, be warned about seeking him out. If people enter his domain he mischievously, and malevolently, schemes to get them lost, especially if they are wandering in the forests and mountains alone. Many a person from the Slavic countries of Europe has a tale to tell about how a *lisovyk* upset their usually good sense of direction and caused them to become uncharacteristically disoriented. They report wandering round and round in circles in spite of having a compass and knowing the area well. They talk about being lured away from their trail, distracted from their destination, unable to find their tent, and terrified by frightening nocturnal noises.

So, what is it that the tales of this supernatural creature have to teach us about the rules of risk-taking? To me they seem to speak as much about journeying through life as they do about journeying into a forest. Beneath the images of the scary *lisovyk* are some important messages about caring for yourself. First, the *lisovyk* stories let people know that it can be dangerous to wander too far into unfamiliar territory. Some exploration may be good and beneficial but take care about how far you can journey safely.

Second, the *lisovyk* warns us that it may not be wise to explore risky places, situations, or experiences alone. Indeed, every hiker or backpacker hopefully knows this. Journeying with a companion or companions not only increases the safety factor, it can also increase the enjoyment and pleasure factor.

Third, the more prepared you are for your journey, the safer and more enjoyable it is likely to be too. Just as when trekking in an unfamiliar forest, you may want to take all-weather clothing, a good medical kit, sufficient water and emergency food, so in journeying through life's risky times it helps to be prepared, to ask what you need to do to equip yourself for the journey ahead.

Finally, to me, the *lisovyk's* message is not designed to frighten us off visiting unfamiliar territory completely but rather to say, "When you do, take care. Explore how you can risk while minimizing potential dangers and maximizing your safety. Look after yourself. Take care of you . . . and enjoy."

SELF-CARING

11 On Being a Positive Thinker

No pessimist ever discovered the secret of the stars, or sailed to an unchartered land, or opened a new doorway to the human spirit.

Helen Keller, writer

Introduction

For a long time we thought that to 'get rid of' a problem we had to know and understand that problem well, that we had to analyze it and scrutinize it, at length. We aimed to eliminate the problem through knowing the problem. However, positively oriented theorists and researchers have thrown that hypothesis into question. By building greater levels of positivity we outweigh negativity. Positive thoughts, feelings, and actions act effectively to dissolve, melt, or undo negative thoughts, feelings, and actions.

I have a childhood memory of the first thing my father used to do when we went to our beach house for the summer holidays. He would tap his knuckle up the corrugated rungs of rainwater tank to hear how much water was there for our holidays. The tank could be full of air or full of water, or have various levels of both. In reflection, it seems to me that, as human beings, we are a bit like that rainwater tank. We have a certain capacity for thought, feelings, and actions. While that may not be as finite as the tank, the parallel is that we can fill our psychological space with negative experiences, positive experiences, or various levels of both. If our emotional rainwater tank is filled with the negative, there is little room for the positive. Conversely, if we build the positive it displaces the negative in much the same way as the rain waters filling the tank displace the volume of air.

How does this work? If we are feeling joy and excitement it is unlikely we will be feeling flat and depressed at the same time. If we are relaxed and serene, we are not—at that point of time—feeling anxious or stressed. If we are confident and hopeful, we are not simultaneously insecure and hopeless. Of course, the reverse is equally true. Simply put, creating one feeling displaces its counterpart. Think negative or pessimistic thoughts and you displace positive or optimistic thoughts. Create positive or optimistic thoughts and you displace negative or pessimistic thoughts.

The stories here show ways and means for tipping your emotional scales toward greater positivity, optimism, and happiness. These are just some metaphoric examples of how to develop acceptance, how to open a new door when an old one closes, how to be focused on the sensations of the moment, and how to accept impermanence. The stories speak about creating a happy and positive self-image and about adopting a forward-looking orientation. They explore how uncertainty and challenge can be strengthening, along with the appreciation of beauty, the journeying through life, and the anticipation of arrival. Building positivity comes from setting your sights on the attainable rather than the unattainable, learning to look forward rather than back, and discovering how to positively anticipate the future rather than negatively revisit the past. Seeing the possibilities of what may lay ahead in life, being prepared for the worst case scenarios, and developing proactive resources, can help us positively equip ourselves for life's seemingly inevitable challenges.

The final story in this chapter explores how someone can turn severe trauma into positive post-traumatic growth by choosing what is controllable, developing a sense of adventure, seeing beauty in the world, maintaining positivity, and channeling a tragedy in both constructive and creative directions.

Story 61

When One Door Closes

Happiness-Enhancing Characteristics

Problems Addressed

> When one door closes
> Frustration of hopes, plans, and goals
> Despair
> A depth of disappointment

Resources Developed

> Learning to accept what cannot be changed
> Finding alternatives
> Letting go of past disappointments
> Discovering new experiences
> Being focused on sensations of the moment

Outcomes Offered

> Acceptance of what cannot be changed
> An openness to new opportunities
> Acceptance of impermanence
> Laughter

POSITIVE THINKING

"When one door closes," said Deb, "another opens." I knew she was being empathic about my frustration and disappointment. I knew she wanted to offer me a glimmer of hope. I knew too that sometimes in the intensity of despair, when someone says something of that nature, no matter how well-intentioned, you might feel like slamming the door in their face. How can a common cliché such as that be expected to alter the depth of such disappointment as I was experiencing?

Deb and I were working as fellow volunteers at the national hospital in Thimphu, the capital of Bhutan, and she had seen part of the emotional rollercoaster ride I had been on over the last few weeks.

I had come back to this Himalayan country, in part, to make a high altitude trek to a remote and holy site tucked high in the mountains near the Tibetan border. After three years of trying, I had recently been told I had become the first foreigner ever granted permission to visit this out-of-bounds destination for tourists.

On the basis of this permission, I booked and paid for flights, arranged visas, confirmed my volunteer commitments, and drove my body into fitness. I got on with the work of organizing transport for the two-day drive to the start of the trail; booking ponies, pony handlers, and a cook to carry our gear and provide our meals; and making lists of the provisions we needed for almost two weeks of self-sufficiency in the wilderness. It was mounting into a big expedition.

Then we heard the news! The first group of local pilgrims for the season had to turn back as the snow was too deep for their ponies to get through. Unseasonal cold and higher than normal precipitation put our plans on hold. I tried phoning contacts in the region and checking the less-than-reliable extended weather forecasts: more snow, thunderstorms, and below freezing temperatures were predicted. While the government had finally come through on the permit, the weather was not so permitting.

It felt like an emotional rollercoaster, an on-again-off-again event. The excitement was building, then crashing. Snow turned into deep impassable mud! We could but wait and hope for drying temperatures.

The days passed, the rains eased, the temperatures rose . . . and with them leeches that crawl their way up your trousers, leap from the bushes to attach on your face, and to fall from the trees overhead to work their way inside your collar. Still, I planned to go the very next weekend, again rescheduling transport, ponies, pony handlers, and cook. My hopes were high. At last it seemed probable.

Then my local traveling companions announced the delays meant they could no longer take further time off work. The emotional rollercoaster came to a grinding halt.

However, because of the collapse of the planned trek, I accepted the invitation of one of the expedition members, Wangchuk, to visit him and his family for the weekend. Wangchuk took me on a hike to Drakapo, a very special and holy site that, after about 12 visits to Bhutan, I had not discovered before and was not listed in my guidebooks. As it hangs from a cliff face, one doesn't approach the monastery directly but by circumambulating it and the cliff in a clockwise direction visiting various holy sites along the way.

First we came to a cave entered by the descent down a steel ladder. At the bottom was an altar with water-filled bowls and burning candles that dimly lit the otherwise pitch black cave. I was glad for the headlamp I constantly carry in my daypack. The cave wove down, then up through body hugging passages, past formations that have taken on religious symbolism. A couple of small diameter tree trunks with narrow footholds notched in them served as ladders to ascend the steep rock faces. Suddenly a hole gapped open beneath me, dropping some thirty feet to a view of the flickering candles we passed below. It took a full leg stretch to a narrow rock lip in the dark to negotiate the gap. *Stay calm*, I try to remind myself. *Take your time. Be mindful.* The exit was a rebirth, an on-your-side, feet first emergence through a narrow slit into the light of day. A small price to pay for an act of devotion that I was told washes away the sins of a past lifetime.

Continuing the ascending circumambulation we found another cliff-face cave with magnificent views over the lush green terraced rice fields of the valley below. Here an elderly lady sat, lighting butter lamps, burning incense, and chanting her prayers. She smiled a smile of red, betel nut-stained teeth and lips, and continued chanting.

We climbed higher through dense decorations of red, green, blue, yellow, and white prayer flags (reflecting the five elements of fire, water, sky, earth, and ether) to a rocky and vertiginous pinnacle that dropped sharply to a panoramic view from the frothing white serpentine path of the Paro River to the steep wooded valley walls, the more distant sharp, black and white summits of Himalayan peaks, and a sky full of racing cumulus clouds.

The disappointments about my planned trek had not entered my mind as I had been enjoying the current circumambulation. Strangely, I came away feeling a real sense of acceptance of it. It was what it was, and that could not be changed. In fact, I felt great.

The door had closed on my planned trek but, as Deb had said, a new door had opened. Then I recalled being at a ward round in the hospital a few days before when the psychiatrist asked how my plans for the trek were going. I shared my tale of frustration, expecting a response of empathic understanding to my bitter disappointment. Instead he and the nursing staff laughed riotously.

"Why do you laugh at my misfortune?" I asked.

"In Buddhism we say that nothing is permanent," he answered. "So if nothing is permanent, you might as well laugh about it."

Story 62

Creating Positive Images

Happiness-Enhancing Characteristics

Problems Addressed

Internal focus
Negative self-perceptions

Resources Developed

Creating a happy and positive self-image
Creating a forward looking orientation
Looking for happiness and positivity

Outcomes Offered

Outward focus
Happy and positive self-perceptions
A forward looking outlook

Walking along my home beach one Sunday morning, I encountered a woman on her hands and knees, scooping up sand with a blue ice cream container and patting it down into a shape. I looked for a child or grandchild but there were none. She was alone in the early morning shadow of the dune, shaping out a female figure. It had modest breasts, maternal hips, one arm bent down onto its hip and the other up to its head. The head was faceless, no eyes, no mouth, no expression. Was it meant to be that way or had she simply not got to the face yet?

I looked at her to make eye contact and exchange the morning greeting that people usually offer each other along our beach but she did not look up, silently patting and shaping the figure's torso.

Further up the beach a series of women, five to 10 yards apart, all bent down in the shadow of the dunes, facing away from the water and the soft morning light that was beautifully illuminating the offshore islands, working sand into shapes. *Was this a sand sculpting class or lesson?* I wondered as I approached the second woman who was also molding a sand figure. With neither breasts nor genitalia it initially seemed non-gender specific but, at a second glance, the beer barrel gut clearly defined it as a male. Again she worked in silence, ignoring my passing and anticipation of a greeting.

Next was a nun in a grey habit, shaping an asexual figure. She looked up but quickly dropped her gaze. Nonetheless, I now began to make sense of all these women and sand figures. Across the road from the beach was as a Catholic center that commonly held silent retreats. Perhaps these morning sand sculptors were in retreat. It seemed probable the sand sculpting was an exercise they had been set as part of the retreat. *Had they been asked to sculpt an image of themselves, to see how they saw themselves?* I wondered.

Further up the beach were sculptures that had been created and then trampled back to beach level under multiple footprints. *Had they been asked to sculpt an image of someone they wanted to get out of their lives? Create the image, and then destroy it?*

Wrapped in my curiosity and guesses, I came to the last woman. She was further down the beach from the others, having chosen a spot where the dunes dipped and the sun shone through the shadows. She sat in the morning light, her figure facing the rising sun while she looked out over the sea to the brightly illuminated islands. Her sculpture had a face with a pair of shell eyes and a seaweed mouth that twisted up in a smile. *Yes*, I thought, *if you are going to create an image of yourself or someone important in your life, why not create a happy and positive one. If your image is not happy at the moment, why not look forward to how you want it to be in the future? If you are going to create an image of another, why not look for the happiness and positivity there?*

She looked up as I walked by. With the eye contact, I said, "Good morning." She nodded a silent smile in response.

Story 63

Sailing a Solo Sea

Happiness-Enhancing Characteristics

Problems Addressed

> Limitations to creativity
> Resigning from a job
> Facing a challenge
> Loss of security

Resources Developed

> Discovering turbulence, uncertainty, and challenges can be strengthening
> Discovering the beautiful
> Appreciating the solo journey
> Learning to anticipate the arrival
> Accepting the scary
> Opening up to opportunities of discovery

Outcomes Offered

> Happy journeys
> Happy arriving

Recently I received an email from a colleague who for the whole of her professional life had been an academic, a university lecturer in psychology. She loved her work, loved her research, and had climbed to the level of professor but found that working in a rather conservative school imposed severe limitations to her creative ideas. She had discussed with me her thoughts of resigning and working in her own practice. It would be a challenge. She would be throwing away the security of a permanent job with a stable income for an uncertain financial future. She was the prime income earner for the family and had the usual commitments to a mortgage, school fees, and young mouths to feed. For her own happiness, and ultimately that of her family, she decided to give up her salaried position.

In her email, she said, "After all these years, I am looking forward to the end of university. I feel thankful to be casting free of the university island even though it means I am now adrift at sea on my life raft. I hope to see new land soon."

She gave me an eloquent metaphor to reply to. "I am glad," I responded, "to hear that you have cast free and will finally be adrift of university island. Not all seas are turbulent," I continued. "Some can be very tranquil. Though at times we often encounter some turbulence in the journey of getting to where we want to go. Turbulence, uncertainty, and challenging times can help strengthen us."

"All seas are dotted with lands. Some are big and some small. Some are barren and some are fertile. Some are challenging and some are tranquil. In fact, there are many beautiful islands out there and many exciting lands on which to arrive."

"In addition, journeying solo isn't necessarily a bad experience either. Personally, I have had the joy of sharing travels through life and have also made many journeys solo. Solo can feel a little scary at first but it does open up many opportunities for discovering things about yourself that you may otherwise never have discovered. If I had a choice, I know I would certainly prefer to be journeying alone in my life raft than not at all. So let me wish you happy journeys, wherever the winds and your own steering may take you . . . and happy arrivals too."

Story 64

Wanting What You Can Have

Happiness-Enhancing Characteristics

Problems Addressed

Limited choices
Wanting the unattainable
Lack of thought management
A formula for unhappiness

Resources Developed

> Learning to want the attainable
> Learning to achieve the attainable
> Learning to look forward rather than back
> Learning to anticipate what lies ahead

Outcomes Offered

> Satisfaction
> Contentment
> Joy
> Attainment of the achievable

"I want my mummy." The whining, tearful, three-year-old voice came from the child seat in the back of the car. I had just dropped my daughter at work and was looking after my grandson for the day. His mum had to go to work. In that she had no choice. My grandson could not go to work with his mum. In that he had no choice. The cause of his unhappiness was clear. It was his desire for something he could not have that was causing his misery. But how do you explain that to a three-year-old who is not capable of comprehending it and who has not yet learnt how to assess and adjust his thinking?

I could have simply said, "There is no point in wanting what you cannot have," but would that have been speaking from an experience that he, at his tender young age, did not yet have? I would be offering a concept that a three-year-old mind could not comprehend—a child reacting out of his immediate experience. Likewise, there was no point in trying to reason with someone who could not yet understand or accept a rational argument. What was I to do?

As I drove on, contemplating this and listening to the tearful demands from the back seat, I remembered a cartoon I once saw in a newspaper. In the first frame, one character was asking the other, "If you could have anything in the world, what would you want?"

"A ham and cheese sandwich," came the reply.

"What!" exploded the first character. "Talk about a failure of imagination. You could have wished for a million, trillion dollars, your own private Pacific island, or the most luxurious mansion in the world."

In the last frame, the second character was holding a sandwich in his hands while in the speech balloon above his head was the response, "Yes, but I got what I wanted."

As we were headed to my grandson's swimming lesson, I wondered how he could direct his thoughts toward wanting what he could achieve. I began to talk about the lessons, about his teacher, about the things he might be doing in today's class.

Soon, he too was talking about swimming, his hopes, his expectations. His voice settled, the tears dried, he began to anticipate what lay ahead. He began

POSITIVE THINKING

to want what was attainable. His attention shifted from past unhappiness to anticipations of future pleasure.

Wanting a mummy you can't have right there and then, a million dollars that may not fall from the heavens into your lap just when you want it, the love of a partner who can't or won't give it, a goal that you have made no efforts to achieve, or any other unrealistic, unattainable desire, is an almost guaranteed formula for unhappiness. Conversely, wanting the attainable, the ham and cheese sandwich, or the forthcoming swimming lessons, can lead to satisfaction, contentment, and joy.

As he leapt from his car seat, my three-year-old grandson couldn't wait to grab his swim bag from the trunk and head in to his swimming lesson. That was a want he could—and did—achieve.

Story 65

Better to Have It and Not Need It

Happiness-Enhancing Characteristics

Problems Addressed

> Lack of necessary resources or skills
> Lack of preparedness
> Reactivity to life
> Stress
> Depression
> Unhappiness

Resources Developed

> Looking forward to the future
> Seeing the possibilities that may possibly occur
> Being aware of the worst-case scenarios
> Being prepared for the worst-case scenarios
> Learning to plan ahead
> Being proactive

Outcomes Offered

> Preparedness
> A proactive perspective
> Greater control
> Enhanced happiness

There was something Trapper Rick said that I would like to share with you. I was up in the fjords of northern British Columbia to hopefully see and photograph both grizzly and black bears when I met Trapper Rick. Rick was a guy who had been brought up through the school of hard knocks. He had learnt to survive in the wilds of civilization and now, for many years, had survived a rather solitary life in the wilds of the backwoods. In doing so, he had developed his own home-spun philosophy and said several things that struck me with their wisdom.

We pulled our fiberglass boat into the jetty to pick up Trapper Rick from his float home. He was wearing a brown knitted lumberjack hat with fold down earflaps, a much-stained cream, windproof jacket, and unlaced boots, their soles separating from the upper. In his hand he preciously carried a hard, black, watertight plastic case like many photographers use to protect their camera and lens. He tapped it affectionately and reassuringly. "Rosemary," he said.

Angus, our guide, had already told us that Rosemary accompanied Rick all the time. She even goes to town with him and, at times, has gotten both her and him into trouble. But who or what Rosemary was remained a mystery. When asked, Rick simply and philosophically said, "Better to have it and not need it than need it and not have it." And conversation ended over the roar of the outboard as we accelerate up the inlet.

We stepped ashore at a rough wooden dock on our way to his forest cabin. Here, Rick opened his case . . . and we got to meet Rosemary. She was a heavy looking, long-barreled Colt 45. He strapped her into a leather holster, under his jacket, on his left-hand side.

Regardless of whether I, or you, agree with people's right to bear firearms, I had to agree with Rick's philosophy that it is better to have something and not need it than need it and not have it. As I reflected on my own life, I realized I have purchased and carried a knife with me when scuba diving in the hope that I would never need it. It was bought to give myself the reassurance that if ever I needed to cut free of entangling ropes or weeds I would have the necessary means of escape. Likewise I have purchased lifejackets to wear when I am sailing or kayaking, again, in the hope of never needing them but knowing that if the worst-case scenario develops they are there, and I am prepared. When trekking in remote areas I always carry a medical kit sufficient for almost every eventuality. The kit is not inexpensive but again I work on the principle that it is better to have it and not need it. Mostly I end up disposing of the medicines because they pass their expiry date before I ever use them—an outcome I am happier with than being ill enough to have had to consume them.

So Rick's statement echoed a truth for me. It seemed to be about looking forward, about looking to the future, about seeing the possibilities that may possibly occur. It was about being prepared for the worst-case scenarios because if we see what *can* happen then we can be prepared for what may happen. His statement was about awareness and preparedness for the eventualities that life can inevitably, unexpectedly hurl at us.

I never got to ask Trapper Rick whether he had always held this philosophy or whether it was something that had developed over time. Had he initially gone into the backwoods thinking and planning ahead or did he initially blunder in, learning from experience along the way? Had he approached the backwoods like some people approach life, charging in then being reactive to whatever happens? Or had he approached it as some others approach life, planning ahead, being proactive, looking for the potential possibilities?

I would like to have known, for through my life and observations as a psychologist it has been my experience that people who don't plan for the possibilities and eventualities, who react to whatever life throws their way—as it does and will do—tend to be more stressed, more depressed, and less happy. In contrast, those who think ahead, plan for the possibilities and eventualities, and have both an awareness and preparedness for what may happen feel more in control of their lives and, consequently, feel happier.

Another thing Trapper Rick's statement had me thinking was that *what* we are better to have and not need is both individual and contextual. What is relevant to my needs as a person and the situations in which I find myself? For Rick, living in the backwoods with bears that have been known to attack and kill humans, it was Rosemary. For me, it was a knife while scuba diving, a life-jacket while boating, and a medical kit while trekking remote areas. We each need to ask: *What resources do I need for my journey through life? What skills are helpful for me to develop to enhance my happiness? What are the things that, as Trapper Rick said, are better to have and not need than need and not have?*

Story 66

On Being a Positive Role Model

Happiness-Enhancing Characteristics

Problems Addressed

> Unexpected tragedy
> Loss
> Grief
> Unwelcome and unwanted adversities
> When life is unfair

Resources Developed

> Choosing to control what you can
> Developing a sense of adventure
> Seeing beauty and good in the world
> Learning to grow beyond tragedy
> Keeping your mind oriented to the positive
> Channeling tragedy constructively and creatively

Outcomes Offered

> Personal control
> A better, stronger, wiser person
> A happy, healthy, functional, meaningful life

Can you even begin to imagine what it would be like to have your spouse or life partner murdered? I certainly find it hard to imagine. Sure, loss and grief are inevitable parts of our life experience—things we can't escape—but to have that loss and grief associated with the suddenness, violence, and brutality of murder is another thing altogether. That, unfortunately, is what happened to a colleague of mine. As if that wasn't enough, life heaped even more seemingly undeserved and unwelcome adversities on her shoulders. Was it not enough to leave even the psychologically strongest person feeling shattered?

My colleague, however, has moved from surviving to thriving. She has gone on to complete a PhD and publish three psychology books. She has dedicated her life to helping others work through their problems, and finds happiness when her life experiences inspire others to greater happiness. How does someone do this? How does someone not only deal with such severe tragedy but move on to a happy, healthy, functional, and meaningful life?

I guess if you want to know something like that it helps to ask . . . so I did. She answered, "I would make a great positive psychology guinea pig. I actively use my own positive psychology research to guide my thoughts."

When I then asked, "What are some of those thoughts that guide you?" she was very clear and explicit in her answer.

"Although we can't control many things in life, it helps to remember that there are a lot of things we *can* control," she said. "It's all about our personal control. For example, we cannot control whether the day is sunny or raining but we can control what we do with our day and how we enjoy it."

"A sense of adventure also helps. When you have lost everything, what is there left to lose? You are free to take risks, adventure, explore, and do things differently. This could involve visiting new places, creating new experiences, or reaching out to new people."

"Yes," she continued, "life can be unfair. It can be tragic. There are lots of unkind, selfish, corrupt people out there. But there is also a lot of beauty and good in the world. That is worth seeing and worth fighting for."

"A psychological tragedy can also be a spiritual opportunity," she added. "When you do something greater than yourself, it helps you to grow and move beyond the tragedy, becoming a better, stronger, wiser person.

"Then, it helps not to complain all the time but to keep your mind oriented to the positive—just like the story in your book, *101 Healing Stories*, illustrates. One tale talks about two people who visited Africa. One sat watching the stunning wildlife while the other person, who only complained about all the negative things in her day, totally missed out on experiencing all the beautiful things around her."

"Finally," she concluded, "I guess you can either channel depression and tragedy destructively—by drinking, doing drugs, and shutting the world out. Or you can choose to channel tragedy constructively and creatively. I chose to express my energy creatively . . . and wrote a book. By making choices that move you forward, you win."

POSITIVE THINKING

What an amazing person, I thought, to be able to build such positivity out of such tragedy, and then to be able to see and explain the processes so clearly. But there was something in her statement that I had to disagree with. It was not that I didn't find her and her ways of managing such adversity a true inspiration. She certainly is inspiring. It was not that I didn't admire her as someone who truly practices what she preaches. It was not that I didn't see her ways of handling severe adversity as hopeful, practical, clear, and useful for others.

"What I have to disagree with," I said, "is that you described yourself as a great positive psychology guinea pig. I don't think you are a guinea pig. I think you are an amazingly great positive psychology role model. And I hope that, as you share your experiences, others may find your example a useful model on which to build their own happiness and positivity."

12 On Being Emotionally Positive and Engaged

There are only two ways to live your life. One is as though nothing is a miracle. The other is as if everything is.

Albert Einstein, physicist

Introduction

Martin Seligman, who has been hailed as the father of positive psychology, describes five core components of happiness and well-being (Seligman, 2011). For these he has developed the anagram PERMA: Positive emotions, Engagement, Relationships, Meaning, and Accomplishments. This chapter includes metaphors for communicating these first two components: positive emotions and engagement. Then, in the next two chapters we will deal with relationships, before a chapter on meaning. Metaphors covering accomplishments have already been covered in Chapter 1, On Being a Goal-Setter and Goal-Achiever, and Chapter 2, On Finding and Using Strengths.

Positive emotions are essential in our life if we are to experience happiness and well-being. They include pleasure (which is usually seen as the satisfaction of bodily needs like hunger, thirst, sex, and taking a long sleep after a hard day) and enjoyment (which comes from creativity and intellectual satisfaction). Feelings of peace, gratitude, satisfaction, inspiration, hope, curiosity, and love also fall within this category. While these are often short-term, temporary sensations and not necessarily a part of enduring happiness, positive emotions are important for enjoying one's self in the here and now. For a more lasting, long-term experience of happiness, positive emotions are seen as a part of the whole parcel that includes all the other components of the PERMA anagram.

Discovering the ability to create and experience positive emotions is a powerful tool for enhancing happiness. For someone who is significantly depressed—in that dark night of depression—to see the glimmer of just one star, briefly smell the fragrance of a single rose, or admire the colors of only one beautiful bird and, therefore, experience joy, is a potent discovery. Once a person knows, first, that they can experience it, second, that they can enjoy it, and, third, that it may be possible to experience more of it, such pleasure may be a potent point of change.

Engagement or flow refers to a high level of absorption in a situation, task, or project. It is this sort of experience we have all had when totally engaged in a movie, a concert, a good book, a sporting activity, a hobby, or sex. The characteristics of this experience are a high level of concentration, and a deep, effortless involvement. Tasks that are engaging have clear goals, present a challenge, and demand a high level of skill. In doing them we commonly feel a strong sense of control, lose awareness of self, concentrate intensely on the present, and often experience an alteration in the passage of time. Such engagement not only feels good but has us functioning at optimal levels. Achieving it is both natural and common especially when people are engaged in activities that they love, are good at, and give them a sense of accomplishment.

The following stories offer pathways and process for attaining and maintaining pleasure and engagement.

Story 67

Finding and Enjoying Pleasure

Happiness-Enhancing Characteristics

Problems Addressed

Repetitive, worrisome thoughts
A formula for depression

Resources Developed

Discovering the capacity for fun
Discovering the ability to be absorbed
Rediscovering past positive experiences
Committing to pleasurable activities
Learning to change experience

Outcomes Offered

More pleasurable life experiences
A sense of control
Creation of a more positive and pleasurable life

Janet was struggling with repetitive, worrisome thoughts. They were present whenever she had time to herself but at their worst at night. She could fall asleep in front of the television or while reading a book but as soon as she put her head on the pillow the thoughts rushed in like a tsunami. It didn't matter what they were. They could have been thoughts of a broken relationship, lost job, aging parent, drug-addicted child, a rocky marriage, hefty mortgage repayments, or whatever. In her worries she had stopped caring for herself. She was experiencing an almost guaranteed formula for depression.

How could she begin to find more pleasure and enjoyment in her life? I wondered. We know that a pleasurable life is one that is rich in positive emotions about the past, present, and future. Unfortunately, Janet's wasn't.

Research shows us clearly that the more positive emotions you have, the less you feel depressed or anxious. As building more positive emotions in effect overturns the detrimental effects of negative emotions, I wondered, *How could Janet build more pleasant emotions and thoughts and, in turn, let go of her negative emotions and thoughts?*

"What do you do for fun?" I began to enquire.

"I don't," came the reply. "I've been too worried to feel like having fun."

Fortunately, pleasure is a natural human emotion we have all experienced at some time to a greater or lesser degree . . . and are capable of experiencing again. So I asked, "What have you done for fun in the past?"

"I used to go out for a movie or coffee with my girlfriends."

"What else?" I enquired.

"I used to do embroidery, making patchwork quilts for my grandchildren and family."

Like with her worries, it really didn't matter what Janet's particular pleasurable experiences were. Whether embroidery, patchwork, grandkids, movies, coffee, or whatever it was for her, if she could enjoy such pleasurable absorption in the past, I wondered what she could do to capture those feelings in the present and into the future.

"What do you see yourself doing in the future that might also be absorbing, fun, enjoyable, or pleasant?" I asked.

"I have a room set up for sewing. I just haven't used it for a while. Perhaps I could set aside time to do so. I could also renew contacts with my friends or at least accept invitations when they call to ask me out," she replied.

Janet made a commitment to seek out and engage in the particular pleasurable activities she had enjoyed in the past and could anticipate enjoying in the future. She set aside time to spend in her sewing room engaging in needlework and came back to the next session telling me how much she had enjoyed it.

Another week she accepted an invitation to a movie with her girlfriends. Fortunately they chose a comedy and, she told me with a smile, that she found herself laughing out loud—something she had not done in a long while.

"Were you aware of those repetitive, worrisome thoughts while you were laughing at the movie?" I asked.

She hesitated for a moment before replying with a sound of surprise, "No."

"And what about while you were doing the embroidery?"

"Oh, I can always be absorbed in that," she said.

At times, when there are things we cannot change or alter, we know that worrying doesn't help . . . but often we still do it. If the circumstances are not likely to change, then we need to ask how we can change our experience about them.

Janet discovered that by creating more pleasurable experiences in her life it was possible to at least temporarily escape her previous worrisome thoughts.

POSITIVITY & ENGAGEMENT

She began to regain a sense of control about creating a more positive and pleasurable life. As she had discovered, the more time she allowed for positively absorbing fun thoughts and experiences, the less time she had for the old negative ones.

Story 68

Focusing on Sensory Pleasures

Happiness-Enhancing Characteristics

Problems Addressed

Depression
Lethargy
Social withdrawal
Loss of interest
Sensory or stimulus deprivation

Resources Developed

Learning to appreciate visual pleasures
Learning to appreciate auditory pleasures
Learning to appreciate pleasures of smell
Learning to appreciate taste pleasures
Learning to appreciate pleasures of touch
Discovering change is a process

Outcomes Offered

The discovery of new possibilities
Engagement in pleasurable sensory experiences
Sensory awareness and enjoyment

Depression has been described as a state of sensory or stimulus deprivation, and that is exactly what Brendon was experiencing. He was reluctant to get up in the morning and face the day. He couldn't be bothered going to work. He had ceased contacting friends. Spending most of the day in bed reading or playing solitaire, he had lost interest in almost everything. He had stopped doing the things that brought him pleasure and enjoyment. He worried about all the things he needed to be doing but was not doing. His senses received little stimulation, seeing only the four walls of his home; hearing only the familiar sounds of his home or passing traffic outside; smelling only the household aromas so familiar that he didn't even notice them; touching no one or feeling the temperature of the day. His senses were certainly deprived of stimulation.

Brendon didn't know or appreciate that it is our senses of sight, sound, smell, taste, and touch that put us in contact with the world and potentially pleasurable stimulations. How could someone so withdrawn, depressed, and sensory-deprived as Brendon now was become aware of, and focus on, pleasurable, sensory experiences that might enhance his sensory stimulation and, in turn, lift his depression? That was the challenge for him and me.

I gave him a copy of the Sensory Awareness Inventory to complete in our session (Burns, 2014)—a little tool I developed to help people be in touch with and savor the pleasures of their senses. The Inventory simply asks people to list things they get pleasure, relaxation, and enjoyment from in each of their five senses: sight, sound, smell, taste, and touch as well as in the things or activities they do.

As Brendon expressed the doubt that he would not be able to do it—stating there was nothing he enjoyed in the present—we sat and went through it together.

"If there is nothing in the moment, what things have you enjoyed looking at or seeing in the past?" I enquired. When he began to recall a few, I pressed, "And what visual things can you imagine yourself enjoying in the future?"

Gradually we stepped through each of his senses. "What sounds bring you enjoyment and pleasure?" "What smell sensations do you find calming or pleasurable?" "What tastes give you joy or satisfaction?" "What tactile or touch sensations are soothing, relaxing, exciting, or pleasurable for you?"

Change is a process and doesn't always happen suddenly or instantly. As the old Chinese philosopher said, "The journey of a thousand miles begins with the first step." Without those first steps we took as a child, or the falls that we suffered in doing so, we could not now know the pleasures of playing sport, dancing, cycling, walking along a beach, hiking through a forest, or simply jumping for joy. Each new step Brendon took was yet another step forward.

Discussing and completing the Sensory Awareness Inventory together had Brendon thinking about, remembering, and recalling past, positive experiences in each of his different sense modalities. He had a glimpse of what it was like for his mood to lift briefly—a time in which he felt better and more energized. It was just a fleeting change but fleeting enough to enable him to see that change was possible—a glimmer of hope in his otherwise dark world.

Building on this, I asked Brendon to select one pleasurable item from his inventory for him to do each day. To help him be open to discovering new possibilities, I asked him to add new items of pleasure to his inventory as he discovered them, and to keep it in a visible place—like on his fridge door—so as to remind him to find and engage in pleasurable sensory experiences each day.

For just as depression has been described as a state of sensory or stimulus deprivation, so happiness, at least in part, can be seen as a state of sensory or stimulus awareness and enjoyment. As Brendon experienced more joy and pleasure he gradually felt less sadness and depression. And that was a big step forward.

POSITIVITY & ENGAGEMENT

Story 69

Playing with Sea Lions

Happiness-Enhancing Characteristics

Problems Addressed

When nothing seems to be going right
When feeling out of your control
At a point of choice
Hesitancy

Resources Developed

Learning the value of exercise
Learning the value of getting into nature
Being in the moment
Being aware of pleasurable sensations
Experiencing a window of joy
Finding the potential for pleasure and joy

Outcomes Offered

Greater relaxation and happiness
Pleasure and joy
Creation of possibilities

Have you ever known those times when nothing seems to be going right, when your best laid plans are falling apart, when things seem out of your control or when the proverbial hits the fan? I was there a while ago and knew I needed to do something about it. At such times in life we have a choice: give into it and sink into despair, or find a way to change either the circumstances or how we feel about them. I guess we all have different ways of doing that, different things that work for us. In fact, one of life's important learnings is to know what works for us and what doesn't—and how we might use it for our well-being.

Experience has taught me that one such thing is to get physically active. I don't need science to tell me . . . but it does. If you want to lift your mood, exercise can be as good as or even better than taking anti-depressant medication. And it doesn't take a lot. Exercising for just 10 minutes per day, five days per week can reduce the severity of depression by up to 50%.

I have learnt that burning up some of the energy of my negative feelings helps shifts my head into a different space. Getting into nature, to take a walk through the woods, a stroll alongside a stream, a swim in the ocean, or a kayak paddle to one of the islands in the bay near my home, is especially beneficial. Nonetheless, just knowing what works doesn't necessarily mean we do it. If

I ask myself, *Do I feel like changing into paddling gear, wheeling the kayak to the beach, and launching into the cold water?* the answer would probably be a strong *No*. However, if I ask, *Do I know that going for a paddle is likely to benefit me and my feelings?*, I usually answer in the affirmative and set about heading to the beach.

One day—when feeling down and knowing I needed to do something—I wheeled my kayak to the beach and pointed the bow toward Seal Island. On reaching the shelter of the island's bay, I drifted along with the shore current watching the sea lions snoozing on the beach. Suddenly, one popped his head up beside the kayak and eyeballed me with his large, brown, puppy-like eyes. He dived under the kayak, bobbed up on the other side and studied me. Then he swam to the bow, did a duck dive, flicking up his rear flippers to splash me with water, like a kid playfully asking you to come play.

At first, I hesitated to hop in the water with him. While I had safely swum with sea lions before, I was out here alone, a long way off shore. When another kayaker paddled into the bay, his presence allowed me to feel safe enough to drop the anchor, pull on my mask and snorkel, and slip overboard.

Immediately, the sea lion swam up to me and started twisting in underwater somersaults. Awkwardly, I tried to mimic his 'aquabatics.' Soon two more equally playful sea lions came to join us. Together we swam, twisted, turned, and somersaulted. Time stood still. I was, as the common expression says, in the moment. I had briefly stepped out of my world and into theirs. I was part of their energy and their playfulness. I was aware of nothing but my own immediate, pleasurable senses. It was only later I realized the worries that had plagued my head as I pushed off from the shore had totally evaporated. I was giggling out loud through my snorkel.

The sea lions' energy eventually outstripped mine. Reluctant to leave such a window of joy in my seemingly current world of worries I hauled myself onto the kayak to return to shore. Back there I knew things would be no different from when I had left. The plans that were falling apart had not miraculously reunited and there were things that, realistically, remained beyond my control—but I *felt* different. I felt more relaxed, I felt happier, I felt a smile on my face.

As I may not always be able to go swimming with sea lions when I want or need, I need to ask myself, *What else can bring me such engaged pleasure? What are the things I can do that allow me to be absorbed and enjoying? Where and when can I allow myself the pleasure of such enjoyable experiences?*

By taking the opportunity to engage in what I knew worked for me, what had the potential to bring me pleasure and joy, my feelings and thoughts changed. Even if only temporarily, I now knew it was possible.

POSITIVITY & ENGAGEMENT

Story 70

Stopping to Savor the Roses

Happiness-Enhancing Characteristics

Problems Addressed

Overwhelmingly complex issues and worries
Disempowerment
Lack of joy and pleasure
Ruminative worries
Avoidant behaviors
History of abuse
Depression

Resources Developed

Pleasure and enjoyment
Engagement, focus, and absorption
Sensory awareness
Sensate focusing
Mindfulness

Outcomes Offered

Pleasure
Engagement
Mindfulness
Laughter

I have to confess that there have been times in my career when I have felt stumped. Times when a person's story has been so overwhelmingly complex and complicated that I found myself asking, "Where do I begin?" And, if I am asking that question, then the person experiencing it has probably asked the same question many times over and felt even more disempowered than me by the lack of a clear answer. That's how it was with Mary when she told me about her diffuse symptoms, lack of joy, forgetfulness, pain, obesity, a gambling problem, ruminative worries, avoidant behaviors, an unhappy marriage, a history of abuse, children at risk of a fatal disease, a dying father, two automobile accidents, the death and illness of several family and friends, and so the sad list went on.

Many of those things in Mary's story could not and would not alter. There were things that had happened in the past, things that were happening in the present, and things that could realistically happen in the future. Battling to change what could not be changed had not proved to be successful—and was the basis of her feelings of helplessness and hopelessness. There was no point in either of us persisting in a path that had already proven to be unproductive.

Looking for alternative directions, I began to wonder, *Was it possible to help her create at least some positive, pleasurable experiences? Could she find some joy amidst the pain—a glimmer of hope, a light at the end of a long, dark tunnel?*

Exploring when Mary felt at her most relaxed and happiest, she described how she enjoyed tending her roses. As the research shows us that pleasure and enjoyment come when we are engaged, focused, and absorbed in pleasurable experiences I asked Mary to imagine herself tending to her roses, particularly observing the pleasures she experienced in each of her sensory modalities: her sight, smell, sound, taste, and touch sensations.

"When you *look* at your roses, what brings you pleasure?" I enquired. "Imagine the shapes, shades, colors, tones, and movements that you enjoy." What were the variations she could appreciate even in a single petal or leaf? What sights brought her greatest enjoyment?

After giving her time to think on, recall, and discuss these, we then moved on to her sense of smell. What fragrances brought her pleasure, enjoyment, and comfort? Could she detect the fragrance of the roses when she stepped into the garden? Could she notice the differences of fragrances between different roses or even different flowers on the same bush? Did she, literally, give herself time to stop and smell the roses?

Step by step we worked our way through each of her senses. Were there sounds that she associated with her roses? Like holding a seashell to your ear, you may never know there are sounds there unless you stop to listen: The flutter of a leaf in the breeze, the sound the wind in the bushes, the buzzing of a bee or hum of an insect.

One may not normally link the sense of taste with roses but still I wanted Mary to examine all her pleasurable sensory experiences with roses. "Have you noticed if you can taste the fragrance of the roses on your tongue or palate?" I asked. "Have you ever placed a petal on your tongue or bitten into it to experience the taste?"

"And what tactile sensations do you enjoy about your roses? What does the touch of a petal feel like against your skin or held gently between your fingers?"

We psychologists call this process sensate focusing or savoring. For Mary it simply meant that she was invited to be very specifically mindful and aware of the pleasurable sensory experiences she enjoyed—and to enjoy them more. The detailed questions opened possibilities for her to revisit her own pleasurable experiences and explore how she could continue to enjoy them, intimately, into the future.

Mary subsequently wrote to me about her trip home following that first appointment. She used the journey to visualize making her husband rose petal sandwiches, marinating his meat in rose perfume, rose petals in the stew, lighting rose candles, sprinkling rose petals all around the room, and added, "some other ideas that I won't write down." After getting off the train she found herself laughing out loud while walking down the street. Concluding her letter, she said "I found a freedom of spirit that hasn't been there for a long

POSITIVITY & ENGAGEMENT

time. Thanks for letting me find my own way through it. The rose petals are a great idea."

(For a full description of Mary's case and the therapy offered, see Burns, 2007.)

Story 71

Being in the Flow

Happiness-Enhancing Characteristics

Problems Addressed

> Disappointment
> Unhappiness
> Desire for optimal performance

Resources Developed

> Finding a challenge
> Developing clear goals
> Seeking clear and immediate feedback
> Building a deep, effortless involvement
> Building a sense of control or mastery
> Experiencing the loss of self-awareness
> Experiencing how time stands still

Outcomes Offered

> Optimal experiences
> Satisfaction
> Contentment and happiness
> Absorption and engagement
> Being in the flow

A highly competitive rally car driver once consulted me requesting assistance with hypnosis to enhance his racing performance by being totally engaged and mindful. Do you know the experience he requested? Are there times when you have been so totally absorbed or engaged in a hobby, sport, or other activity that you have switched off from the things around you and been totally 'in the zone' as athletes often refer to the experience?

Guys engrossed in watching their team playing on TV, teenagers totally unresponsive when playing a video game, or someone involved in reading a novel all display the phenomena—often to the frustration of anyone wanting their attention. Well, you may be surprised to learn that researchers have studied this phenomena, particularly Dr Csikszentmihalyi (pronounced Chick-sent-me-hi) and call it 'Flow.' Csikszentmihalyi says this is often a sign of when we are at our best, when we are performing optimally, and when we are likely to be happy. The times when you have been so totally involved in playing sport, making love, undertaking an exciting work challenge, absorbed in a concert, or 'switched off' in a state of meditation that you are no longer aware of the sights, sounds, or sensations around you, or even the passage of time.

My rally driver wanted to learn how to acquire these characteristics of being in the flow. To do so, first, he would need to be involved in *a task of challenge and skill* for him—as he already was.

His request for assistance with hypnosis was to help build the second characteristic of flow: his *concentration* as he was hurling a high powered car, at high speeds, around rough gravel roads without knowing exactly what lay ahead. This demanded extreme concentration.

He had *clear goals*, a third component of flow. He wanted to be the best rally driver in the nation and had his sights set on competing at top international levels.

A fourth characteristic of flow is that it provides us with *immediate feedback*. My rally driver knew immediately how well or how poorly he was performing. His awareness and skills were highly fine-tuned and I was impressed as he described how he used them.

I remember him describing how he applied his newly learnt hypnotic skills in a recent rally. Unlike us suburban drivers who drive cars around the corner, rally drivers don't. They slide their car sideways into the corner so that they can quickly accelerate straightforward out of bend, and this is all done at the highest speed possible. The slightest under- or over-estimate, the misjudging of the curve, or the failure to see a rock or rut on the road in those microseconds of cornering could be fatal.

By slowing his thoughts, my driver said that he was able to concentrate on each corner as if viewing a slow motion movie. He could see each rock and rut, he could estimate the angle of bend, he could calculate the amount of slide, and know both when and how rapidly to accelerate. Unknown to him he was in fact describing other characteristics of flow: a *deep effortless involvement* in what he was doing; a clear and confident *sense of control*; and a *sense that self had vanished*. In addition, his experience was that *time had altered*. It had gone into slow motion. He expressed his own surprise that he was able to slow his thoughts so markedly and appear to be so much in control of his decisions and actions in such a fleeting time.

While he showed me what I believe is a very clear example of being highly engaged in an optimal experience, I appreciate that such high action sports are not for everyone. So I wonder what the times are when you have experienced similar things in a sport, a hobby, or an activity. When have you undertaken a *challenge*, with *clear goals*, that has given you *clear and immediate feedback* about your involvement in that activity? When did you engage in something *with deep, effortless involvement* and felt a *sense of control or mastery* in what you were doing? When were the times you have experienced the *sense of self vanishing*, or noticed that *time appeared to stand still*?

POSITIVITY &
ENGAGEMENT

These are the times when you engage in optimal experiences, the times when you are absorbed and involved, the times you are likely to feel satisfied, and the times when you are contented and happy in yourself. When are those times for you? And how can you create more of them?

Story 72

Counting Your Blessings

Happiness-Enhancing Characteristics

Problems Addressed

> Depressive feelings
> Depressive thoughts
> Ruminations
> Negative emotions
> Anxiety

Resources Developed

> Gratefulness
> Counting your blessings
> Appreciation of events, experiences, and people
> Gratitude exercises
> Gratitude journal

Outcomes Offered

> Pleasure
> Engagement
> Meaning

Clara was depressed. She had dragged her body into my office, dumped it heavily into the chair, and sat expressionless, her eyes gazing at the floor. The letter of referral from her psychiatrist diagnosed her with a major depressive disorder and obsessive ruminations of delusional intensity when very unwell. Treatment efforts with cognitive behavior therapy medication and electro-convulsive therapy had, in his words, "failed to modify the ruminations."

If all these efforts to *stop* her being depressed had failed, I wondered if efforts to help her *start* feeling happier might be more productive. At the moment it seemed like she was experiencing a host of negative emotions. Was it possible to help her build more positive emotions? Would the building of the positive help her to outweigh the negative, depressive feelings and thoughts?

A pleasurable life is one that is rich in positive emotions about the past, present, and future. The more a person experiences, and is grateful for, positive emotions, the lower their levels of negative emotions such as depression and anxiety. To create, and experience, a brief moment of pleasure is often an easier task than to get rid of the depression, or instantly find a deep and abiding happiness. So what would best help Clara build more positive emotions?

There is a lot of evidence in the happiness research that shows taking time to acknowledge the things you are grateful for, count your blessings, and appreciate the events, experiences, and people in your life can add to the creation and maintenance of happier feelings. If you are grateful for the job you have you are likely to feel happier at work. If you consider your spouse to be one of your greatest blessings, you are likely to enjoy a happy relationship. If you are appreciative of simple everyday events, your life will be more fulfilling and rewarding.

On the basis of this evidence, I could have asked Clara to engage in several different gratitude exercises. I could have asked her, for example, to visit someone who'd been especially kind and helpful to her and expressed her gratitude in person. I could have asked her to write a letter expressing her thankfulness and appreciation, perhaps personally delivering and discussing the letter with that person. I could have asked her to express gratitude to someone in a concrete way by sending a thank-you card, a bunch of flowers, or a box of chocolates.

I could have asked her to establish an ongoing practice of expressing gratitude by actively watching for things that others do that are helpful, kind, and considerate—and to thank them overtly. I could have asked her to observe any ungrateful thought that she may have had during the day (such as "My husband forgot to put out the rubbish again") and substitute that with a grateful thought (such as "He has been loving, caring and supportive for the last 20 years of their marriage"). I could have asked to keep a daily gratitude journal, recording and reflecting on those things that she was appreciative of during her day.

What I in fact did was ask Clara to engage in two exercises. "First," I asked, "write down just three things that you feel grateful for or acknowledge as a blessing in your life each day. Second, when you and your husband go to bed at night, ask him about the three things that he was grateful for in the day, and discuss your mutual blessings."

The list of daily blessings Clara brought to the next session included things like being appreciative of her husband's cooking, enjoying a picnic with her grandkids in the park, and feeling grateful for the days it rained in our drought-stricken state. I could visibly see her mood lift as she shared and talked about the things that she felt grateful for.

Researchers have shown us that people who engage in these gratitude exercises for one to 12 weeks report being significantly happier, and continue to remain happier for as long as six months after they complete the exercise. For Clara—whose depression was deep and long-standing—I am sure that neither of us expected it would instantly rid her of all of her symptoms. However, it did show her that pleasure and positive feelings were possible even in the depths of her unhappiness. Combined with other exercises to help her build more positive emotions, become more engaged, and find greater meaning in her life, Clara began to feel happier—and it showed.

After a total of five weekly sessions, she was seen again for a follow-up session after three months at which time she announced, "The depression has gone," but acknowledged, "though I still get days of feeling anxious." Clara was beginning to learn that it was possible to have pleasurable experiences in her life and that those pleasurable experiences could outweigh or undo her previous depressive thoughts. Instead of her life being filled with worries and despair, it was now much richer in pleasure, engagement, and meaning.

(For a full description of Clara's case and the therapy offered, see Burns, 2010.)

13 On Being in Social Relationships

A journey is best measured in friends rather than miles.

Tom Cahill, writer

Introduction

We humans are social beings. We live in couple relationships, family relationships, social relationships, community relationships, and work relationships. As a result of being social, interactive beings, our ability to create and maintain warm, caring, empathic relationships is one of the essential building blocks for future psychological and social maturity as well as happiness. Both research findings and real life experience show that people who have meaningful, positive relationships with others are happier than those who do not. In other words, relationships really matter in the happiness stakes.

When children develop empathy, caring, and compassion for another person, they are less likely to engage in violence, aggression, or other conduct disorders. Learning positive relationship skills is also healthy, both emotionally and physically, as it improves immune system functioning and lowers rates of cancer, cholesterol, and premature death.

Studies examining 'very happy people'—the top 10% of people who rated themselves as happy—reveal that relationships again stand out as a core happiness factor. The majority of the happiest people have five or more good friends. They are social people who joined social groups, experienced quality relationships, and built social support networks.

The stories in this chapter look primarily at social relationships but also touch on romantic relationships as the processes for selecting, building, and maintaining such relationships have many similarities. They seek to address questions like, How do you build reciprocal relationships that involve giving and receiving, and working together cooperatively? How do you learn to create and maintain good social relationships? How do you learn and follow the rules of the relationship? How do you come to appreciate that "no man is an island"—that we are all interrelated? How do you go about finding and selecting the attributes in a potential life partner? And given that we are all individuals, how do we work cooperatively with others for our mutual benefit?

Story 73

An Unexpected Lesson

Happiness-Enhancing Characteristics

Problems Addressed

Need of support
Need of a role model
Need of a reciprocal relationship

Resources Developed

Learning to look after and care for others
Learning that good relationships are reciprocal
Learning to give and receive
Learning about working together
Becoming wiser, stronger, and better equipped

Outcomes Offered

Reciprocal relationships
Life experiences live on
Acceptance of unexpected learnings

Sometimes there are unexpected gains from attending a conference: benefits that go beyond the lectures, latest research, new approaches, or even the collegiate networking.

A few years back, I was invited to present at a conference in South Africa that was temptingly accommodated within a wildlife park—one of those invitations you don't have to contemplate long before accepting. At six in the morning and again after the presentations at the approach of sunset, we participants had the opportunity to join an animal-watching safari. Each trip we trundled through the jungles and savannahs in the back of an open vehicle, sighting giraffes, zebras, hippopotamus, rhinoceros, lions, monkeys, and elephants. It was on one of these trips that our local guide, Moses, pointed to three elephants that ambled across the dirt road in front of us and said, "*Askaris.*"

In attending the conference, I had expected to learn not only from the well-known colleagues who were leaders in their specialties but also from the new, younger students who can often propose fresh ideas and insights. I had not expected to learn something of such importance from my safari guide.

"What does *askaris* mean?" I asked Moses.

"They are bull elephants," he explained pointing to the stunningly huge and beautiful creatures crossing our path. "See how the two smaller ones are flanking the largest?" The big bull's long, curved tusks stretched almost to the ground. I was thankful we were on a private reserve where those magnificent tusks were hopefully out of reach from ivory poachers. "It is the younger ones who are the *askaris.*"

"It is actually a Swahili word," he continued, "that means guard or sentry but has a couple of meanings. It's more modern meaning has a military context. This evolved during the colonial times and it spread into common use across most of the African continent. You could hear it used to refer to native African soldiers who were employed in 'white' armies. But here, in South Africa, it took a more specific meaning during our period of apartheid. Here *askaris* referred to 'black' personnel who worked as undercover agents for the 'white' government."

"What you are seeing with the elephants is closer to its original meaning. The role of the *askaris* is to look after and take care of the older, more important one. They flank him as his protectors. At a time when his senses begin to dull with age, they are there for him, becoming his eyes and his ears."

"Like with any good relationship," said Moses with a quiet sense of wisdom, "it is reciprocal. Both give and receive. The older bull receives protection, support, and caring, while giving of his experience and wisdom to the younger. He is like a sage or tutor to them. As the younger bulls give by looking out for their elder so they also receive what they learn from him, from the life experience he passes on to them. They are a team. By working together, they survive where they might not if they were to go it alone."

"As one grows weaker, the others grow stronger and the lessons of surviving well are passed on. When the old bull dies, the younger ones will have learnt much to prepare them for a good life. They will be wiser, stronger, and better equipped. His journey will not have been in vain. He and his life experiences will live on in them."

I watched the two elephants flanking their elder as they wandered off slowly toward a water hole. And found myself wondering, *Who do I see as my sage or wise tutor? Who do I see as the person I want to learn most from? Who provides me with support, caring, and protecting? Who do I have, or want to have, such a reciprocal relationship with? And do those things need to come from someone externally? Are there caring, protective parts of me that I can tap into when needed? Is there wisdom and experience that I have built up and can draw on in times of need?*

If I reflect back to that conference, I have to confess there is not a lot that I remember from the formal presentations but I sure do remember Moses and his lesson about the *askaris*.

Story 74

Building and Maintaining Social Relationships

Happiness-Enhancing Characteristics

Problems Addressed

Lack of friendships
Loneliness
Lack of information about how to establish friendships

Lack of information about how to maintain friendships

Resources Developed

Learning to build more relationships
Learning to accept invitations
Committing to following up new contacts
Joining mutual interest groups
Reconnecting with an old friend
Talking to a stranger, safely

Outcomes Offered

Expanded social networks
Happiness
Greater life satisfaction
Enhanced emotional well-being

"How do you establish and maintain friendships?" It is a question that interests me, a question that I have asked friends, clients, colleagues in my workshops, and listeners on my radio talkback program. The answers I get are often varied and diverse but come down to some core underlying principles—principles that have been confirmed in research.

There seems to be little question that relationships are an important, if not the most important, source of our happiness, life satisfaction, and emotional well-being. This is not surprising as there is truth in the statement that no man is an island. We are social beings, we need to relate with other people and we need to relate with other people well for our own quality of life.

Some of my colleagues, researching what factors contribute to our happiness, did something interesting. They pulled out the top 10% of happy people, describing these as "very happy people." Then they looked at what were the contributing factors to the happiness of those very happy people. One thing stood out, and stood out clearly. Very happy people have good networks of friends, with 50% of this group having five or more close friends. They joined social groups, they had loving relationships, and they built social support networks. They spent more time with other people than the research subjects who fell in the "happy" group, let alone the "unhappy" group. Overall, loneliness seems to be associated with life dissatisfaction whereas social ability is correlated with life satisfaction.

Hopefully, we know this from our own experience. How often have you heard people say after going through the breakup of a relationship, experiencing a period of trauma, or being severely challenged, "I wouldn't have got through that if it hadn't been for a loving family and friends?"

With this background knowledge, I am interested to ask people, "How do you establish and maintain friendships?" The answers vary but do come down to one core principle: I put in the effort to connect and maintain those connections with others.

One guy, after the breakup of his marriage and the inevitable falling away of what were mutual friends, found himself very lonely and decided he needed to create new friendships.

"How did you do that?" I asked him, curious about how he went about building new relationships.

"First, I decided to accept every invitation to go to a party or social function," he said. "Second, I made a commitment to meet and talk with people I didn't know. And, third, I decided to follow-up contact with at least one person. Whether it was male or female, whether it had the potential to be romantic or just a friendship, I would swap phone numbers with someone and agreed to meet for a coffee, walk, or at another party. Each person I met had their own network of friends, so meeting just one person introduced me to a number of others."

Others have found they can build new friendships through joining mutual interest groups, regardless of what they may be—a dance school, gym, bushwalking club, men's shed, embroidery class, book club, choir, wine tasting course, or any of the many, many other things in which they may have a personal interest.

Instead of seeking new friendships some people told me they had sought to reconnect with an old friend whose company they had previously enjoyed but for various reasons had drifted apart. This they had done in many different ways: making a phone call, writing a card, sending an email, or posting a letter.

Finally, some told me that they made the effort to talk to a stranger, safely. Engaging in pleasantries with a checkout operator or shop assistant may not form the basis of an ongoing relationship but may help the social interactions of the day be more enjoyable. Speaking with people while out walking the dog, playing with kids in the park, sitting next to you on the bus, or any other circumstances helps add to life's enjoyment and may open opportunities for new friendships.

So, while we know friendships and social relationships are good for us, I find it interesting to hear all the various ways that people establish and maintain those networks of friends. "How do *you* establish and maintain friendships for you?"

Story 75

In Sand or Stone?

Happiness-Enhancing Characteristics

Problems Addressed

Abuse
Hurt
Challenges to relationships

Resources Developed

Empathy
Altruism
Generosity
Forgiveness
Acceptance of individual differences
Granting the freedom to be
A healthy level of compromise
Letting things go
Gratitude
Strengthspotting

Outcomes Offered

Acceptance
Freedom to be
Healthy compromise
Gratitude
Strengthspotting
Creation and maintenance of positive relationships

I recall once hearing a story about two friends who were taking an extended walk along the beach. At some stage in their journey they got into a rather heated argument. One of the friends became so enraged that he shouted abuse at the other. The one who was shouted at felt extremely hurt. Nonetheless, he said nothing. Instead he stopped, knelt down in the sand and wrote, "TODAY MY BEST FRIEND SHOUTED ABUSE AT ME."

There is good evidence from recent research on well-being that the most significant determinant of our well-being is our network of close relationships with other people. In general terms, the more connected we are with others in our social relationships and friendships, the better off we are in regards to our happiness.

Qualities like empathy, altruism, and generosity contribute to us forming and keeping good relationships. A number of my colleagues have also taken an interest in forgiveness and the effect this has upon our friendships. While the results show that better mental and physical health are related to forgiveness, we don't have a clear understanding of exactly why or how this works.

Yet other colleagues question whether forgiveness is really as beneficial to a relationship as some think. Obviously, at times forgiveness—such as in an abusive relationship where continued forgiveness has not resulted in a change of behavior—is not the answer. There one needs to be making choices that are both protective and practical.

Sometimes I wonder about the concept of forgiveness. If I say *I forgive you* is it like saying *I am right and you are wrong*? Does it seem like putting oneself in a position of power, authority, and superiority? Culturally, we usually associate someone like God or a high being as the one who does the forgiving. For me to forgive seems to impose an unequal power structure to the relationship.

After all is it not *me* feeling hurt about what the other has done? And, if so, should it not be me looking at how to change myself or the relationship to achieve a better outcome?

I also wonder. Are relationships not better off where we can acknowledge and accept our unique individual differences? Are relationships not healthier where we grant our friends and partners the same right to think, to feel, and to act with the freedom that we would wish for ourselves? Do relationships not require some healthy level of compromise? If we can see the other as an equal, acknowledge and accept our differences, permit each other mutual freedoms and appreciate the need for some shared compromises, maybe there is no need to forgive but rather to let go of what has happened.

The story I began to relate did speak of forgiveness but I suspect the true sense was of letting things go, of putting them in the past, of leaving them behind.

After resuming their walk along the beach in silence, the friend who had shouted at his best mate eventually asked him, "After I hurt you back there, you wrote in the sand. Why?"

His friend replied, "When someone hurts us, we should write it in sand. That way the winds and waves of forgiveness can erase it. Then it will have gone forever."

As they continued along the beach they came upon a stream that needed to be crossed. The friend who had been shouted at was not a good swimmer, got swept away by the current, and was struggling to avoid drowning. The friend who got angry saw his mate's predicament, dived in the water, pulled his friend from the stream, applied resuscitation, and saved his life. After the friend had recovered from his near drowning, he picked up a hard stone and carved into one of the softer beach rocks, "TODAY MY BEST FRIEND SAVED MY LIFE."

Showing and expressing gratitude helps us both form relationships in the first place and then maintain them once established. People tend to connect positively with grateful people, in part, because gratitude enhances greater levels of liking and inclusiveness in friendships and, in part, because it boosts essential relationship qualities like sensitivity and concern. In romantic relationships, people feel more committed where there is a high level of gratitude. Once married, relationships are described as more satisfying when partners show gratitude and appreciation of each other. Having and expressing gratitude in relationships tends to reduce aggression, build trust, and enable people to feel more socially confident.

If this is so, it begs the question *How can I feel and express gratitude in my relationship?* Well, being a strengthspotter is a good starting point. Ask yourself about the qualities and strengths you see in the other person. What are those strengths? What are the things you like about that person? What are the qualities that attracted you to them in the first place? What are the things that they do well? What do you admire in them? What are the things about your relationship with them that enhances the quality of your life?

Next, don't just take them for granted. Make a mental note of them. Keep a diary about the things you appreciate in both that person and that relationship. Maybe take time to reflect on how that friend and friendship enhance your own well-being.

And then express them. Let your friends know the things you appreciate about them. Tell them what you are grateful for in the relationship. Pat them on the back for their achievements. Send them a card as a note of thanks. Even a simple gift, like a bunch of flowers, a bottle of wine, or a box of chocolates is a way of showing appreciation and gratitude. These things help create, develop, and maintain positive relationships.

Carving a message of gratitude in the beach rocks was another example told in our story. The friend who had saved his best mate from drowning asked, "After I shouted at you, you wrote in the sand. That I understand, but now you write on a stone. Why?"

The rescued friend replied, "When someone does something good for us, we should engrave it in stone. There, neither wind nor waves remove it. The memory and gratitude remain."

Story 76

No Man Is an Island

Happiness-Enhancing Characteristics

Problems Addressed

> When no man is an island
> Depression
> Lack of affection, love, caring
> Feelings of being unloved or rejected
> Feelings of worthlessness

Resources Developed

> Making choices
> Discriminating between the person and his actions
> Differentiating feelings and reason
> Recalling past positive associations
> Seeing and responding to the big picture
> Seeing the potential light at the end of the tunnel

Outcomes Offered

> Appreciation of connections
> Greater relationship happiness

"No man is an island," I can vividly remember a client whom I shall call Kay once saying to me. "And no man's depression is an island either," she continued. She was clearly letting me know that her husband's depression powerfully affected her, their family, and those near and dear to him as well.

When depressed, a person simply isn't as affectionate, caring, loving, understanding, or supportive. Being wrapped in their own emotions and feelings, they are less aware and responsive to the feelings of others. This was tough for someone like Kay who felt unloved or rejected. In her words, she said, "He made me feel worthless."

I guess there is no need to mention the specific reasons why her husband was so depressed. They can vary from person to person. What mattered for Kay was the effect his depression was having on her and their family of three children. Feeling that she was unable to take anymore herself, and not wanting to put the kids through anymore, she left him on two occasions but after short periods went back.

I was curious. Why had she gone back when faced with such a choice? Separation is never easy but neither is attempting to resume a relationship with someone so down. How had she made the choice? How had she managed to make that choice work for her?

First, she seemed to discriminate between the person and his actions. She said, "While I didn't hate him, I did hate what he was doing and how he made our life hell. He didn't mean it. It wasn't my husband."

Second, she differentiated between her feelings and her reason. She *felt* anger and frustration about what he was doing. He was making their lives hell and didn't appear to be doing, or want to do, anything to pull himself out of his misery. Naturally, she wanted to protect herself and her kids from that. But, on the other hand, she *knew* that he didn't mean it, that her husband was not the sort of person who, in his normal state of mind, would consciously or deliberately want to inflict such pain on her or the children. "He would put us before everyone and everything," she commented.

Third, she could recall past positive associations with him and their relationship. "There was none of this when I first met him," she said. "He has always been loving and affectionate. He really is a caring and considerate person."

Fourth, she let me—and more importantly herself—know that she could see and respond to the big picture of their relationship rather than just the specifics of the current situation. "Like all relationships," she said, "we have had our ups and downs but overall it has been good. I would say it is 80–90% good. We have to remember those times and learn how to ride out the not-so-good times when they do inevitably occur, like now."

Finally, she could see the potential light at the end of the tunnel. She held hope, based on her knowledge of the past, that things could and most likely would be better. "If he can feel better as he has done previously, if we can get well in our relationship and if our family can be happy as we have been in the past, then we know it is possible again."

Not everyone may make the same choice as Kay or follow exactly the same processes. Nonetheless, I could not help agreeing with her that no man—nor his depression or happiness—is an island . . . and that there may be ways to find a happy or at least happier ending.

Story 77

Dropping Sticks

Happiness-Enhancing Characteristics

Problems Addressed

> Desire to find a life partner
> Partner selection based on infatuation
> Past disastrous relationships
> Repeated past patterns of relationships

Resources Developed

> Looking for desired partner qualities
> Learning to ask helpful relationship questions
> Looking for desired relationship qualities
> Assessing compatibility
> Assessing a partner's abilities
> Making informed choices about a partner

Outcomes Offered

> New relationship assessment
> Informed relationship choices
> Enhanced chances of a relationship working well

"I am dropping sticks," said Peter with a smile as if I should know what he was talking about . . . and I thought I did. "I read one of your books that told a Native American story of how a female eagle selects her mate." I nodded as he continued. "To find her life partner, she picks up a stick, carries it up into the air and, when her potential suitor is following, drops the stick to see if he will catch it. She keeps repeating it with heavier and heavier sticks until she finds the partner who is up to her challenge. As you know, she wants someone who will be able to pluck her young eaglets from the air if they fall from their cliff-edge nest when first learning to spread their wings. It impressed me. She didn't select on momentary infatuation but by looking at the partner qualities she wanted in the future of her relationship."

Peter had been through a series of disastrous relationships and didn't want to repeat the patterns of the past. "We guys have a reputation for thinking from a little lower than our navel, don't we?" he commented. "We look for someone who is beautiful or sexy. We get sold this image from movies and

TV: you meet someone attractive, fall into bed but no one tells you if they live happily ever after, if it is even possible to do, or how to do it."

"So, how are you dropping sticks?" I asked.

"Well, the eagle in the story *knew* what she wanted in a partner. That is the first thing. I realized I needed to ask myself, *What do I want in a partner? What do I want my relationship to look like in the future? What are the things that will make a relationship sustainable in the long-term?* Like the eagle, I need a clear vision of the qualities of my future partner as well as of our relationship."

"Then, the eagle tested her partner. When I say *I'm dropping sticks*, I mean I am asking more questions than I ever did before . . . and different questions. Rather than just get together and see if it works or not, now I want to know more about how compatible we might be. What are her past patterns of relationships? How was her parents' relationship? How does she handle conflict in a relationship? How does she handle her partner being under stress? What are her hopes for a relationship? Does she want children? Would she put children or career first? Do we share life's core values? Do we value similar things in the big picture of life?"

"Another thing the eagle story taught me is that she (the eagle) was active in her assessment. She deliberately did things that allowed her to actively observe her potential partner closely and carefully. She didn't rely on the rose-colored glasses of romance but went about creating situations that would allow her to truly assess her partner's abilities to be the mate she wanted. Following her example, I too have been using another way of 'dropping sticks.' How does a potential partner relate with my friends and family? How does she behave toward young children? How does she manage stress or challenging times? How dependent or independent is she? Does she express her feelings or bottle them inside? What happens when we have a difference of opinion? Are we able to communicate openly and honestly about such things? How does she go about problem-solving? How do we problem-solve together?"

"I realize we can't predict the future and never know what may happen around life's next corner but to me the eagle story seems to say we can, and should, make informed choices about selecting a partner. If we do, I believe we have a much better chance of the relationship working and working well. That's why I'm 'dropping sticks.'"

Story 78

Four Faithful Friends

Happiness-Enhancing Characteristics

Problems Addressed

Tackling a task
Independence versus cooperation

Resources Developed

> Building cooperative endeavors
> Making offers to help others
> Discovering how individual skills can contribute to a whole
> Learning the values of friendship
> Accepting differences

Outcomes Offered

> Cooperation
> Consideration
> Friendships
> Acceptance of differences

At the end of a study tour of colleagues that I had lead into the tiny little Himalayan country of Bhutan, the group presented me with a painting as a thank-you gift. Knowing my interest in stories they had chosen a painting of Bhutan's national story, entitled the Four Faithful Friends. The story tells a tale of a pheasant, a rabbit, a monkey, and an elephant. On reaching home I found a spot to proudly hang it on the wall. When my grandson next came to visit he looked at the painting and asked me about the story. Though I have since heard several different versions of it, the story I related to him went something like this.

One day a beautiful pheasant, with long, colorful feathers, found a seed that it decided to plant. As she was unsuccessfully scratching away to dig a hole deep enough for the seed, she was startled by a long-eared rabbit who hopped up and asked what she was doing.

"I am good at digging," said the rabbit acknowledging one of its strengths. "Is there anything I can do to help?"

"Thank you kindly," answered the beautiful pheasant who waited for the rabbit to dig a deep enough hole before dropping in the seed and standing back for the rabbit to cover it over and tamp it down with his back feet.

Seeing all this activity a brown-furred monkey swung down from his tree to enquire what was happening. "Can I help too?" he asked.

"With your longer arms could you carry water up from the stream to water it and give it life?" requested the pheasant.

Delighted to help his friends, the monkey watched and watered the seed, especially throughout the dry season, until they all began to see the first shoot of green life springing from the dark soil.

Curiously observing his forest friends tending to the seed, and now young seedling, a wrinkly-skinned elephant swayed by to investigate the activities. "Maybe I can stand guard so that no one will dare eat or damage it while it is growing," he offered.

Each of the four friends utilized their individual, personal strengths to nurture the seed, in their own ways. They dug a hole, dropped in the seed, covered it over, watered it, and guarded it as it grew from a young sapling into a tall, strong, mature tree. It hardly seemed any time at all before its branches were drooping with rich fruit.

As they had worked cooperatively together planting and caring for the tree, now the four friends formed a pyramid so that they could reach up into the tree and harvest the fruit. After clambering onto the back of the elephant, the monkey helped lift the rabbit onto his shoulders. Taking its position on the back of the rabbit, the pheasant topped the pyramid. With this ladder of friends, they were able to reach the fruit and harvest enough for them to all have a good feed.

After I had told my grandson this tale he looked studiously at the painting. "But the bird could have flown up into the tree and got the fruit by itself," he said. "Monkeys climb trees so it could have got the fruit by itself, too. And the elephant could have reached up with its long trunk to take the fruit."

At first I thought, *cynical kid*, then as I thought about it more I realized he was right. Yes, the bird may have been able to fly up into the tree, the monkey could climb the branches, the elephant could reach up with his trunk, and, maybe, all the rabbit had to do was wait until the ripe fruit had fallen to the ground. *Perhaps*, I thought, *that is the true essence of the story. They could have done it by themselves but they* chose *to do it cooperatively—as friends.*

14 On Improving Loving Relationships

Love is that condition in which the happiness of another person is essential to your own.

Robert A. Heinlein, writer

Introduction

Just as social relationships are an essential and core element of life satisfaction (See the Introduction to Chapter 13), so are intimate, loving, and romantic relationships. Our survival and well-being as a newborn is dependent on an intimate, physical, and loving relationship with our mother. From the cradle to the grave, we need, desire, and crave affection, intimacy, and love. We spend a lifetime seeking and striving for continuing relationships with peers, friends, colleagues, and, ultimately, a life companion with whom we can share love. Achieving it is beneficial for both our health and happiness.

Indeed, one of the best things you can do for your physical health is to have a good, loving, intimate relationship. If you do, you are likely to live a longer and healthier life. Having the consistent support of a loved one bolsters the immune system, reduces blood pressure, and enhances recovery from coronary bypass surgery. If you are married, you are three times more likely to live an extra 15 years than if you are not married. The presence of an intimate, supportive relationship also buffers you against premature death from cancer and reduces the likelihood of both heart and infectious diseases.

Psychological health is another winner if you have a close, loving relationship. Good intimate relationships are the best and strongest predictor of happiness and life satisfaction—even more so than an education, a good job, an expensive home, a portfolio of wise investments, or a bank vault full of money. Recovery from trauma and avoidance of depression is significantly better for those in loving relationships than those without. Intimacy builds resilience to stress and trauma, it reduces susceptibility to depression and anxiety, and it enhances our feelings of happiness and well-being.

How do you achieve this? How do you create and maintain a relationship by building pleasure and enjoyment for the self, for the other, and for the couple? How do you have fun in a relationship? How do you explore ways to help the romance linger? How do you understand and differentiate the concepts of love and attachment? How do you deal with the age-old dilemma of whether it helps to listen to your heart or your head in relationship issues? How do you help heal a wounded relationship and laugh again? These are some of the questions addressed in this chapter with its stories focused on enhancing romantic and loving relationships.

Story 79

Helping a Relationship Dawn Anew

Happiness-Enhancing Characteristics

Problems Addressed

> Problems of the past
> Ongoing, insoluble issues
> Helplessness
> Frustration
> Irritability and verbal aggression
> Relationship issues

Resources Developed

> Revisiting initial attraction
> Finding pleasurable sensory awareness
> Creating more individual pleasure
> Creating more partner pleasure
> Creating more mutual experiences of pleasure
> Exploring how to continue mutual pleasure

Outcomes Offered

> Beauty, pleasure, and sensory awareness
> Creation of joyful, love-based, effective relationships
> Renewed relationship pleasure and satisfaction

"I see what you're getting at," Malcolm said to me. "If we attend to something we enjoy, like watching a sunset, it can help our relationship dawn anew." The imagery of his words stuck in my mind.

Malcolm and Belinda had been together for 10 years and, seemingly, were doing all the right things to have their relationship work but were constantly stuck in problems of their past relationships and ongoing, insoluble issues of a blended family from which they felt helpless to escape. In their frustration, Belinda felt anxious, said her head "was about to explode" and had been diagnosed with high blood pressure. Malcolm became irritable and verbally aggressive. Their relationship was being affected. And they found their way to my office.

The contexts in which couples often create and build loving relationships are often based in nature. They 'get away' for the weekend, picnic in a park, camp in the woods, watch a sunset, court under a full moon, or stroll hand in hand along the seashore. Such contexts facilitate the creation of shared positive experiences and emotions, and can go on to sustain and enhance the quality of continuing couple and family relationships. This had previously been the case with Malcolm and Belinda but, in feeling they had to be constantly dealing with all the insoluble 'issues,' pleasure had slipped from their agenda. The question was how could they reconnect with the pleasures of their relationship?

To help Malcolm and Belinda make that reconnection, I invited them to individually complete an inventory listing their pleasurable experiences in the five basic sensory categories of sight, sound, smell, taste, and touch. A sixth category on the inventory asks people to list the activities, the things they do, that bring them relaxation, enjoyment, or pleasure.

Once they had each completed the inventory I enquired, first, how could they create more pleasure for themselves as *individuals*? What items from the inventory could they use to alter unwanted thoughts or experiences and create more pleasurable states of thought and experience?

Could Belinda, if starting to feel anxious, pause to watch reflections in still water, listen to the sounds of a babbling stream, or enjoy the fragrance of the woods? Could Malcolm, when he found his irritability rising, listen to the sound of breaking waves, smell a freshly mown lawn, or enjoy the tactile experience of patting his pet dog.

Second, how could they use this information *to please their partner*? If wanting to show love and caring toward Malcolm, could Belinda use items on his inventory to suggest they watch a sunset together over the ocean, walk barefoot in the rain, or silently recline on a rock near the roar of a waterfall? If wanting to give Belinda pleasure, could Malcolm sit with her and listen to the sounds of birds in a national park or serve her a meal of garlic prawns on a table decked with candles and carnations?

Third, I wondered aloud, how they could use their lists to create *mutual experiences* of joy and happiness? Could they plan a different pleasurable activity to share together each day for the following week? Could they plan more extended enjoyable activities for the weekend? Bonding in a relationship can take place simply from the process of discussing, planning, and anticipating such positive events, as well as in putting them into action.

Finally, I requested Belinda and Malcolm to ask themselves some questions after engaging in each of the above activities. What did we gain from doing that, as individuals and as a couple? If we did benefit, how could we do more? What similar, or different, things can we do for fun again? When is it going to be convenient to re-create such an experience?

Bringing beauty and sensory awareness into life is what makes it rewarding, happy, and healthy, and may even facilitate feelings of love. Love, after all, is about beauty, aesthetics, sensuousness, joy, and common shared experiences. Being in touch with positive, natural experiences can help create joyful, love-based, effective relationships . . . and the resources for doing this are often readily available at a neighborhood park, on a local beach, in your own back-yard, or through a kitchen window.

It was, on discovering this that Malcolm said, "I see what you're getting at. If we attend to something we enjoy, like watching a sunset, it can help our relationship dawn anew."

Story 80

Doing It for Fun

Happiness-Enhancing Characteristics

Problems Addressed

A deteriorating relationship
Loss of intimacy
Loss of having fun
Loss of love-making

Resources Developed

Learning to have fun
Engaging in playfulness

Outcomes Offered

Restoration of fun in a relationship
Restoration of fun in life

She was alone in my office. "I asked, even begged, my husband to come but he firmly said there was no way he was going to see a shrink," she explained. Her concern was that their relationship was gradually deteriorating, had lost intimacy, and they were no longer having fun or making love together.

Being at home all day, looking after the house and the kids, she looked forward to her husband coming home to share some support and conversa-tions but he was generally tired, flopped in front of the TV, opened a beer, and hardly spoke a word. They would sit silently over the meal, he would flop back in front of the TV and, when it came to bed time, he would roll over with their backs facing each other, not even touching.

There was something I wanted to say to this woman but did not want, or dare, to say it in my own words. Instead I said, "As you have been telling me about your situation, I have been recalling a case by a colleague, Dr Milton Erickson. I don't know how but maybe you might make some sense of it."

With that I walked across to my bookcase, pulled off a copy of Jay Haley's *Uncommon Therapy*, flipped through to the appropriate page, and began to read the case as described by Erickson. He told how a 30-year-old university professor met and married a 30-year-old single woman. Given their ages, they planned to have a family as quickly as possible but after three years were still childless, despite medical examinations and advice. Erickson described them as extremely prudish and embarrassed, using a most stilted and formal language.

The husband explained, "Because of our desire for children we have engaged in the marital union with full physiological concomitants each night and morning for pro-creative purposes. On Sundays and holidays we have engaged in the marital union with full physiological concomitants for pro-creative purposes as much as four times a day. . . . As a result of the frustration of our philoprogenitive desires, the marital union has become progressively unpleasant for us, but it has not interfered with our efforts at procreation; but it does distress both of us to discover our increasing impatience with each other. For this reason we are seeking your aid, since other medical aid has failed."

The wife spoke in a similar pedantic language but with even greater embarrassment.

Erickson said he could correct this but it will involve shock therapy—not an electric or physical shock but a significant psychological shock. He then left them alone for 15 minutes to discuss their willingness to receive a rather severe psychological shock. On his return, the couple affirmed their willingness to accept anything that might help resolve their problems.

Erickson explained that the psychological shock would involve their emotions and be a definite strain upon them. He suggested that they reach down, hang on tightly to the bottom of their chairs and listen well to what he said. After he delivered the shock, he advised they were to leave his office and return home, maintaining an absolute silence all the way. During that silence they would discover a multitude of thoughts rushing through their minds. Upon reaching home, they should maintain silence until after they had entered the house and closed the door. Then they would be free!

"Now hang tightly to the bottom of your chairs," he said, "because I am now going to give you the psychological shock. It is this: For three long years you have engaged in the marital union with full physiological concomitants for procreative purposes at least twice a day and sometimes as much as four times in 24 hours, and you have met with defeat of your philoprogenitive desires. Now why in hell don't you fuck for fun and pray to the devil that she isn't knocked up for at least three months. Now please leave."

After reading this story to the woman with the intimacy problems she left. The next week, she returned—with her husband. She explained the evening after our previous session her husband arrived home, flopped in front of the TV, opened a beer, and hardly spoke a word. As had become usual, they sat silently over the meal, he flopped back in front of the TV and, when it came to bed time, he rolled over with his back facing her, not even touching. Then he asked, "What did your shrink say?"

She replied, "He said we should fuck for fun."

He replied, "That's not a bad idea."

I think he was willing to come and see a therapist who made such suggestions to his wife—suggestions of putting fun back into their relationship and lives.

Story 81

How Do You Make It Last?

Happiness-Enhancing Characteristics

Problems Addressed

> Changes in romantic relationships
> When initial feelings fade
> Hedonic adaptation

Resources Developed

> Learning to create variety
> Learning to cultivate appreciation
> Creating more positive events and emotions
> Learning to do something different
> Keeping aspirations reasonable
> Spotting and valuing partner strengths

Outcomes Offered

> Maintenance of relationship vitality
> Commitment to creation of positive events and emotion
> Creation of variety
> Reasonable aspirations
> Cultivation of appreciation

This morning I picked up the latest professional journal to arrive in my mailbox. Interestingly, an article explored just what we have been talking about. None of us are alone in experiencing the fact that romantic relationships change. Hopefully, we have all experienced the initial exhilaration of a new relationship that is marked by high levels of attraction, passion, joy, excitement, and novelty. However, once that fades, how do you keep the relationship going? Is it possible to maintain those initial feelings or are all relationships inevitably destined to boredom? If possible, what can a couple do to preserve and protect their romance?

Scientists give fancy labels to common things like the fading of romance. They call it hedonic adaptation, meaning that we quickly adapt to the stimulating, exhilarating feelings of initial romance, that initial excitement fades. When a couple first comes together, they experience of host of new positive changes in their life, such as going out on dates, having weekends away, meeting new people, experiencing stimulation of their senses, and engaging in the arousal of love-making. These experiences bring with them a host of positive emotions, such as heightened energy, increased excitement, greater affection, and enhanced enjoyment. The combination of these positive experiences and positive emotions leads to greater perceived levels of happiness.

Problems begin when dating goes by the way, weekends away diminish with work demands and kids, and conversations get repetitive. Love-making grows more routine and perhaps time-pressured. While the early stimulation and excitement of a relationship may fade, the desire for it doesn't, and this is when a partner may wander—again seeking the thrill of initial arousal.

Can the romance last? And, if so, how? This morning's journal article assured me that there are two key factors that may help counterbalance this process of growing stale in the relationship: variety and appreciation.

Variety is the spice of your relationship. The more variety of positive experiences that we can introduce into a relationship, the longer it stalls the adaptation. Instead of going to the same old restaurant every Friday night, try a new place and new cuisine on a different night. Instead of following the same weekend routine, break out and do something different. Find a new hobby or activity that you can engage in together. Extend the number and variety of friends with whom you can share novel, stimulating conversations. Engage in exciting activities like rock climbing, skydiving, or riding a rollercoaster to arouse physical and sexual attractiveness. The positive benefit of these activities is likely to rub off in a positive way on your partner and relationship.

To assist variety, keep your aspirations reasonable. As we increase positive experiences, we are likely to want even more. Such escalating aspirations can become difficult to achieve and therefore lead to disappointment and dissatisfaction with the relationship. For example, it's easy for a partner to feel that she may deserve more of his time than she is getting. Aspiring to things that are unrealistic, perhaps given his work load, is only likely to lead to her feeling disappointment and, in turn, dissatisfied with the relationship.

Cultivating appreciation—of life and of your partner—the journal article assured me would extend feelings of romance. People who appreciate their partners and, in turn, feel appreciated are more committed to the relationship and more likely to remain in it. So how do you achieve this? Well, it seems it's not enough just to be appreciative but that appreciation needs to be expressed. Your partner needs to *hear* how much he or she is valued. Express the things you are grateful for in your partner and your relationship by counting the blessings that you share together, writing a letter of appreciation, sending a grateful email, or bringing home a bunch of flowers with an appreciative note. Look for and acknowledge their strengths, qualities, and abilities. Spotting and valuing the strengths you see in another helps strengthen the relationship.

When I finished reading the article it was with a sense of hope. Maybe it is possible to maintain some of the spark, exhilaration, and vitality of a young relationship. It doesn't come without work, dedication, and commitment but by creating positive events and emotion, bringing variety into the relationship, keeping aspirations at a reasonable level, and cultivating appreciation, it is a realistic hope.

Story 82

Love and Attachment

Happiness-Enhancing Characteristics

Problems Addressed

> Attachment
> Break-up of a relationship
> Grief
> Emotional suffering and pain
> Confusion about the nature of love

Resources Developed

> Clarifying the differences between attachment and love
> Understanding the nature of separation and detachment
> Discovering freedom
> Learning about the true nature of love

Outcomes Offered

> Freedom
> Independence
> Acceptance of the other person
> Compassionate, selfless love

Trulku Jamyang Rinpoche is a young yet wise monk I met during one of my visits to the Himalaya. 'Trulku' is a title that indicates he is recognized as the reincarnation of a high order lama. 'Rinpoche' is a title meaning 'precious one,' perhaps a little like 'reverend' in Christianity.

While there, I attended a talk given by Rinpoche and heard him speak about emotional attachment as being a major cause of human suffering. Later in reflecting on this, I could see the wisdom in his thinking. If you are attached to a job and you get fired, you are likely to experience a feeling of grief. If you are attached to your home, your car, or your material possessions and you lose everything in a stock market crash, you are likely to feel a lot of pain and grief. But how does this work in relationships, I wondered. Do love and attachment not go together? If you are in love do you not invest a lot of emotional attachment into the relationship? Do you not both give up some of your independence and become, at least to some degree, dependent on the other? Tossing these questions around in my head, I decided to email Rinpoche and ask him.

"Let me tell you the meaning of Attachment and Love," he wrote in reply. "Attachment is not Love. Imagine if two people are physically attached, perhaps like Siamese twins. When one person sits, the other has no choice but to sit. When one person walks, the other has no choice but to walk. And when one person falls down, the other will also fall down—naturally, because they are attached. However, if they are surgically operated on and become two separate individuals then real freedom appears for both of them. Now that they are separated when one falls down the other does not have to fall but is there to help the first get up again."

"Being separate individuals is to be detached and Detachment is FREEDOM," he continued with capitalized emphasis on the word freedom. "Only when one is detached from the other, can he help the one who has fallen because he is standing and not fallen with the other."

"Similarly, if people are attached in feelings, when one is happy the other is happy but when one cries the other also cries, when one is tense the other is also tense, when one is angry the other also gets angry. Therefore, Attachment is *not* Freedom because both people go into the same feeling when they are attached. In order to love and care freely we need to be free from Attachment. Only then if one cries the other does not need to cry but is there to help wipe away the tears of their loved one. On the other hand, if both are emotionally attached, if both cry together, then they need someone else to be there to wipe away their tears."

"Detachment certainly doesn't mean that you have to be to be cold or devoid of feeling toward your loved one. However, to be free of the situation, you need to step back, be neutral and see the situation in a cool way without emotional investment or disturbance. Only an undisturbed mind can clearly see and have the best solution for every good or bad time."

"Love then is not Attachment," he concluded. "Instead, love means to be detached, to be free and independent from both the happy and unhappy scenarios that occur in a relationship. Only when we accept life's scenarios for what they are can we then try to solve any problems that may arise. Love also means accepting the other person as he or she is. This means accepting them for what they have been in their past and what they are now *and* it also means working to bring about a better future. That is true, compassionate, and selfless love."

Story 83

Do You Listen to Your Heart or Head?

Happiness-Enhancing Characteristics

Problems Addressed

Do I listen to my heart or my head?
Mixed negative emotions
Ruminative worries
Ambivalence between intuition and reason

Resources Developed

Understanding the nature of intuition
Understanding the nature of reason
Doing an emotional cost-benefit analysis
Doing a rational cost-benefit analysis
Learning to step back and think
Seeking impartial feedback

Outcomes Offered

A cost benefit analysis
A balance of heart and head
A consonance of intuition and reason

Joe asked a not an uncommon question, especially in the area of relationships: "Do I listen to my heart or my head?" Two years prior his partner had suddenly packed her bags and left during a stressful time. He had loved her dearly, had believed that they would be together forever, and had taken out a large mortgage to purchase a home in which they would live. Just when things seem to be falling so nicely into place, and he felt so happy, she left—without so much as a word of conversation about why.

Joe felt hurt, confusion, bewilderment, anger, love, and a depth of grief he had never previously known. He spent his days and sleepless nights in unrelenting ruminative worries but, as she had requested, made no further contact.

Then, about two years later, they bumped into each other. Joe's heart did a flip when he saw her. She reached out and took his hand and told him how much she missed him, how unhappy she was without him. Could they catch up again for a coffee, a walk, or a movie, she asked.

That was when Joe asked, "Do I listen to my heart or my head?"

He continued, "Some friends and books say go with your feelings, be in the moment, act on your intuitions. Others say think the situation through rationally, act out of reason. What am I to do? My heart says that I have loved her more than anyone else in my life and would love to be back in a relationship with her. My head says she has walked out three times before, and could do it again. My head rings alarm bells at me like crazy."

Joe's dilemma is not unique. From the early Greek philosophers to most recent research in cognitive psychology, we know thoughts and feelings can run in opposite directions when faced with making choices, judgments, and decisions. Intuition—relying on our immediate feelings, our gut instincts, and what feels good at the time—is emotion-based rather than thought-based. It comes from 'being in the moment' without regard of the information of the past or the prospects for the future. It is the if-it-feels-good-just-do-it response. Intuition is what gets us into a relationship without weighing up the consequences, what has us breaking up the relationship in the heat of an argument without seeing the good in the big picture, and what has us falling back into a relationship without regard for the mountain of information we have acquired in the past about the relationship.

Decision-making is based in reason: where we weigh up the information we have and take a rational, considered, and deliberate perspective on all the information we have available.

Intuition is where, in the heat of an argument we scream at our partner to get out of the house and never come back—because it feels right at the time. Reason is where we sit back, allow the heat of the moment to pass, and begin to assess the big picture of the relationship: Is what we have good overall? Do we generally get on well together? Are these things worth hanging on to despite the current heat-of-the-moment feelings?

I handed Joe a paper and pen, and asked him to write a column of all his *feelings* to support them getting back together. Then, list in a column beside it all his feelings to oppose them getting back together.

When he had done this, I asked he do the same exercise with his *rational thoughts*. What rational thoughts would support him getting back into the relationship? What rational thoughts would oppose him getting back into the relationship?

"You mean you want me to do a cost-benefit analysis for both my heart and my head?" he asked in astute observation. In his language that is exactly what I was asking.

If Joe hadn't already been doing so I would also have asked him to talk with a psychologist, counselor, or impartial friend as it often helps to verbalize problems that have been running around in your head, get them off your chest, stand back and take a look at them through the eyes of someone else, and consider the perspectives another person may bring to the problem.

Of course, heart and head are not autonomously separate units. They are wrapped up in the same body, in the same person. Intuition involves some thought, and reason is not necessarily devoid of feeling. Sometimes it is a matter of balancing both intuition *and* reason. Intuition alone can lead us along a false path, and reason alone does not necessarily meet our emotional needs. However, if we step back to think about the situation, do a cost benefit analysis—as Joe described it—and talk it out with someone who might be more objective, we are likely to make better and more informed decisions when faced with that age-old question, "Do I listen to my heart or my head?"

Story 84

We Will Be Laughing Again

Happiness-Enhancing Characteristics

Problems Addressed

> Relationship challenges
> Extramarital affair
> Ambivalent love

Resources Developed

> Learning about the positivity ratio
> Building greater positivity
> Expressing affection
> Expressing admiration and appreciation
> Reconnecting with initial attraction
> Using the 'seven second hug'

Outcomes Offered

> Helpful healing and restoring strategies
> A healed relationship
> A happy relationship
> Laughing again, together

Friends and colleagues of mine in Portugal kindly contributed a chapter to one of my previous books in which they discuss the case of a couple in a very fragile relationship. They asked the couple, if they looked ahead to a time when they could see the relationship back on a healthy track, what would be different. Both husband and wife agreed, "We will be laughing again."

The husband had an affair when his wife was seven months pregnant with their first child. She found it hard to forgive and forget. He wanted to put the incident behind them and restore the marital relationship. For three years it limped on with mixed emotions of guilt, doubts, sadness, anger, despair . . . and ambivalent love. Both affirmed their deep love for their son—a prime reason for them remaining together—and the desire for their relationship to be back on a positive, enjoyable keel.

How could they best achieve that goal? Fortunately, there is a strong, growing body of research that shows what works well for the creation and maintenance of positive relationships. Relationships are one of the prime factors for us leading a happy, satisfied, and flourishing life. However, it is not just having a relationship—as this particular husband and wife were discovering—but also the quality of the relationship that matters.

How could they now enhance the quality of their relationship? Researchers talk of a positivity ratio: the balance of negative compared to positive experiences in a relationship. Generally, if a couple encounters one negative experience, it needs to create three to five positive experiences to rebalance the scales. Of course, the weight of each negative experience can vary. Something like an extra marital affair while your spouse is pregnant is a pretty hefty negative weight to counterbalance. For this couple they would need a heap of heavily weighted positives to restore a healthy ratio.

To build greater positivity in a relationship, it is often the small things that count. Happy couples commonly ask their spouse when they part in the morning (such as going to work) about at least one thing that person might be doing during the day at work or at home. When they reunite at the end of the day, happy couples reconnect with what has been called 'low stress conversations.' They don't jump into weighty discussions about the hassles at work, the problems with the kids, or the heavy issues about their relationship. They talk more about their pleasant and positive experiences, perhaps setting aside times for when the other issues can be dealt with in effective, problem-solving ways.

Happy couples express and show affection towards their partner. If you are expressing just five or more minutes of affectionate behavior every day your relationship is in a healthy position. Significantly less than five minutes per day and it's likely to be on a downhill slide. Having weekly 'dates,' going out together, and ensuring that you have pure time with each other are other factors that enhance your positivity ratio.

Expressing your admiration and appreciation of your spouse goes a long way to heightening the positivity stakes as well. It is easy to get focused on the little, niggly issues in a relationship that annoy us. Does he squeeze the toothpaste tube in the middle rather than at the bottom? Does she stack the dishes on the dish rack the wrong way? If we see the negatives, we feel the negatives . . . and our relationship suffers. On the other hand, if we look for our partner's strengths, qualities, and resources, the relationship is likely to be stronger and happier—as long as they are expressed as well as observed them.

Sometimes it can help to reflect on and reconnect with the reasons that you came together as a couple in the first place. What attracted you to each other? What were the positive feelings and experiences that consolidated your connection? How can you reconnect with those experiences or create more positive experiences in your relationship now?

Another positivity builder that I have heard a colleague (a medical practitioner and sex therapist) speak about is what she calls the seven-second hug. She says that it takes at least seven seconds of hugging for our body chemistry to experience the feel-good aspects of the hug. It is not my area of expertise to know the details of the physiology here but it seems to me like a good excuse to enjoy lingering, affectionate hugs with your spouse or loved one.

Science and experience both affirm that it is possible to have a happy, lasting relationship, that damaged relationships can be healed, and that there are a number of helpful and effective strategies for healing and restoring relationships. Indeed, it is possible—and important—for a couple to be laughing again.

(For a full description of this couple's case and the therapy offered, see Perloiro, Neto, & Marujo, 2010.)

15 On Finding Meaning and Wisdom

We do not receive wisdom, we must discover it for ourselves.

Marcel Proust, writer

Introduction

Wisdom *is* primary happiness, according to the long-held philosophy of Aristotle. Some scientists have agreed, calling wisdom the supreme source of happiness while others have questioned whether having a well informed and wise view of reality may reduce happiness or even lead to despair. Fortunately, studies have tended to support Aristotle's view and shown a positive relationship between wisdom, meaning, and happiness. For our lives to have a sense of well-being, they need to have meaning and purpose. For most people, purpose and meaning comes from serving a cause greater than ourselves, believing in something bigger than us—be it a deity, a religion—or having a purpose to serve humanity in some way.

Meaning and purpose lead to greatest well-being when grounded in knowledge and wisdom. But what is the difference between wisdom and knowledge? And is there not a paradox here? Science has placed strong emphasis on knowledge, on cutting through superstitions and beliefs to find the facts or reality. It is based in logic, reason, experimentation, and validation. On the other hand, philosophy from the times of the ancient Greeks and before has emphasized wisdom as a basis for cutting through ignorance and thus enhancing our quality of life. While wisdom and knowledge can—and perhaps should—go hand in hand, and while it is hard to imagine having wisdom without sound knowledge, we often encounter problems when knowledge is present but wisdom isn't.

Take for example a person who has the clear and sound knowledge that smoking, illicit drug use, excessive alcohol consumption, bulimia, or anorexia can be extremely destructive of your health and well-being. For that person to continue in those patterns—given that knowledge—is not something most of us would consider wise. Ask any counselor or therapist about this and I am sure you will get a similar answer: giving people information alone is generally not sufficient for them to wisely modify their patterns of behavior.

Shifting from knowledge to wisdom involves several important steps. First, we need to acknowledge or accept the information. Second, we need to incorporate that knowledge, take it on board, and find personal meaning in it for ourselves. Third, we need to act on it. Knowledge that does not lead to informed action is useless knowledge. Finally, wisdom is further developed from an openness to learn from the successes and failures that derive from the informed actions we take.

Story 85

Three Questions

Happiness-Enhancing Characteristics

Problems Addressed

  Uncertainty
  Indecision
  Doubt
  Avoidance behaviors
  Unanswered questions

Resources Developed

  Learning to ask questions
  Discriminating helpful from unhelpful answers
  Discovering compassion
  Dealing with potential threats
  Accepting our own abilities

Outcomes Offered

  Appropriate, helpful, and caring behaviors
  Positive evaluation of others
  Opportunity-based action

Once there was a young man plagued with uncertainty, indecision, and confusion. He didn't know what was the right thing to do, or even if there was a right thing. If he planned to do something, he questioned when was the best time to do it or who should he be doing it for. *Whatever I do could be wrong*, he thought to himself . . . and so he didn't do much at all. He avoided action, avoided people, and felt unhappy in himself. Fortunately, he had enough awareness of his situation to see that he needed to do something about it if he wanted life to be different.

"If only I had the answers, if someone could tell me what I should do," he thought, "then I would always know what to do." He was looking for a formula, a script, or a recipe for life that would guide him, unvaryingly, at all times and in all situations.

Fortunately, he was bright enough to realize that if you want the right answers, you need to ask the right questions. There was no point asking himself questions like, *Why me?* for which there was no clear or useful answer. So he thought to himself, *What questions do I need to ask?* He wrote down a list of possibilities and, after some consideration, settled on three questions that he decided to ask his friends. Surely they could give him the answers that he sought.

"What is the right thing to do?" he asked first. To his surprise, there appeared to be no single answer. One friend who was a businessman answered, "To make lots of money." A priest friend said, "To spread the word of the Gospel." A social worker friend said, "To help others who are less fortunate," while a policeman friend said, "To enforce law and order."

"Who is the most important person to do things for?" he asked next . . . and again got a mix of responses. "You have to look out for Number One—if you don't, no one else will," said some. Others replied, "You have to put others first. Happiness comes from being compassionate."

"When is the best time to do things?" he enquired and once more received a variety of replies. "You have to be in the moment," said his more new-age friends. "You need to plan in advance if you are to achieve what you want," said the businessman. "No, pray for God's guidance on the best time," answered the priest.

Realizing that such mixed answers had not been helpful, he decided to seek the advice of a wise man who lived on a mountain on the other side of the woods. Having made his way through the woods and up the mountain, he found the old man slowly building himself a new hut for the winter. Eagerly, the young man asked the elder his questions. But the wise man went on laboriously lifting rocks and placing them on the growing wall, ignoring the young man's questions.

After a while, not knowing what else to do, the young man offered to help lift and place the stones. Having thus labored for a while, he again asked his questions. However, before the wise man could answer, a huge bear emerged from the woods and charged at the young man. Seemingly at the last minute, it stepped on an old, rusty hunter's trap, fell to the ground, hit its head, and was knocked unconscious.

The young man's heart went out to the bear and so he approached cautiously, released the trap, and treated the wound. That night both the young man and the wise man cared for the bear. By the morning it had improved greatly. If the bear could have spoken, it would probably have expressed its gratitude to its carers, apologized for the attack, and explained that it had been chased by hunters and only wanted to protect itself by frightening off a perceived threat.

After the bear had left, the young man felt surprisingly at peace. He felt a kinship with both the wise man and the bear but he still didn't have the answers he sought. So again he asked his three questions of the wise man.

"Oh, but you do have the answers," said the wise man. "You saw the appropriate, helpful, and caring thing was to help me build my hut yesterday. You saw me as an important and valued person in that you put aside your own urgent questions to assist someone else. And you chose that the best time to act was when the opportunity presented itself."

"Then you saw that the appropriate, helpful, and caring thing was to assist the bear when it was trapped and in pain. Even though it had posed a threat to you, you acted from your heart, treating an aggressor as an important other. And once again you chose that the best time to act was there when the opportunity presented itself."

"So, that is why I say you do have the answers," assured the wise man.

Story 86

The Bread of Life

Happiness-Enhancing Characteristics

Problems Addressed

Desire to learn
Confined to one approach or recipe
Lack of empowerment

Resources Developed

Understanding the workings of process
Learning to start at the beginning
Learning by practice
Discovering mistakes and 'failures' are opportunities to learn
Keeping notes of learning experiences
Learning by trial-and-error

Outcomes Offered

Appreciation of process
Expanded skills
Enhanced empowerment

I enjoy making bread. Perhaps it has something to do with it being a creative process. Perhaps it is because it has a history, connecting the baker with millennia of bakers who have worked such basic ingredients into such a stable part of our diet. Perhaps it is to do with the balance between the certainty of science and the uncertainty of never quite knowing how it will turn out until it has turned out. Maybe it is that once you have a basic recipe, you are free to experiment. Maybe it is in the sharing, making something that looks and tastes good for those you care about. Perhaps it is because it wins me accolades from appreciative tasters. Or, maybe it is simply that I enjoy the process in itself.

There are many reasons that we do the things we do and, when we enjoy something, we often want to find out more about it. So it was that I picked up a book on the science and art of bread-making by Emily Buehler. As I read the Introduction, it seemed to speak to me about more than bread-making, and I am interested to know what you might make of it. Here is what it said.

"The obvious way to make bread is to find a recipe . . . and follow it. Chances are it will work well enough, but making bread this way confines the baker to one recipe, gives him or her no understanding of how to fix problems that arise, and perpetuates the myth that he or she needs a 'good recipe' to begin with. In short, following a recipe is not an empowering way to make a loaf of bread."

"The alternative method . . . is more akin to what our ancestors have done, working with basic recipes to learn about the process of bread-making, with the benefits of decades of scientific research enabling us to understand the inner workings of the process. Think of the method as starting at the beginning—each time you make the dough you see what happens to it and learn something new about the process. That information will help you learn faster and understand how and why bread 'works.'"

"Reading about bread will not be enough though; the only way to get to know bread and dough is to get your hands in—practice. Do not be intimidated—mistakes and 'failures' are just opportunities to learn. (Besides, messed up bread often still tastes good!) Take data when mixing your dough. . . . Remember what the dough feels like. Write notes for the next time in order to remember what to do the same or what to do differently."

"Good bread is not the result of one brilliant mind; it came about by trial-and-error, over the centuries. And it was done by ordinary people; it does not require special talents or an advanced degree. Re-learning the process from the beginning is surprisingly simple. In this day, making bread 'by hand' might seem like a lost art, but it remains accessible to anyone who wishes to try it."

As I read, I thought, *Maybe that is why I enjoy bread making so much. Maybe it is also why we have the expression, 'the bread of life.' Perhaps the process of bread-making and bread speaks to us about life itself.*

Story 87

Appreciating Beauty

Happiness-Enhancing Characteristics

Problems Addressed

Failure to perceive beauty

Resources Developed

Learning to ask, "What is beautiful in my life?"
Learning to pause and enjoy beauty

Learning to create more appreciation of beauty
Learning to savor beauty
Learning to share beauty with others

Outcomes Offered

Awareness of beauty
Appreciation of beauty

I was recently sent a story that reminded me of something a colleague, Michael Ventura, recommended all therapists should ask their clients. His recommended question is one I think we should also ask ourselves: *What is beautiful in your life?*

He said that a psychology of beauty is a psychology of experience, a psychology that appreciates and teaches an aesthetic of experience. For our very lives depend upon the way we are capable of experiencing beauty in each other and as well as ourselves.

The story that reminded me of this was about a man who sat at a metro station in Washington, DC, and started to play the violin. It was a cold January morning. He played six Bach pieces for about 45 minutes. Being rush hour, it was calculated that thousands of people went through the station during that time, most of them on their way to work.

Three minutes went by before a middle-aged man noticed there was musician playing. He slowed his pace and stopped for a few seconds before hurrying on to meet his schedule.

A minute later, the violinist received his first dollar tip when a woman threw the money in his hat. Without stopping to listen, she continued to walk by.

A few minutes later, someone leaned against the wall to listen to him briefly but the man soon looked at his watch and started to walk on. Assumedly, to pause any longer he would have been late for work.

The one person who paid the most attention was a three-year-old boy. His mother tugged him along, hurriedly, but the child stopped to look at the violinist. Finally, the mother pulled harder and the child continued to walk while turning his head back all the time. This action was repeated by several other children. All the parents, without exception, forced them to move on.

In the 45 minutes the musician played, only six people stopped and stayed for a while. About 20 gave him money but continued to walk by at their normal pace. He collected $32. When he finished playing and silence took over, no one noticed. No one applauded, nor was there any recognition.

Now here is the interesting part to the story. None of the by-passers knew that the violinist was Joshua Bell, one of the best musicians in the world. Not only that, he played one of the most intricate pieces of music ever written. And to top it off it was played on a violin worth $3.5 million.

Just two days before playing in the subway, Joshua Bell had played to a sold-out theater in Boston where the seats averaged $100 each.

Joshua Bell's incognito performance in the metro station was organized by a newspaper as part of a social experiment about perception, taste, and the priorities of people. The experiment took place out of context, in a commonplace environment, at an inappropriate hour, and when people are pre-occupied with other matters. Do those times and places distract us from perceiving beauty? How easy is it for us to fail to appreciate the beauty around us? Do we miss recognizing beauty and talent in unexpected contexts?

The author of the story concluded: If we do not have a moment to stop and listen to one of the best musicians in the world playing the best music ever written, how many other things are we missing?

And this brings me back to Michael Ventura's question, *What is beautiful in your life?* I wonder if you have ever stopped to ask this and, if not, if it would be helpful for you to do so now. It may be helpful now or sometime soon to jot down on a piece of paper the things and people that you find beautiful. It may be helpful to stick that paper on a refrigerator door or dressing table mirror that you can frequently revisit to remind yourself of the things that are beautiful in your life.

Once you have asked, and answered, this question, I think it opens up even more questions:

> *Having discovered what is beautiful in your life, how can you allow yourself to pause and enjoy that beauty?*
> *What can you do to create more time to appreciate that beauty?*
> *How can you find both time and ways to savor that beauty even more?*
> *How might you share that beauty with others?*

I would also like to extend Ventura's comment to say, "Our very lives depend upon the way we are capable of experiencing beauty in each other and ourselves . . . And in our world."

Story 88

What Is Wealth?

Happiness-Enhancing Characteristics

Problems Addressed

　A limited view of life
　Need of another perspective

Resources Developed

　Learning to look at things differently
　Expanding limited perceptions

Perceiving things from a different perspective
Reaching alternative conclusions

Outcomes Offered

Alternative perspectives
New awareness
Wisdom

Once there was a wealthy father who was concerned that a privileged upbringing might give his son a limited view of life. He decided his son needed to see how the other half lived. To do this, he asked his personal assistant to find a very poor family who would be willing to allow him and his son to visit and stay with them.

After weeks of searching she found a very poor farming family who lived in an impoverished country area and organized for her boss and his son to live with them for a couple of days and nights. At the end of the visit, as they were driving back to their expensive suburban mansion, the father asked his son, "What did you think of our stay on the farm?"

"It was great, thanks, Dad," came the reply.

Keen to see if he had achieved the mission of his visit, the father asked, "Has it helped you to see how poor people live?"

"Sure has," answered his son.

"Well, tell me about it. What did you learn?" enquired the father.

"I learnt," his son responded, "that while we have a swimming pool fenced into our backyard, they have a creek with swimming holes, a Tarzan rope hanging from a tree, and rapids they ride on old car tubes."

"We have one dog that lives in a kennel. They have four that live with them."

"Our large house stretches almost to the borders of our small piece of land. They have a small house on open fields that stretch beyond sight."

"Our patio looks out on a neatly mown lawn whereas they view their garden, fields, trees, and hills to the very horizon."

"Spotlights turn our yard into day at night. They have nothing but thousands of twinkling stars to light their night."

"We have to drive to the supermarket to buy our vegetables but they grow theirs right outside the back door."

"We have servants to serve our meals and clean our house. They serve each other and clean up together."

"Our property has walls that fence others out and us in. Their fences contain milking cows and woolly lambs."

"We have security alarms, barred windows, and locks to protect us while they have family and friends to protect them."

The father looked at his son in absolute amazement.

"Thanks Dad," the boy added. "I never realized how poor we are."

Story 89

Once Broken

Happiness-Enhancing Characteristics

Problems Addressed

Anger
Stress and tension
Anger affecting others
Diminishing happiness
Anger affecting a relationship

Resources Developed

Learning that anger drives action
Learning to manage angry thoughts and feelings
Acknowledging once broken things may not be fixable
Learning from experience
Ensuring similar patterns do not continue into the future

Outcomes Offered

Experience is the best teacher

A wife was concerned about her husband's anger. He was a good provider and a successful businessman. They did not want for anything—at least in a material sense. Their home was filled with luxuries that most others could only dream of. Their walls were decked with art by the masters. Their rooms were filled with collectible antique furniture and bric-a-brac. All she wanted was for her husband to better manage his anger.

When stressed or tense, he would explode. When things didn't go his way, he would explode. When people didn't live up to his expectations, he would explode. His explosions were loud, threatening, and abusive—and getting more frequent and more intense. He seemed less able, or inclined, to control them and, in turn, they were affecting her and the family.

She was frightened when he was angry and was getting worried that he seemed less and less happy. Knowing he wouldn't seek help for himself, she went to see a therapist who her friends had recommended as a wise counselor. If she didn't, she feared their marriage would soon break apart.

At the wife's request, the counselor made a home visit but, on meeting him, the husband was immediately on the defensive. "Why have you invited him here?" he shouted at his wife. "There's nothing wrong with me. I can look after myself." Then, sweeping his hand angrily towards the door, he ordered the counselor, "Get out of here."

However, as he swung his arm toward the door he unintentionally struck an antique Chinese vase that was the prize of his collection. Helpless to save it, he watched, as if in slow motion, it crashed to the floor and disintegrated into hundreds of pieces.

Now, even more angry, he yelled at his wife and the counselor. "Look at what you've done. You made me break a priceless piece of history."

The counselor was wise enough to hold his tongue and not point out that *they* had not broken the vase nor *made* the husband do anything. It was his own anger that drove his action. He would never learn to manage it until he learnt to manage his angry thoughts and feelings that led to such behaviors.

Instead the counselor said, perhaps referring to more than the vase, "If something is broken, it needs to be fixed. Do you have some glue? Let us put it back together."

The husband was still angry but he couldn't argue with the reasoning. It was what he would say to his own employees. So, together, he and the counselor sat on the floor, recovering each shard, finding their rightful place, slowly trying to piecing them back into what they had been.

When the vase had somewhat resumed its original shape, the husband, alternating between anger and disappointment, looked at all the fractured lines that now crazed the no-longer so priceless and valued vase and said, "It is ruined. It will never be the same."

"You are right," agreed the counselor, "Once something is broken, you may or may not be able to put it back together again and, even if you can, it will almost certainly never be the same again."

Still angry but now directing it a little more toward himself, the husband announced, "If only you had never come then I would never have broken such a priceless and beautiful vase."

"That may be true," affirmed the counselor, "but it seems to me that both of us can go on regretting what has happened or learn from it to ensure that similar things do not happen again in the future."

"I felt so mad," acknowledged the husband. "Now I have lost something I had worked so hard for and longed to have for so long."

The wise counselor again held his tongue and did not point out the parallel he saw with the man's marriage. Instead, he said, "Yes, sometimes when we act out a temporary feeling we can cause something valuable to be damaged, permanently."

The husband nodded quietly in agreement. As he carefully picked up the flawed and fractured vase, to return it to its former pride of place, it was apparent the message had not escaped him. While he had lost a priceless possession, I would like to think that every time he looked at it there would be a reminder that he had also gained a priceless learning.

MEANING & WISDOM

Story 90

Do You See the Pest or the Pleasure?

Happiness-Enhancing Characteristics

Problems Addressed

Difficult to change thoughts
Negative thinking
A problem-focused view

Resources Developed

Looking from a different perspective
Reexamining old views
Stepping out of long-held, global views
Looking specifically
Acknowledging perception determines experience
Learning it may not be either/or but both

Outcomes Offered

New perspectives
Appreciation of beauty
Open mindedness

Have you ever had a thought you thought you couldn't change? Have you gotten stuck with a negative thought and not even been aware there may be other ways of thinking? I certainly have. And, to my surprise it was a non-psychologist friend who unwittingly showed me how it was possible to develop different thoughts.

Where I live and frequently go walking in Australian forests, there is a pest that is invading our native woods, spreading on mass and preventing the growth of native plants. It is the introduced Watsonia. Over time I have developed now long-established, negative thoughts and associations with it. This bulbous plant was introduced into Australia more than 150 years ago as a garden ornamental but escaped the domestic garden beds to colonize roadside verges, national parks, and native forests. Being a sun-loving herbaceous perennial it found itself at home in Australia and has spread like wildfire.

I am not alone in ripping these plants from the ground as I walk the forest trails. There are several action groups that spend their weekends and spare time targeting problem areas with sprays and mattocks to either kill the plants or scoop their bulbs from the soil. Locally they are known as the 'Watty Whoppers.'

The Watsonia is a tall plant and, I have to confess, it throws a rather pretty pink flower that is somewhat gladiola-like. Nonetheless, my biased perceptions have led me to miss the beauty and latch on only to its negative qualities. That is until I went walking with a friend, a silversmith who creates jewelry from natural objects. As we walked past a cluster of Watsonia and I was cursing them under my breath, she paused, bent down, and pulled a semi-exposed, dried bulb from the ground. She began to peel back the fine lattice-like patterns of the onion-style layers of bulb, holding each delicate layer gently in her hand and carefully cradling them back to the car. Initially, I could not see what she saw in this intrusive pest of a weed.

When I met her next she told me that she had carefully picked soil from the bulbs' latticed layers with a needle, washed them gently, strengthened them with lacquer, taken casts of them, burnt out the lattice and filled the casts with silver. Then she pulled out the fine, pure silver replica. I was stunned by its beauty . . . and caught in a dilemma. Here was something I had long hated and wanted to rid the world of—or at least the part of my beloved world that it threatened. And yet here it was replicated as something of exquisite beauty.

She asked if I would collect more for her on my walks. Helping to rid the forests of Watsonia bulbs fitted comfortably for me but what I had not expected was that I began to appreciate the beauty in the bulbs. I guess I had never before really stopped to look at them, let alone see them from the eyes of an artist. What would she see as beautiful? What would she want to cast into fine jewelry?

As I looked at them from this perspective, I began to discover that no one bulb was the same. There were small ones and big ones. There were flat disc-like ones and ones like the domes of an orthodox church. There were tight lattices and broad-patterned lattices. Each being as unique to the bulb as a finger print is to a person.

Now I was in a conflict. Was this object I had long grown to detest a pest or a pleasure? Was it a beast or was it beautiful? Did I hold to my old views or did I alter them with this new perspective?

What was most interesting for me was how I came to have that new perception. I had to have a willingness to see something through someone else's eyes and not just the eyes of my own pre-conceptions. I needed an openness to look at something from a different perspective. I had to step out of my long-held, global view that Watsonias are all bad, and look more specifically at the beauty that they can hold. And I needed a willingness to incorporate that new perspective.

How did I do that? Well, first, there is no doubt that Watsonias are both a threat and, a growing threat, to our native forests. For that reason I would be happy to see them eradicated from where they do not belong. Second, there is no doubt that they have an intrinsic beauty not only in the flowers that make them popular for domestic gardens but also in the uniquely intricate and pretty latticing of the bulbs. Prior to the walk with my friend, Watsonias were a pest that held no beauty, at least for me. For my friend, unaware of their impact on the forests, she saw no negative in them, just a beauty that she could creatively transform into art. Is there any clearer example of how it is not the object, person, or event itself but the way we perceive it that makes a difference to how we experience and react to it?

So where am I with Watsonias now? Maybe it is not a matter of either/or. Maybe it is not a matter of black and white. Maybe it is not a matter of right or wrong. Maybe it is a matter of both. Watsonias are a threat to our forests *and* they can be a treat to the eye. They can be both pest *and* pleasure.

16 On Being a Problem-Solver

> We cannot solve life's problems except by solving them.
>
> M. Scott Peck, author, psychologist

Introduction

Having good problem-solving abilities is one of life's essential skills. Good problem-solvers feel more in control and more empowered when problems—as they inevitably do and will—hit us unexpectedly. People with poor problem-solving skills are more likely to feel powerless, helpless, and hopeless when life's going gets tough. Without good skills to resolve problems in practical and productive ways it is easy to retreat into depression, explode in rages of anger, turn to substances to escape reality, or contemplate suicide as the only way out.

If there is one guaranteed certainty in life it is this: you won't get through your journey on this planet without having problems. Some may be small while some will be absolutely gigantic. Some people seem to be ground into despair by the problems they encounter while others seem to take them in their stride and grow from the experience of dealing with them. What makes the difference? Well, it is obvious it is not the problems we encounter in life but rather how we go about resolving these problems that makes the difference in terms of our happiness and well-being. Developing and practicing good problem-solving skills helps ensure a more secure and happier existence.

Problem-solving is a process and skill that people can learn and develop. While there are many different ways to solve any potential problem, all involve active steps that a person needs to undertake to reach a resolution. If you read the literature on problem-solving, you will find various recommendations, but what is indisputable is that problem-solving is a process and that process involves steps such as clearly identifying the problem in an objective and unemotive way; examining it from different perspectives to find possible effective solutions; and then identifying the goals you have in resolving that issue. Once this is done it is possible to look at the various alternative outcomes and reach an effective solution. Here you may engage in some brainstorming to look at creative alternatives, bounce possible solutions off other people, seek professional guidance, or observe how others manage similar problems. Having done this you may select a possible alternative that is most relevant, realistic, and manageable, and then test it out. It is only in the implementation of that possible solution that you are going to learn if it works or not. Such feedback will provide you with valuable information on how to evaluate if that particular problem-solving skill is helpful or not. Such effective evaluation, first, helps us from blundering on in ineffective ways and, second, helps equip us to better manage life's next set of inevitable problems.

One effective way of learning problem-solving skills is to observe how good problem-solvers go about practicing their own skills. What do they do? How do they do it? The following stories will hopefully provide you with examples, ideas, and possibilities.

Story 91

Choosing What We Listen to

Happiness-Enhancing Characteristics

Problems Addressed

Facing challenges
Listening to the negatives
Self-doubts
When thoughts become beliefs and beliefs grow into certainties

Resources Developed

Setting personal challenges
Learning from failures and successes
Discovering strengths and abilities
Being encouraged by challenges
Learning not to listen to negative thoughts
Focussing on personal goals
Assessing risks
Learning to proceed with self-caring caution
Becoming aware of personal strengths

Outcomes Offered

Attention to helpful thoughts
Achievement

Once upon a time there were four competitive frogs who were always setting challenges for themselves, learning from their failures and successes, discovering their strengths and abilities. They had previously had jumping competitions, swimming competitions, croaking competitions, and, of course, frog-leaping competitions. One day one of them announced, "Why don't we have a climbing competition? We have never done that before. Let's see who is first to the top of the castle tower?"

The date was set, the word began to spread, and, on the day, a large crowd had gathered, along with the usual news reporters. The mayor fired the starting pistol and all four frogs leapt away from the starting line simultaneously.

The huge crowd, like with the first human attempts to climb Mt Everest and send a rocket to the moon, did not believe it was possible. "It's too high to make it," someone shouted. "You'll never get there," said someone else. "It's far too difficult. It's too dangerous. You could die," called others.

The first frog heard the doubts before the challenge even started. He wondered if they were right. *Was it too difficult? Was there risk of injury, harm, or even death if he fell?* He had begun to take on the doubts, questioning his own ability. Now he was on the tower it seemed like they could be right. Leaping from stone to stone up the rock face of the tower was not easy. The edges were narrow, the risk of falling was high, and he started to get scared. He felt a slight slip of his foot, and his doubts turned to certainty. *They were right. It was too difficult. He could die.* With these thoughts in mind, he turned around, retreated to the starting line, and withdrew from the race.

At first, the second frog was spurred on by his friend's retreat. With only three in the competition his chances had improved. He pushed himself harder, taking each stone, each leap, one at a time, as he drove harder and higher . . . and the shouts from below grew louder.

"No way can you do it," the crowd yelled. "See, one has pulled out already. Give up before you get hurt."

The second frog found himself repeating their words, echo-like, in his head. He knew they were negative and tried to push them from his mind but they kept coming back and back until he, too, had his doubts. His self-doubts turned to beliefs and then into certainties. *There was no way he could do it. The first frog had already pulled out. It wouldn't be too big a disgrace to give up* . . . and he did.

"Two have given up already," the crowd shouted even louder so the two ascending frogs would hear. "No one will make it! It is FAR, FAR too difficult. Give up while you have the chance."

The third frog had been challenged by the crowd's doubts, wanting to prove them wrong, to show them that it could be done, and that he was the one to do it. Now it was down to a one-on-one race, a 50–50 chance. How could he give up, lose face, and retreat back down the tower after coming so far? He tried to tell himself, *Don't listen to the negative thoughts, push them out of your mind*. But it is a bit like the old story of someone saying to you, "Don't think of a pink elephant." Even by telling himself, *Don't listen to the negative thoughts*, the third frog was aware of them, aware retreat was an option, and, he had to admit, he was feeling tired. As the crowd's words echoed in his head, he felt the fatigue growing stronger, sensed the risks were getting higher . . . and he too gave up.

With just one frog left on the wall, the crowd was even more convinced they were right. They shouted still louder and stronger but the fourth frog pressed on, gradually inching higher and higher up the tower. Contrary to everyone's beliefs and expectations, the fourth frog finally reached the top. The crowd was incredulous but still managed a shout of triumph.

When the final frog made it back to the ground, the news reporters rushed to him. The first one pushed a microphone at his face asking, "How were you the only one to make it? Where did you find the strength and determination to reach your goal despite the doubts around you?"

The frog didn't answer. Instead one of the frog's friends spoke for him. "He didn't hear your question. You see, he's deaf."

Story 92

Generating Solutions

Happiness-Enhancing Characteristics

Problems Addressed

> Being only in the moment
> Difficult choices
> Not knowing which way to turn
> Alternatives that hold significant negative consequences

Resources Developed

> Being in the moment
> Developing acceptance
> Facing reality
> Exercising problem-solving skills
> Looking ahead to practical solutions
> Asking questions
> Generating solutions

Outcomes Offered

> A future-orientation
> Enhanced problem-solving skills
> Ability to generate solutions

One of Zen's most retold stories speaks about being in the moment, about savoring even the smallest of pleasures, and enjoying life's little blessings. It is a tale of a man who was walking through the forest when he encountered a hungry, vicious tiger. As the tiger pounced at him, the man fled but unwittingly ran straight to the edge of a high cliff. Faced with a choice of being mauled to death by the tiger or jumping from the cliff, he leapt. As he fell, he grabbed a vine dangling from the fatal precipice. Looking down, he saw another vicious, hungry tiger at the base of the cliff. While he hung in this predicament, two mice emerged from a hole in the cliff and began gnawing at either end of the vine. Just at that moment, the man saw a plump wild strawberry growing on the vine. With one hand he reached out, plucked the strawberry, and popped it in his mouth. It was *so* incredibly delicious!

While the tale speaks so well about being in the moment, is that the whole picture? I have always skeptically wondered, *What happened next?* A Zen master may reply that I was asking the wrong question. "Don't worry about the future. Just be in the moment." But after eating the strawberry, the tigers would still be there, along with the two mice gnawing away at the vine. Once the moment of deliciously savoring the strawberry had passed for our story's character, would the next moment be one of the tigers deliciously savoring him?

From the information we have, the man's post-strawberry position had not changed from what it was before. He had only briefly been distracted from a problem he still needed to solve. Either he had to climb back to the hungry tiger at the top or fall to the one at the bottom. He was caught in one of life's all-too-common dilemmas: not knowing which way to turn when each of the alternatives holds significant negative consequences.

Were I sitting at the feet of the master who told that story I would want to ask him, "What would you say to a mother of three young children, married to an abusive, alcoholic husband, who, on the one hand, needed to leave for the safety of the children and herself but, on the other, felt she couldn't leave because she needed a roof over her head and his income to care for her children? Would a strawberry-like moment really help her or her children? It may briefly allow her to feel a little better but would she not then be back to the cliff-top tiger of her abusive husband and the cliff-base tiger of a homeless life of poverty?"

If I were that mother I may want to ask the master, "Do you face the problem directly and look to work through it, or do you deny it and avoid taking action until the problem finally eats you up? If you choose the first, you need some good problem-solving skills and that means generating possible solutions. Do you assess the tigers, weighing up things such as whether one is weaker or stronger, older or younger, easier to threaten or distract? Do you get a firm grip on the cliff and hang on until one or both tigers give up and go away? Do you look for some loose stones you can throw at one tiger to send it off? Do you not be limited by the seemingly limited choices offered in the story? Instead of seeing only two choices of going up or down, do you look for another option like a route across the face of the cliff to escape the tigers? Do you look for a cave on the cliff where you can shelter for a while, away from the attention of the tigers? Do you call out in the hope that someone will hear you, see your predicament, and offer assistance?"

I can imagine that if the master is truly wise he may say, with a serene smile creeping onto his face, "I see you have found the true essence of the story. While it speaks about being in the moment, about savoring even the smallest

PROBLEM-SOLVING

of pleasures, and enjoying life's little blessings, you have questioned it. In doing so, you have found that being in the moment may be part of the message, as might acceptance, facing the reality, exercising problem-solving skills, and looking ahead to practical solutions. There may not be one answer but many. By asking the questions, you have started to generate the solutions."

Story 93

Problem-Solving

Happiness-Enhancing Characteristics

Problems Addressed

> Limitations imposed by others
> A no-win situation
> Caught in a dilemma
> Ruminative worries

Resources Developed

> Learning to be observant and thoughtful
> Assessing what things cannot be changed and what can
> Being open to different options
> Looking for new possibilities
> Developing flexible problem-solving skills

Outcomes Offered

> Flexible problem-solving skills
> Resolutions for dilemmas
> Creation of win-win situations

How often do we limit ourselves and our problem-solving skills by the limitations that others impose on us?

In an impoverished rural village where arranged marriages were still the common practice, there lived a poor farmer and his family. Life's pressures affect us all in various ways, and this farmer was no exception. The seasons had not been kind to him and over the years he had been borrowing small amounts from a rather unscrupulous village moneylender to maintain his house, keep his farm going, and feed his family. However, with each successive bad season those small amounts had grown to a huge sum that he now had no foreseeable way of repaying.

The moneylender was not only greedy, he was also old, obese, ugly, and uncouth. The farmer had a rather beautiful unmarried daughter. And, I am sure you have guessed it. The moneylender offered the farmer a deal: he would waive the farmer's debt in return for his daughter's hand in marriage.

What a dilemma! The farmer was in a no-win situation. If he didn't give his daughter to the moneylender he would lose his farm, his home, and his only source of meagre income. If he did, he was destining his beloved daughter to a life of misery and unhappiness.

Seeing this, the cunning moneylender said, "If you can't decide then let fate decide. I will put a white pebble and a black pebble in an empty money bag. Your blindfolded daughter can pick a pebble from the bag. If she pulls out the white pebble, she will marry me and your debt will be wiped. If she selects the black pebble she won't have to marry me and your debt will still be wiped. However, if she refuses to do this, I will foreclose on your farm, have you arrested, and sent to jail."

All the farmer could do was to accept the proposal. Fortunately, he and his wife had raised an astute, observant, and thoughtful daughter. She had watched her parents through many tough times. She learnt to assess the things that could not be changed (like the weather, droughts, and floods) and the things that could be changed (such as the way her parents tried to manage them). Her father had often advised her, "When you have limited ways of responding you get limited results. Be open to different options. Look for the possibilities. The more flexible you can be in problem-solving the better your results."

On the assigned day, all the villagers gathered on the pebble path that led to the farmer's house. Like a skilful conjurer, the moneylender distracted the villagers' attention so that he could quickly bend down to pick up two white pebbles from the path. However, the astute daughter was watching his every move. She saw it was two white pebbles that he picked up and put in the money bag. Calling back the villagers' attention, he asked the daughter, "Please step forward, put on the blindfold and select your pebble."

The farmer's daughter had a problem. I wonder how you would have solved it if you were in her position. What were her possibilities?

At least three were obvious. First, she could refuse to take a pebble but that would lead to her family losing the farm and her father going to jail. Second, she could expose the moneylender as a cheat by showing everyone the two white pebbles he had secreted into his bag but that would leave his father still burdened with his debts. Third, she could go ahead a pick a white pebble, sacrifice her own happiness, and save her father from debt and jail.

"Look for the possibilities," she heard her father saying in her mind. Were there more options? A subtle smile crept on her face just before she slipped her hand into the money bag. Fumbling clumsily, she let the pebble fall to the pebble-strewn path before anyone could see what it was. There it was lost among all the other pebbles.

"Oh, how awkward of me," she exclaimed. "Never mind," she said to the moneylender. "If you look at the colour of the stone left in the bag, you will know that I picked the opposite colour."

The moneylender obviously wasn't prepared to admit his dishonestly publically so all he could do was reach in the bag and display the remaining white pebble. The crowd cheered, assuming she had picked the black pebble, freeing both herself and her father.

As she and her father hugged, she whispered, "Thanks to your wisdom, I was able to look for, find, and use possibilities beyond the obvious options."

PROBLEM-SOLVING

Story 94

Managing Thoughts and Fears

Happiness-Enhancing Characteristics

Problems Addressed

A dilemma between thought and feelings

Resources Developed

Focusing attention
Learning to change logic and thoughts helpfully
Realizing there can be choices available in a situation
Learning to act on those choices

Outcomes Offered

Enjoyment of the experience
A process for dealing with dilemmas

I was on a trip to the Bungle Bungles in outback Western Australia when I met Cheryl. Cheryl was in a dilemma. There was something she wanted to do but was scared witless.

Cheryl was one of the other participants on the 4-wheel drive bus trip that I had taken into this remote area. The Bungle Bungles are ancient geological formations that have weathered down into dome shaped, mounds of mountains that dominate the landscape like giant bee-hives. We had spent the morning walking around these towering formations before having the option of taking a helicopter ride over them. Cheryl said, "I want to take the flight but I am scared stiff of flying. I have never been in a helicopter before and don't think I can."

Nonetheless, Cheryl joined those of us in the small group who had opted for the flight and listened as the pilot gave us our flight briefing. To add a degree of difficulty to Cheryl's concerns he advised that they had removed the doors from the helicopter for better viewing and photographing. One would be held into the flying machine by the simple click of one little buckle on a seat belt.

I was in the first flight to go up and certainly felt my own anxiety rise as the pilot made his first steady bank and I saw nothing but air and mountainous formations hundreds of feet below me. The presence of a door between me and potential death would surely have eased the rate of my heart beat. However, when we landed and alighted, I saw that Cheryl was in the next group ready to take off on the second flight.

Later, as we left, I happened to be seated next to her on the bus. She was bubbling with excitement. "I am curious," I said, "as to how people get to do things even when maybe they don't feel up to doing them at times. Do you mind if I ask how you decided to make the flight?"

"I thought about it," she said. "I thought I may never get back to this area again. I realized it was a once-in-a-lifetime opportunity. I knew that I really wanted to do it. I just needed to bite the bullet and do it."

"But *how* did you do it?" I asked again.

"Well, I sure felt anxious, with the noise and the vibration as the pilot started the engine and we began to lift off the ground, but then the scenery was so spectacular that I forgot for a while how I was feeling. When he made the first turn, I again became anxious, but I started to remind myself that I came up here to see the scenery. Let me enjoy it."

Then she added something that seemed important to me. She said, "I focused my attention on the rocks, their colors and their formations, on the gorges that had been cut away by millennia-old streams, and on the unique palms that grow deep in some of the gorges. When the pilot made another turn I found myself getting anxious again and each time I had to bring my attention back to the scenery, to remind myself why I was taking this flight." And then she said something that was perhaps even more important.

However, it was not just in her words. She had also been *doing* something that was important. First, she had made a decision to shift her thoughts of fear to being aware of this once-in-a-lifetime opportunity. Rather than listening to the fear and apprehension that would have stopped or inhibited her from gaining this experience, she listened to the thoughts that offered the potential of a new experience. Second, she realized that there were choices available in the situation. She could choose what she attended to and what she didn't. She could be selective as to whether she put her attention on what was fearful and scary or what was potentially exciting and enjoyable. Third, she acted on that choice. She consciously made the effort to take her thoughts away from her fears and to tune into the experiences that were pleasurable. If they drifted back to the fears, she brought them back to the pleasure. If they drifted back again, once more she brought them back to the pleasure. In doing so, she not only had the enjoyment of the experience, but she learnt a way or process for herself to be able to deal with anxiety, conquer a challenge, and feel the elation of doing so.

The something she said that to me sounded so important was this: "Yes, I felt scared *and* I allowed myself to enjoy it."

Story 95

Choosing How We Do It

Happiness-Enhancing Characteristics

Problems Addressed

Unwanted or undesired responsibilities

Resistance
Lack of perceived choice

Resources Developed

Finding where we have a choice
Learning that thoughts can be chosen
Learning that emotional responses can be chosen
Discovering thoughts that are helpful to choice
Utilizing the 'Taran choice'

Outcomes Offered

Empowerment to make wise choices
Considered choices
Happy choices

I am sure you have heard the saying, "Out of the mouths of babes." It is often used when kids unexpectedly say something wise, profound, or humorous. I guess wisdom and insight can come from many sources other than just wise elders, astute therapists, or learned teachers. Perhaps we just need to be open to hearing, acknowledging and utilizing them when they are offered.

One night I was babysitting my seven- and three-year-old grandsons while their parents went out for a not-often-chance to have a restaurant meal together. As I was stepping the boys through their pre-bed bathroom routine of having a bath, brushing teeth, going to the toilet, etc., the elder started to object to something. I no longer remember what it was about. Maybe I had gotten the routine a little different to mum and dad's usual pattern. I tried to find out what I needed to adjust but in his growing tiredness he did not verbalize the problem. He just continued to object. In the end, I said, "Look, we are going to have to do this before you go to bed. If we have to then we might as well do it happily."

At that point, three-year-old, Taran, put his hands on his hips, looked at me in his most defiant stare, and retorted, "Or we can do it sadly!"

Out of the mouth of a babe came a concept that was wise, profound, and challenging. Yes, we could do it happily, or we could do it sadly. *He is right*, I thought. Sometimes we may not have a choice about doing something. Sometimes there simply is no room for negotiation. Sometimes in life that is just the way it is, whether it be a part of our work role, our parental obligations, our personal or social relationships, or our living by the laws of society. However, we do have a choice about the way or ways we respond.

If we are required to do something at work that we may not want to do, for example, we may have limited choice. If it is part of our job description and we want to keep our job for the benefits it provides, then we may need to undertake particular tasks despite the fact that they seem undesirable to us. Here we have what I have come to think of as the 'Taran choice': Do I do it sadly or do I do it happily? Do I find the things in the task to moan and complain about or do I think of the things I might enjoy in the task and the big picture benefits of the job? How can I adjust my attitude to help me feel worse or better about it? What particular attitude or way of looking at it is the more beneficial in helping me to get the task done easily and enjoyably?

There are so many things that we *have* to do in life—compromising our wants in a relationship, getting to work on time, filling out our tax returns, sticking to the speed limit, abiding by the law—that I am sure I don't need to expand on all the examples for you to think of examples in your own current experience.

"Yes," I found myself responding to my grandson. "You are right. We can choose to do this happily or sadly. Which would you prefer?"

Story 96

Which Thoughts Do I Attend to?

Happiness-Enhancing Characteristics

Problems Addressed

> Emotional baggage
> Negative past memories
> Second guessing
> Ruminative, unwanted thoughts
> Inner critic

Resources Developed

> Asking if thoughts are worth listening to
> Choosing when to listen, and when not
> Evaluating self-talk
> Learning internal experience is changeable
> Learning to recall positive memories
> Discovering you are more than your past

Outcomes Offered

> Greater self-esteem
> Thought management skills
> Enjoyment of the present
> A future orientation
> Enhanced peace of mind

"How do you know if your thoughts are worth listening to?"

I was recently watching a video of my colleague and friend, Dr Michael Yapko, working with a client called Mike. Mike described carrying a lot of emotional baggage for the last 35 years of his life and not being able to break free of his negative memories of the past. He spoke of being beaten and abused as a kid by his father, pushed downstairs, hit by belts and boots, and called every name you could imagine. He ran away from home and spent his youth being shuffled from foster home to foster home.

"With that background how does that affect the choices you make today?" Dr Yapko asked him.

"I keep second guessing myself," answered Mike. "I am not sure which way to move without constantly replaying things in my head. They always keep coming back. I feel like I am stuck in a gutter. I get caught up in them." Mike explained that, when he focused on his negative recollections of the past, they built up to the point that he would have to leave work, finding himself crying for long times. He described the negative thoughts as sticking on him "like a magnet."

That was when Dr Yapko asked, "How do you know if those thoughts are worth listening to? Have you ever had the experience of realizing they are not helpful to you?"

"Words that people say can hurt worse than punches," replied Mike.

"What if someone criticizes you, how do you know whether to take it seriously?" enquired Yapko.

"I don't."

"We all replay the bad things that have happened, the self-criticisms we generate," explained Dr Yapko. He went on to add, "When I am lecturing to a group of hundreds of people, I often ask them, 'Who among you has good self-esteem?' When hands go up, I ask them, 'Do you have an inner critic, a voice inside your head that says rotten things, puts you down, and says mean and horrible things to you?' Every single one says, 'Yes.' So I ask them, 'If you have a voice that says rotten things to you, how can you have good self-esteem?' And the interesting reply—always a little bit different—is, 'I don't listen to it.' When I ask them, 'How do you not listen to it?' that's when I start to learn all different kinds of strategies. One person may say, 'I picture it on a volume control knob and I just turn the volume down.' Somebody else may say, 'I picture it as a barking dog tied to a tree and I keep walking.' Somebody else may say, 'I have another voice on my shoulder that says good things to me.' But the interesting thing is that every single person has that inner critic or critical voice. It is just a matter of whether they listen to it or not."

Then addressing his question directly to Mike, Dr Yapko asked, "Do you evaluate the things you tell yourself?"

"I try to but it always comes back," said Mike.

"They will always come back," responded Yapko. "The question is what you do with them when they come back. When bad memories come back you can do one of two things. You can focus on them or not focus on them."

"It's not easy to forget it or let it go when those thoughts are so negative."

"No, it's not," responded Yapko empathically, "but it is a skill worth developing."

While we are absorbed in negative thoughts it is hard to see other options, other possibilities, or other ways of thinking. But the good news is that there *are* alternative ways of thinking about things.

First, it helps to know that while the world around us may not change, internal experience is imminently changeable. We don't have to be stuck with unwanted thoughts, feelings, or actions.

Then, it may be beneficial to allow and allocate yourself time to recall nice memories, good people, and the small, pleasant things you had forgotten.

Using the past to predict our future can be a pretty shaky foundation for our thoughts. Because something has happened one way in the past doesn't mean it will go on happening that way in the future. As Dr Yapko said to Mike, "You are more than your past."

Enjoying and savoring the simple, pleasurable experiences that we are capable of helps shift thoughts from the worrisome past to the pleasures of the present.

Looking ahead to the ways you want your future to be different from the past can alter thoughts in more positive directions. "The best way to predict the future," Dr Yapko told Mike, "is to create it."

As I turned off the video, I thought to myself, *What a useful question. How do I know which of my thoughts are worth listening to? Of all the millions of thoughts that go through my head, 24/7, is this particular one really worth attending to?*

PROBLEM-SOLVING

17 On Being Happy

We have a natural right to achieve as much happiness as possible.

Dalai Lama

Introduction

"Infinite happiness," promised the electronic sign in front of a phone shop in my local shopping mall. Curious about how one may acquire infinite happiness I read on. It continued, "Join our $60 plan." *Do they really expect anyone to believe that purchasing a phone plan will give you infinite happiness?* I found myself wondering.

Society, culture, and commerce have created, and maintain, many myths and misconceptions about what facilitates happiness . . . and what doesn't. But how do we sort the wheat from the chaff? How do we differentiate the evidence from the myths? How can we be genuinely happy?

I have to confess the title to this chapter is simplistic. Tell anyone who is severely depressed, "Be happy," and you could deservedly expect an irate string of abuse in reply. It is not that people do not want to be happy but rather that they are not, at this point in time, aware of, accessing, and/or utilizing the skills, resources or pathways to find, enhance, and engage in greater levels of happiness.

Society offers us many quick-fix formulae for happiness in the knowledge that this is our ultimate desire for life: Infinite happiness is a certain cell plan; owning a dog; cleaning your home with a certain product; having a beautiful woman or rich man; etc. But happiness is not formulaic. What works for one person may not for another. If I say happiness for me is swimming with sea lions near my home, this may seem like a nightmare for someone who is fearful of the sea, large animals, or uncontrolled experiences. However, if we explore the process we get closer to an understanding of happiness. In accord with Seligman's PERMA model (2011), I gain pleasure from the activity of swimming with sea lions. It is an engaging, mindful experience in which cares and other 'issues' fall from my thoughts. I am in a relationship with the sea lions and nature. It has meaning and purpose and leaves me with a sense of accomplishment.

Happiness is a *process*, a state of mind and being, in which the content may vary for each individual. It may be experienced in gardening, playing bridge, engaging in rewarding work, showing compassion to others, being in a positive relationship, or collecting butterflies. As I once heard the Dalai Lama say, "Because I like chilies doesn't mean you have to like chilies." Our individual pathways to happiness are, indeed, just that: highly individual.

Fortunately, science is helping us to validate some of those processes and it is these that have been the topics of each of the preceding chapters. In this chapter I offer some summating stories about the processes for experiencing greater happiness and well-being.

Story 97

A Tail of Happiness

Happiness-Enhancing Characteristics

Problems Addressed

The pursuit of happiness
Endlessly chasing happiness
The paradox of pursuing happiness

Resources Developed

Enjoying the pleasures of being in the moment
Setting goals, plans, and hope for the future
Savoring or being mindful of sensory pleasures
Enjoying friendships and loving relationships
Benefiting from exercise and activity
Practicing relaxation, meditation, and mindfulness
Being caring and compassionate
Learning that helping others to be happy helps oneself to be happy

Outcomes Offered

Mindfulness of pleasure
Health and well-being
Compassion
Peace and contentment
Happiness

A young puppy once asked its mother, "I have heard you and other adults talk about happiness. What is this happiness and where can I find it?"

Where do you find happiness? the mother wondered, asking herself a question she had never stopped to ask before. Then she thought, *We dogs wag our tails when we are happy.* Happiness is indeed visible, we show it on our faces, express it in our behavior, and hear it in our voices.

So she answered her puppy, "Happiness is in your tail."

Soon after, the puppy started to chase its tail. Constantly, it was running round and round in circles, tripping over things, knocking things down, and generally making a nuisance of itself. No longer could his mother bear it.

Forgetting what she had previously said, she asked the puppy, "Why are you constantly chasing your tail?"

"I want to be happy," came the reply, "and you told me that happiness is in my tail. So I am chasing my tail. When I catch it, I will have happiness."

The mother dog smiled—and probably wagged her tail, too. "Perhaps I should have been clearer. Our tail *expresses* our happiness, it shows it to us and others. Seeing our tail wag, others may then wag theirs. That's a way to spread happiness but happiness itself comes from within us. It is in the ways we think, the ways we feel, and the ways we behave. However, it is like our tail because whenever we try to catch it, it seems out of reach. The harder we pursue it, the more it avoids us and we never get hold of it."

"On the other hand, I find that when I get on with my life, when I am savouring my food or the variety of scents in the air, when I am in the company of other dogs, running free, relaxing, thinking pleasant thoughts, seeing the pleasure I bring to our owners, then I feel happy."

Now, I guess the mother dog had never heard of positive psychology or read the research into the factors that contribute to our happiness and well-being but she sure made a pretty good summation of them. In talking about getting on with life, she was describing what researchers have shown to be the values of enjoying the pleasures of being in the moment *and* having goals, plans, and hope for the future. Her reference to savouring both food and scents speaks of being aware and mindful of sensory pleasures. Enjoying the company of other dogs highlights a social factor. One of the defining features of the very happiest of people is that they have both a greater number and greater quality of good friendships, while people in loving, long-term relationships tend to live longer and healthier.

The mother dog's mention of running free illustrates the benefits of exercise and activity to our state of happiness. Exercise not only reduces depression but also directly enhances health and well-being. Her talk of relaxing with pleasant thoughts has scientific support showing how the regular practice of relaxation, meditation, and mindfulness also creates states of well-being like peace, contentment, and happiness. Bringing pleasure to others, such as the mother dog's owners, being caring and compassionate towards others, has long been a core of most religious traditions and is now being endorsed by research. Helping others to be happy helps oneself be happy.

"When I do these things," said the mother dog to her puppy, "like my tail, happiness just follows me wherever I go."

Story 98

Lighting Up the Darkness

Happiness-Enhancing Characteristics

Problems Addressed

> Not knowing what an experience is like
> Limited range of experience
> Curiosity
> Desire to experience something new
> Self-doubts

Resources Developed

> Being open to possibilities
> Moving from here to where you want to be
> Discovering that things can be different
> Learning that positive emotions undo negative emotions

Outcomes Offered

> Brighter and more cheerful
> Relaxation and peaceful feelings
> Happiness

How could an eagle know what it is like to swim around a coral reef or a sea-slug know the experiencing of soaring on a thermal a thousand feet up in the air? If you haven't had an experience, it is hard to know what that experience is like. If you haven't had an experience for a long time, it may be hard to remember what that experience is like. That's how it was for a hidden cave that resided deep beneath the earth. With just a narrow twisting tunnel for an entrance, light had never found its way into the depths of the cave. Consequently, the underground cave had never seen light and had no idea what it was. The word 'light' meant nothing to the cave and the concept it conveyed was not even within the cave's realm of imagination. In its depth of darkness it had limited chance of experiencing the joy of light.

One day, the sun sent an invitation to the cave. "Please come and visit me," it read. The cave had to admit that it was curious about what it might be like to experience even a little light in its life. It had to admit that it even felt a desire or longing to know what that light might feel like, to experience something new and different from what its experience had been so far.

Now, like the cave, you may wonder how, seemingly trapped in the depths of darkness, seeing no way out or up, if it could ever get to visit the sun high in the sky. To be honest I am not sure either but I guess it first had to be open to the possibility that it could somehow move beyond its current situation, and that it was possible for things to be different. I guess it also had to find the ways or means to be able to make that move. How did it get from where it was to where it wanted to be? Through the magic of stories, things can just happen, but it was important for the cave to explore those questions, to find ways to bring light into its life.

When the cave got to visit the sun, it immediately felt different. Feelings of cold, damp, dark, and loneliness that it had just taken for granted, or assumed was how it was meant to be, seemed to evaporate. In the presence of the sun, the cave was warm, comfortable, cozy, and secure. Not recalling that it had ever seen, felt, or experienced such light before, the cave was amazed how different life could be. But then it had self-doubts. It was all right for the sun. He was naturally bright and cheerful. It was the way he had always been. It was his job. For the cave it was different. It felt like life had always been dark and gloomy. It was easy for the cave to assume that was the way it was and the way it would always be. Then it realized: *Right now it isn't. If things can be light, bright, and cheerful for just this moment, is it possible for life to be lighter, brighter, and more cheerful in future moments, too?*

Appreciative of the sun's invitation that had allowed him to experience something so new, the polite cave apprehensively invited the sun to pay it a visit sometime. It was apprehensive because it had few friends and rarely invited guests to visit. It also felt ashamed. How would the bright and cheerful sun feel in the cave's dark, gloomy abode?

Well, one day the sun did come to visit. Darkness was as foreign to the sun as light had been to the cave. It was intrigued by what this word 'darkness' meant and what the experience of it would be like. As it approached the entrance tunnel, a slight glimmer of light, like a thin torch beam, found its way into the cave. The closer the sun approached the more it began to light up the darkness inside the cave. It was subtle rather than sudden but the cave not only let it in, it found itself anticipating it and welcoming it. Already the cave was wondering why it had not invited the sun into its world and life before.

As the sun finally emerged from the tunnel and entered the cave, it filled the cave with brightness and joy. I guess the cave was discovering for itself, and in its own way, what a colleague of mine, Dr Barbara Fredrickson, has spent her professional life researching. She has discovered that the more positive emotions you create, the more you displace negative emotions in much the same way as light entering a cave dispels the darkness. Like the cave, the more we invite and create relaxing, peaceful feelings into our lives, the less we feel stressed and anxious. The more we invite and create happy feelings into our lives, the less we feel sad. Just as it is possible to replace darkness with light, so it is possible to replace sadness with happiness. Like the cave, we can do so, first, by being open to the possibility, second, by inviting more positive emotions into our lives, and, third, by actively creating more positive experiences for ourselves.

Looking around, curiously wanting to see what darkness was like, the puzzled sun asked the cave, "Where is the darkness?"

Story 99

Eliminating Sadness or Creating Happiness?

Happiness-Enhancing Characteristics

Problems Addressed

Unhappiness
Asking unhelpful questions
Being past-oriented
Externalizing problems
Aiming primarily at eliminating problems

Resources Developed

Creating happiness is different from eliminating unhappiness
Creating more positive experiences and emotions means less negative ones
Learning to ask the most helpful questions
Shifting from external to inner control
Moving from understanding to action

Outcomes Offered

Being happier in the present and future
Being action-oriented
Being personally responsible for one's happiness
Asking questions that empower toward happiness

"What makes me unhappy?" It was Robert's first question on our first meeting.

"Wrong question," I replied . . . and Robert looked startled. I guessed that for several decades he had been asking the same question and for several decades he had been failing to come up with any helpful answer.

Why did I say that he was asking the wrong question? Well, first, it seemed to me, his question was past-oriented. It had him looking back on his history, seeking an explanation of what had been rather than looking forward to how he might change things for the better.

Second, he was just over 60 years old and said he had been suffering from unhappiness for as long as he could remember. If after all those years of searching for an answer to his despair, in philosophy, religion, medicine, and therapy, and not finding it, why should anything be different now?

Third, he appeared to already have a good understanding of the basis of his unhappiness. He spoke of a "very domineering mother," parents with high expectations of their children, three highly successful older siblings, four failed attempts at university degrees, recent retirement from a life-long job behind the same desk as "a paper-pusher," and the absence of "an intimate relationship" since the age of 18 years.

Fourth, in asking what *made* him unhappy he was externalizing the problem rather than taking responsibility for his own happiness.

Finally, his request of me as a therapist focused on the negative. He wanted to know what made him *unhappy* rather than what he could do to be *happier*.

"What should my question be then? How do I stop being unhappy?" he replied after a few thoughtful moments.

"Well, it's a better question," I responded, "but still a wrong question," . . . and again he paused.

His new question had moved from one seeking understanding to one of action but still it wasn't the most helpful question he could be asking. Aiming to get rid of a symptom or unpleasant feeling is something I have written about as a goal of neutrality. It is problematic aiming to simply eliminate a problem—in four ways.

First, if a person like Robert has had a long history of sadness or despair and a long history of unsuccessful attempts to change things, it is unlikely that he or she is going to hold any great hope or belief that yet another attempt will suddenly bring about a miracle—even though it may be desired, and desired strongly.

Second, his desire to stop being unhappy—to be devoid of a particular feeling—was aimed at an unattainable goal. There is no such thing as emotional or experiential neutrality. We are never devoid of feeling, psychologically or physically. Feelings are constantly present and constantly varying, even when we feel 'normal.' Therefore, to make the absence of feeling his goal was impossible and hence destined to failure from the beginning.

Third, not only is a goal of neutrality unattainable, but it may also be detrimental for a person. We have good evidence that setting unattainable, unworkable, and inappropriate goals can lead to frustration, disappointment, and even greater levels of depression.

Finally, unpleasant emotions such as anxiety, grief, and depression can serve useful functions for us at times by helping us cope with stress, loss, and plain old rotten experiences. To suggest that one might remove a symptom that has such function or that has been a primary, familiar way of coping in the past can be both frightening and scary for that person.

Early in my career, I had accepted that helping a person eliminate their anxiety, depression, or relationship problems would result in them being happier. Unfortunately, I was proven wrong. In many cases, this was not the outcome. Gradually, I discovered that to help a person become happy is a different process from helping a person get rid of their unhappiness. Eliminating the negative doesn't necessarily create the positive, whereas creating the positive may help eliminate the negative. The more positive experiences and emotions a person creates, the less negative ones they maintain.

"Then what should I be asking?" Robert enquired. "What can I do to be happier?"

Robert's question had shifted from one that sought an explanation of what *made* him unhappy in the past to what *he could do* to be happier in the present and future. It had moved from understanding to action. It had shifted the responsibility for his happiness from external factors to his own personal control. It was a question for which he could find answers, a question that could empower him to be happy.

"That sounds like a more practical, more helpful and more answerable question to me," I said with an affirming smile. "What is your answer?"

Story 100

You Are What You Think

Happiness-Enhancing Characteristics

Problems Addressed

Lack of happiness
Lack of happy thought patterns
Depressive thought patterns
A sense of hopelessness

Resources Developed

Developing a sense of perceived control
Thinking optimistically
Building positive self-esteem
Fulfilling personal goals
Developing 'cognitive hardiness'
Discovering everyone can learn to think in happier ways

Outcomes Offered

Happier thought patterns
Increased levels of happiness and well-being
Maintained levels of happiness and well-being

"It's the way you *think* that makes you happy," said my colleague, psychologist Dr Julie-Anne Sykley. "It is not your age, your gender, your job, your hobbies, your income, your education level, or the things you possess. It is your mind."

Julie-Anne should know. She has researched and written a doctoral thesis about the thought processes involved in happiness and psychological well-being, and applies them in her own life. She maintains that just as certain ways of thinking can create and keep us stuck in a state of depression, so there are special ways of thinking that can increase our feelings of happiness.

Curious to discover what she had discovered in both her research and life I asked Julie-Anne, "Tell me about your research. What *are* those certain ways of thinking? What are the special thoughts that increase our happiness?"

"Well, there are five major patterns of thinking that determine psychological well-being," she replied, "and all five are related to perceptions of personal control."

The first she described as the most significant thought that determines happiness is a sense of perceived control. When you believe *you* have a reasonable amount of personal control over your world, it appears that you do. If something bad happens you might not be able to control those negative events but you *can* control your thoughts and feelings about them. It's not so much the negative event that matters, but how you *react* to that event that can make all the difference between happiness and misery.

Second, she pointed out that happy people tend to think optimistically. They look on the bright side of life and seek out the positives rather than dwelling on bad things. It is the age-old glass-half-full example. Optimistic thinkers will consider how lucky they are to have half a glass to drink while pessimistic thinkers will believe how awful it is that their glass is half empty.

Positive self-esteem is the next important style of thinking held by happy people. This means valuing your strengths and knowing that you can control them. Dr Sykley gave the example of an overweight person who thinks "I can lose weight because I am positive and determined when I put my mind to it." Such a person will be happier and more likely to succeed at their goal than someone who thinks "Nothing will work because I am fat and lazy." Adopting an I-will-take-action-to-do-it approach to life can work wonders.

A fourth pattern of thinking is that happy people feel as if they are fulfilling their goals. Unrealistic, unachievable, and high expectancy goals (such as "I want a partner with perfect looks, body, and personality") are likely to lead to feeling bad and disappointed. On the other hand, realistic, achievable, and practical goals (such as "I want to spend time with someone who is a nice person") are more attainable and, therefore, more likely to attract feelings of well-being.

Finally, happy people also have what Dr Sykley calls 'cognitive hardiness.' By this she means having a sense of control, commitment, and challenge towards life. When hardy people are exposed to stressful events, they will make efforts to control that stress and think about it positively and creatively. Less hardy individuals, however, believe they have no control over stressful events. This makes them prone to depression, anxiety, and physical illness. While a less hardy person thinks 'Life is full of problems' and suffers emotionally and physically as a result, a hardy person thinks 'Life is an adventure' and feels happier for it.

"My studies," Dr Sykley summated, "basically showed that the main cognitive determinant (perceived control) is regulated or mediated by the other four cognitive factors (optimism, self-esteem, goal-fulfillment, and hardiness) that we could call 'positive appraisal.' In other words, a sense of control and a positive appraisal of life leads to psychological well-being—feeling happy, healthy, and satisfied with life."

"Interestingly, this positive style of thinking (having a sense of control and positive appraisal) happens to be the exact opposite of the negative thinking style found in depression. A sense of hopelessness—which is clearly the absence of perceived control—is a well-known predictor of depression and even suicide. Depression also features a pessimistic world view, a low self-esteem, a lack of fulfillment, and a sense of disengagement from life."

For me, the reassuring news to stem from such positive psychology research is that everyone can learn to think in happier ways—to strengthen their sense of personal control over life, think more optimistically, value themselves more positively, set fulfilling goals, and think resilient thoughts. The clear message from our research is this: making positive changes to our thinking will increase and maintain feelings of happiness and well-being.

"That's why," concluded Dr Sykley, "it's not what you do, what you have, or who you are but the way you *think* that makes you happy."

Story 101

Everyone Has the Potential to Be Happy

Happiness-Enhancing Characteristics

Problems Addressed

Depression
Difficult challenges
Loss
Lack of the affection

Resources Developed

Discovering the purpose of life is to be happy
Building positive human relationships
Practicing altruism, love, and compassion
Practicing smiles
Taking constructive action
Developing inner peace

Outcomes Offered

Happiness comprises many factors
A balance between a good brain and good heart
Happier days, happier lives
We all have the potential to be a happy human being

Some years ago I was privileged to be invited to participate in a symposium on Eastern and Western concepts of the mind with His Holiness, the Dalai Lama of Tibet. For me, coming from a culture in which depression rates are rapidly on the rise, I sought to enquire how the Dalai Lama and his people could maintain their sense of happiness in face of the adversities they had suffered. I had heard him say, "Take my own example. I have lost my country." His life has not been without significant challenges: the military occupation of his country, the flight for his life across the world's highest mountain range, the genocide of innumerable Tibetan people, the incarceration of his supporters, and some six decades in exile. Nonetheless, he speaks of losing his country with less angst than what I might experience at misplacing my cell phone when needing to make an urgent call. More than that, he appears to be the very epitome of happiness.

I was keen to ask him, "What might we learn from your example to help others attain happiness?"

The Dalai Lama replied contemplatively, "I believe that the very purpose of life is to be happy. From the very core of our being, we desire happiness." As he continued his reply, he clearly acknowledged that happiness is not a singular entity to be possessed like a new car, a fashionable dress, or some other acquisition. He portrayed it as a combination of many factors.

"First," he said almost apologetically in reference to a social factor, "there is something not very profound. Tibet has a small population in a large area. Quarrels, killings, and bad things do happen," he acknowledged, "but, basically, the human-to-human relationship is positive. Generally speaking, as human beings, people are friendly. That is always there."

It came as no surprise that the Dalai Lama considered the basic tenets of his own religious and philosophical beliefs were a significant element of happiness. "Then, no doubt, one factor is Buddhism in general but particularly Mahayana Buddhism. The key teaching is altruism, infinite altruism, so I think that also makes a difference," he stated, implying that happiness was not to be found in a selfish pursuit of individual well-being but was more likely to emerge through selfless thoughts and actions based in care and consideration.

"The source of all happiness," he continued, "is love and compassion, a sense of kindness and warm-heartedness towards others. I believe that we can all achieve such peace and happiness, because we all possess some basic good human values. For example, if we can be friendly and trusting towards others, we become more calm and relaxed. We lose the sense of fear and suspicion that we often feel about other people. When we are calm and relaxed we can make proper use of our mind's ability to think clearly, so whatever we do, whether we are studying or working, we will be able to do it better."

Making his next point, the Dalai Lama said, "Since we are not solely material creatures, it is a mistake to place all our hopes for happiness on external development alone. During discussions I have had with concerned scientists, it has emerged that the main cause of the depression in the developed world particularly is not a lack of material necessities but feeling deprived of the affection of others. With the rapid advances made by civilization in this century we have laid undue emphasis on material development alone. We have become so engrossed in its pursuit that, without even knowing it, we have neglected to foster the most basic human needs of love, kindness, cooperation, and caring.

Yet the development of human society is based entirely on people helping each other."

"So you see if we realize the fact that material things will not bring peace of mind, and we are still content, that is genuine contentment, isn't it?"

"In my own case, I am a Buddhist monk. Although I cannot practice satisfactorily, I try to practice as a Buddhist monk with a smile." The Dalai Lama's words were not mere words. His infectious smile is something he both wears and shares.

Nonetheless, it seemed to me he saw happiness not just as the product of an attitude of mind but also as the product of constructive action. "It is clear that our own actions and emotions play a significant role (in being happy)," continued the Dalai Lama. "Negative actions always bring pain and sorrow, but constructive actions bring us pleasure and joy. If I think about my experience today, it is mainly due to my own previous actions. If my actions have been negative, some pains and some uncomfortable things are likely to happen today. The basic source of today's experience is my own experience and my own past actions. So, I cannot blame anybody else for these things."

But how did he make the shift from the adversities of the past to currently having a happy state of mind? I wondered.

"The most important thing is transforming our minds, for this is the key to developing inner peace. Since we desire the true happiness that is brought about only by a calm mind, and since such peace of mind is brought about only by a compassionate attitude, we need to find out how we can develop it. I believe that even if only a few individuals are able to create mental peace and happiness within themselves and act responsibly and kind-heartedly towards others, they will have a positive influence in their community."

In summing up, the Dalai Lama reiterated with a smile, "So you see there are many factors. I believe every individual human being has this potential to be a wonderful human being with a wonderful human heart. If you create a balance between a good brain and good heart you get happier days, happier lives. . . ."

I think everyone has the positive potential to be a happy human being."

PART THREE

 Creating Your Own
Happiness-Enhancing Stories

A Guide to Creating Your Own Happiness-Enhancing Stories

I have been privileged to meet many amazing people during my life but the most amazingly happy man I have ever met is someone I doubt you have ever heard of.

On our first encounter, Pema Tshering sat on the floor at the School of Traditional Arts in Thimpu, the capital of Bhutan, holding a chisel with the toes of one foot while gently tapping at it with a wooden mallet held in the toes of his other foot. His arms were frozen in contorted positions around his body, his head twisted at an angle but his face beamed with a smile as he laughed his way through his work.

Only later did I learn that Pema Tshering was born with cerebral palsy, was abandoned by his parents who could not cope with his disability, and raised by his grandparents who kept putting him down as useless and good for nothing. Unable to cope and seriously depressed, he thrice attempted suicide by hanging.

However, the last time that I sat with him on the floor of his art studio he was a highly independent person, tapping away at his laptop computer with his toes. He took a call on his cell phone, picking it up with a foot and toeing the keypad. He makes his living by carving, drawing, and painting solely with his feet. He cooks and looks after himself in a fiercely independent way. All the while his face beams in a smile, his laughter echoes through his little studio, and his happiness is infectious.

I was curious about how he had managed to be so happy despite the fact that the odds were stacked against him in so many ways. He seemed to epitomize many of the qualities that are affirmed in positive psychology research and that I have wanted to communicate through the stories in this book.

Positive psychology has revolutionized the therapeutic and counseling disciplines at several levels. First, it has created a dramatic paradigm shift from looking primarily at what was wrong with the person to focusing more on what is right with the person. It has shifted focus from the pathological to a person's potentialities. It has moved from exploring weaknesses to discovering and utilizing strengths. It has reversed the previous major mental health trends of analyzing past problems to exploring solutions in the present and for the future.

Second, it has been at the forefront of researching what contributes to and facilitates our happiness, flourishing, and well-being. Here a number of clear and replicable interventions have been found to be soundly evidence-based. If we are to help people move from depression to happiness, anxiety to relaxation, or anger to acceptance we need to have both clear evidence and replicable processes. It is these defined processes that have formed the themes behind each of the preceding chapters.

Adopting this paradigm shift and applying the research findings of positive psychology into clinical practice for the uniquely individual clients that we meet in our office is the real challenge for practitioners. Researchers are interested in the trends that apply for the majority of people. Clinicians have the challenge of adapting and communicating those research findings to a particular person, with a particular problem, and a particular objective or outcome. As I mentioned in the Introduction, by the time the depressed client arrives in our office they have often been given sound advice by caring family, friends, and professionals such as their physician or counselors. That the advice, based in well-grounded research, has not been accepted and applied means we need to move beyond the science to look at the art of effectively communicating the evidence-based interventions in ways that will be accepted by this particular person. This comes down to the art and science of language and communication. It is in this context that metaphors and storytelling offer non-authoritarian and empowering communicative processes that can assist clients find and utilize their own effective therapeutic outcomes.

Learning to create and present metaphors in positive psychotherapy and counseling is really no different from learning any other skill. It follows the same sort of processes by which you have learnt to ride a bike, drive a car, practice counseling, do therapy, or any other of your many acquired life skills.

The examples I have given in this book are simply that: examples. They are to offer you some samples of the happiness-enhancing characteristics of metaphors and how a story can be created to communicate the therapeutic messages that are grounded in the research, evidence, and application of positive psychology.

Those of you who have worked with standardized, formulaic approaches to the treatment of particular issues, such as substance abuse, weight management, anxiety, or depression, know that while these approaches work for some clients some of the time they might not necessarily work for all clients all of the time. Those of you who have worked with clinical hypnosis will know that a hypnotic script may have worked for one person at one time but is not guaranteed to work for a different client sitting in the same room with you at a different time. For therapy to be most effective it needs to be tailored to the needs, problems, resources, and outcomes for each uniquely individual client.

Hopefully, in this book I have provided and modeled some processes and guidelines that will enable you to create and adapt your own stories to meet each new client and each new therapeutic challenge. They are basically twofold:

1. *Undertake a PRO Assessment.*

    This will provide you with the Problems your client wishes to address, the Resources that they have or need to develop to resolve these problems and reach a greater level of happiness, and the realistic, attainable, and specific Outcomes they wish to achieve. This will additionally provide you with the basis and framework on which to work collaboratively with your client in providing any therapeutic intervention and, in particular, creating and offering happiness-enhancing therapeutic stories.

2. *Employ the PRO Approach.*

    Therapy is about facilitating the client's transition from their problems to their outcomes and this usually means engaging their strengths, resources, and abilities in ways that will best assist that transition. Therapeutic stories are no exception. The PRO Assessment will have provided both client and therapist with clear therapeutic goals. The PRO Approach to therapy and metaphors will simply engage what you have already defined in the assessment and translate it into a happiness-enhancing story along the lines, *I once saw a client in a similar position to yourself* (identifying and linking the client with the Problems to be addressed) *who recognized her abilities to undertake certain* (specified) *steps* (developing the Resources) *to reach the goals* (specified) *that she wished to achieve for herself* (attaining the Outcomes).

Let me offer the assurance that you don't need to feel confident in your ability to be able to create an amazing story. I have previously given the example of when I first started to work with metaphors having a client for whom I was able to easily tell a metaphor that matched into her problem . . . but then I got stuck. Where did I go from there? What would be a successful outcome? What steps or processes could she appropriately follow to get to that outcome? In the anxiety of trying hard to make it work I came up with a blank—and felt as stuck as she did.

She went home from that first session with a partial story about a little octopus that found itself stuck in a dire predicament—much as she was. However, to my surprise, she came back to the next session and said, "I know what happened to the little octopus." She found the pathways and outcomes that she needed for herself despite my inability to create the perfect story for her. In doing so, she taught me about the value of (a) engaging clients collaboratively in their own story processes and (b) assisting them to generate their own healing stories. Details of her case can be found in Burns (2010).

Because of clients like her I have discovered you don't have to be a masterful storyteller but rather simply someone who can listen empathically and facilitate the clients' process of changing their old, unhelpful stories to new, happiness-enhancing tales for improving their life, happiness, and well-being. Consequently, in therapeutic storytelling you can feel confident in your client's ability to:

- enjoy listening to stories
- have the ability to learn from stories
- find meaning for themselves in a story
- search for their own strengths, abilities, and resources, and
- seek appropriate resolution through the context and processes of the metaphor.

As my previous books, *101 Healing Stories, 101 Healing Stories for Kids and Teens,* and *Healing With Stories,* have included details about how to create your own healing stories, how to use metaphors effectively, how to avoid some of the potential pitfalls, where to get ideas for the therapeutic metaphors, and how to plan and present metaphors in therapy I will not reiterate these topics here but rather refer you to those sources for more detailed explanations (Burns, 2001, 2005, 2007).

This book is also different from my previous collections of 101 healing stories. Not only does it specifically cover some of the core, documented interventions of positive psychology but it also includes more personal life stories. In previous works I had wanted to demonstrate the diversity of potential therapeutic stories from many different sources. Here I have deliberately chosen to include personal stories because our own life and learning experiences can often hold potent learnings for others—just as others' life stories can hold important messages for us. Nonetheless, care needs to be taken in using personal life stories to ensure that they are:

- crafted for the benefit of the client
- are clearly outcome-oriented
- provide appropriate pathways for the client to enhance their happiness and well-being, and
- follow the PRO Approach (Problem, Resources, Outcomes).

Following these outcome-oriented guidelines, carefully-crafted and therapeutically-focused personal life stories have the ability to enhance (a) the positive, healing dynamics of a quality, collaborative therapeutic relationship and (b) the attainment of desired therapeutic goals. For more guidelines on safely and constructively using personal life stories as therapeutic metaphors see Burns (2005, pp. 253–254).

We have all grown up on stories in all their various forms. We have all communicated through hearing and telling stories. We have all learnt from the important messages that stories share. As such stories provide a means, *par excellence,* to communicate the essential and vital messages of effective therapy. They are not therapy *per se* but the vehicle by which that therapy can be offered to a client in a way that is non-authoritarian, non-judgemental, and allows a person the opportunity of discovering empowered solutions for themselves. In fact, discovering empowering solutions is one of the outcomes of the story I was telling you about my artist friend, Pema Tshering, in Bhutan who carves and paints solely with his feet.

Curious, I asked him. "How did you make the transition from where you were to where you are? How can a person face such significant and unchangeable adversity yet be so genuinely happy?"

Pema replied, "There is a great difference between then and now. Sometimes I am still overtaken by sorrow. Sometimes I appreciate myself as I can do almost anything. I look after myself and found my own personal happiness."

"How have you found your own personal happiness?" I pressed him.

"The Queen Mother found me when I was at home doing nothing," he answered. "She saw how I could use my feet and opened up the opportunity for me to get into the art school where I did a six year apprenticeship." His response highlighted how having someone believe in you and spot your strengths can enable you to also believe in yourself and become aware of your own strengths and abilities. From there Pema began to see opportunities and set goals for undertaking and completing his apprenticeship in fine arts—a process of personal empowerment.

"I have learnt to accept my disability and not dwell on it," he added. Acceptance of what could not be changed was a large step towards his personal happiness. He became mindfully engaged in his painting and wood carving. He reframed his 'disability' as the means for creating his artistic skills and talent.

For me Pema highlights how it is possible to learn from experience. His thoughts are positive and future-oriented, with the dream that one day he will compete in the Paralympics archery. His constant laughter reflects resilient and positive emotions, and his independent lifestyle is a reminder of how he needs to be a constant problem-solver. The qualities he exhibits parallel almost exactly the chapter headings that I have listed in this book.

Each time I return to Bhutan I look forward to meeting him again. Though we don't share the same language and have to communicate through a translator, at another level we connect deeply through laughter, joy, and happiness. It is a privilege to think of him as a friend. Personally he has discovered the processes that our science is now validating for the enhancement of happiness and well-being. He is the most amazingly happy man I have ever met and, like nine-year-old Lucia whose story of overcoming a fear of flying, I told in the Introduction to this book, he reaffirms how changing your story changes your experience . . . and your life. (Pema Tshering's story, My Paralympic Dream, can be found at: https://www.youtube.com/watch?v=0rShkVdJuUM).

A very strong reason behind me writing this book has been to share that message with you and hope that you, in turn, may share it with your clients for

CREATING YOUR STORIES

the enhancement of your happiness and well-being as well as theirs. My hope is that the examples of stories provided in this book will facilitate your search for, recording of, and offering of your own individual stories for your own individual clients. My wish is that you, personally, enjoy many more enriching, enhancing, and happy stories of life, work, and love.

References and Reading Resources

On Metaphors

Blenkiron, P. (2005). Stories and analogies in cognitive behaviour therapy: A clinical review. *Behavioural and Cognitive Psychotherapy*, 33, 1, 45–59.

Burns, G. W. (2001). *101 Healing Stories: Using Metaphors in Therapy*. New York: John Wiley and Sons.

Burns, G. W. (2005). *101 Healing Stories for Kids and Teens*. Hoboken, NJ: John Wiley and Sons.

Burns, G. W. (2006). Building coping skills with metaphors. In M. D. Yapko (Ed.), *Hypnosis and Treating Depression: Applications in Clinical Practice*. New York: Routledge.

Burns, G. W. (2007). *Healing With Stories: Your Casebook Collection for Using Therapeutic Metaphors*. Hoboken, NJ: John Wiley & Sons.

Heffner, M., Greco, L. A. & Eifert, G. H. (2003). Pretend you are a turtle: Children's responses to metaphorical versus literal relaxation instructions. *Child & Family Behavior Therapy*, 25, 1, 19–33.

Kottler, J. (2015). *Stories We've Heard, Stories We've Told: Life-Changing Narratives in Therapy and Everyday Life*. Oxford: Oxford University Press.

Kozak, A. (2009). *Wild Chickens and Petty Tyrants: 108 Metaphors for Mindfulness*. Somerville, MA: Wisdom Publications.

Lyddon, W. J., Clay, A. L. & Sparks, C. L. (2001). Metaphor and change in counseling. *Journal of Counseling & Development*, 79, 3, 269–274.

Malhotra, H. (2014). *Metaphors of Healing: Playful Language in Psychotherapy and Everyday Life Paperback*. Lanham, MD: Hamilton Books.

Otto, M. W. (2000). Stories and metaphors in cognitive-behavior therapy. *Cognitive and Behavioral Practice*, 7, 2, 166–172.

Pernicano, P. (2010). *Metaphorical Stories for Child Therapy: Of Magic and Miracles*. Lanham, MD: Jason Aronson.

Pernicano, P. (2011). *Outsmarting the Riptide of Domestic Violence: Metaphor and Mindfulness for Change*. Lanham, MD: Jason Aronson.

Pernicano, P. (2014). *Using Trauma-Focused Therapy Stories: Interventions for Therapists, Children and Their Caregivers*. New York: Routledge.

Rigby, L. & Waite, S. (2007). Group therapy for self-esteem, using creative approaches and metaphor as clinical tools. *Behavioural and Cognitive Psychotherapy*, 35, 3, 361–364.

Slivinske, J. & Slivinske, L. (2011). *Storytelling and Other Activities for Children in Therapy*. Hoboken, NJ: John Wiley & Sons.

Stoddard, J. A. & Afari, N. (2014). *The Big Book of ACT Metaphors: A Practitioner's Guide to Experiential Exercises and Metaphors in Acceptance and Commitment Therapy*. Oakland, CA: New Harbinger Publications.

On the PRO Assessment

Burns, G. W. (2001). *101 Healing Stories: Using Metaphors in Therapy*. New York: John Wiley and Sons.

Burns, G. W. (2005). *101 Healing Stories for Kids and Teens*. Hoboken, NJ: John Wiley and Sons.

Burns, G. W. (2007). *Healing with Stories: Your Casebook Collection for Using Therapeutic Metaphors*. Hoboken, NJ: John Wiley & Sons.

Burns, G. W. (Ed.). (2010). *Happiness Healing Enhancement: Your Casebook Collection for Using Positive Therapy*. Hoboken, NJ: John Wiley & Sons.

Cheavens, J. S. & Gum, A. M. (2010). From here to where you want to be: Building the bridges with hope therapy in a case of major depression. In G. W. Burns (Ed.), *Happiness Healing Enhancement: Your Casebook Collection for using Positive Therapy* (pp. 51–63). Hoboken, NJ: John Wiley & Sons.

Erickson, B. A. (2010). What's right with him? Ericksonian positive psychotherapy in a case of sexual abuse. In G. W. Burns (Ed.), *Happiness Healing Enhancement: Your Casebook Collection for Using Positive Therapy* (pp. 29–39). Hoboken, NJ: John Wiley & Sons.

Linley, A. (2008). *Average to A+: Realising Strengths in Yourself and Others*. Coventry, UK: CAPP Press.

Linley, P. A. & Burns, G. W. (2010). Strengthspotting: Finding and developing client resources in the management of intense anger. In G. W. Burns (Ed.), *Happiness Healing Enhancement: Your Casebook Collection for Using Positive Therapy* (pp. 3–14). Hoboken, NJ: John Wiley & Sons.

Peterson, C. (2008). *What Is Positive Psychology, and What Is It Not?* Accessed on May 5, 2016, from https://www.psychologytoday.com/blog/the-good-life/200805/what-is-positive-psychology-and-what-is-it-not

Rashid, T. (2015). Strength-based assessment. In S. Joseph (Ed.), *Positive Psychology in Practice: Promoting Human Flourishing in Work, Health, Education, and Everyday Life* (2nd ed., pp. 519–542). Hoboken, NY: John Wiley and Sons.

Seligman, M. (2011). *Flourish*. North Sydney, Australia: William Heinemann.

Snyder, C. R. (1994). *The Psychology of Hope: You Can Get There from Here*. New York: Free Press.

Snyder, C. R. (2002). Hope theory: Rainbows in the mind. *Psychological Inquiry*, 13, 249–275.

Snyder, C. R. & Lopez, S. (2007). *Positive Psychology: The Scientific and Practical Explorations of Human Strengths*. Thousand Oaks, CA: Sage.

Chapter 1: On Being a Goal-Setter and Goal-Achiever

Burns, G. W. & Street, H. (2003). *Standing without Shoes: Creating Happiness, Relieving Depression, Enhancing Life*. Sydney, Australia: Prentice Hall.

Cheavens, J. S. & Gum, A. M. (2010). From here to where you want to be: Building the bridges with hope therapy in a case of major depression. In G. W. Burns

(Ed.), *Happiness Healing Enhancement: Your Casebook Collection for Using Positive Therapy* (pp. 51–63). Hoboken, NJ: John Wiley & Sons.

Emmons, R. (1999). *The Psychology of Ultimate Concerns*. New York: Guildford Press.

Kasser, T. & Ryan, R. M. (2001). Be careful what you wish for: Optimal functioning and the relative attainment of intrinsic and extrinsic goals. In P. Schmuck & K. M. Sheldon (Eds.), *Life Goals and Well-Being: Towards a Positive Psychology of Human Striving* (pp. 116–131). Goettingen, Germany: Hogrefe & Huber.

Little, B. R. (2007). *Personal Project Pursuit: Goals Action and Human Flourishing*. Mahwah, NJ: Lawrence Erlbaum Associates.

Niemiec, C. P. & Ryan, R. M. (2013). What makes for a life well lived? Autonomy and its relation to full functioning and organismic wellness. In S. A. David, I. Boniwell & A. Conley Ayers (Eds.), *The Oxford Handbook of Happiness* (pp. 214–226). Oxford: Oxford University Press.

Sheldon, K. & Hoon, T. (2007). The multiple determination of well-being: Independent effects of positive traits, needs, goals, selves, social supports, and cultural contexts. *Journal of Happiness Studies*, 7, 55–86.

Sheldon, K. & Lyubomirsky, S. (2007). Is it possible to become happier? (And, if so, how?). *Social and Personality Psychology Compass*, 1, 129–145.

Snyder, C. R. (1994). *The Psychology of Hope: You Can Get There from Here*. New York: Free Press.

Snyder, C. R. (2002). Hope theory: Rainbows in the mind. *Psychological Inquiry*, 13, 249–275.

Street, H. (2010). The why, not the what: The positive power of intrinsic motivations in client goal setting and pursuit. In G. W. Burns (Ed.), *Happiness Healing Enhancement: Your Casebook Collection for Using Positive Therapy* (pp. 40–50). Hoboken, NJ: John Wiley & Sons.

Chapter 2: On Finding and Using Strengths

Biswas-Diener, R. (2010a). A positive way of addressing negatives: Using strengths-based interventions in coaching and therapy. In G. W. Burns (Ed.), *Happiness Healing Enhancement: Your Casebook Collection for Using Positive Therapy* (pp. 291–302). Hoboken, NJ: John Wiley & Sons.

Biswas-Diener, R. (2010b). *Practicing Positive Psychology Coaching: Assessment, Activities and Strategies for Success*. Hoboken, NJ: John Wiley & Sons.

Carr, A. (2004). *Positive Psychology: The Science of Happiness and Human Strengths*. New York: Routledge.

Fox Eades, J. M. (2008). *Celebrating Strengths: Building Strengths-Based Schools*. Coventry, UK: CAPP Press.

Fox Eades, J. M., Proctor, C. & Ashley, M. (2013). Happiness in the classroom. In S. A. David, I. Boniwell & A. Conley Ayers (Eds.), *The Oxford Handbook of Happiness* (pp. 579–591). Oxford, UK: Oxford University Press.

Linley, P. A. (2008). *Average to A+: Realising Strengths in Yourself and Others*. Coventry, UK: CAPP Press.

Linley, P. A. & Burns, G. W. (2010). Strengthspotting: Finding and developing client resources in the management of intense anger. In G. W. Burns (Ed.), *Happiness Healing Enhancement: Your Casebook Collection for Using Positive Therapy* (pp. 3–14). Hoboken, NJ: John Wiley & Sons.

Linley, P. A., Willars, J. & Biswas-Diener, R. (2010). *The Strengths Book: Be Confident, Be Successful, and Enjoy Better Relationships by Realising the Best of You.* Coventry, UK: CAPP Press.

Lopez, S. J., Pedrotti, J. T. & Snyder, C. R. (2015). *Positive Psychology: The Scientific and Practical Explorations of Human Strengths* (3rd ed.). Thousand Oaks, CA: Sage Publications.

Rashid, T. (2015). Strength-based assessment. In S. Joseph (Ed.), *Positive Psychology in Practice: Promoting Human Flourishing in Work, Health, Education, and Everyday Life* (2nd ed., pp. 519–542). Hoboken, NY: John Wiley and Sons.

Snyder, C. R. & Lopez, S. (2007). *Positive Psychology: The Scientific and Practical Explorations of Human Strengths.* Thousand Oaks, CA: Sage Publications.

Chapter 3: On Being Empowered

Fetterman, D. M. & Wandersman, A. (2005). *Empowerment Evaluation Principles in Practice: Looking through the Lens of Empowerment Evaluation Principles.* New York: Guilford Press.

Rubin, A. & Babbie, E. R. (2016). *Empowerment Series: Research Methods for Social Work.* Boston, MA: Cengage Learning.

Segal, E. A., Gerdes, K. E. & Steiner, S. (2016). *Empowerment Series: An Introduction to the Profession of Social Work* (5th ed.). Boston, MA: Cengage Learning.

Seligman, M. (2011). *Flourish.* North Sydney, Australia: William Heinemann.

Wallerstein, N. (2006). *What Is the Evidence on Effectiveness of Empowerment to Improve Health?* Accessed on May 5, 2016, from http://www.popline.org/node/175634#sthash.r6vC4GQ2.dpuf

Chapter 4: On Being Accepting

Hayes, L. L. & Ciarrochi, J. (2015).*The Thriving Adolescent: Using Acceptance and Commitment Therapy and Positive Psychology to Help Teens Manage Emotions, Achieve Goals, and Build Connection.* Oakland, CA: Context Press.

Hayes, S. C., Strosahl, K. D., Luoma, J., Varra, A. A. & Wilson, K. (2004). ACT case formulation. In S. C. Hayes & K. D. Strosahl (Eds.), *A Practical Guide to Acceptance and Commitment Therapy* (pp. 59–73). New York: Springer.

Hayes, S. C., Strosahl, K. D. & Wilson, K. G. (1999). *Acceptance and Commitment Therapy: An Experiential Approach to Behavior Change.* New York: Guilford Press.

Hildebrandt, M. J., Fletcher, L. B. & Hayes, S. C. (2007). Climbing anxiety mountain: Generating metaphors in acceptance and commitment therapy. In G. W. Burns (Ed.), *Healing with Stories: Your Casebook Collection for Using Therapeutic Metaphors* (pp. 55–64). Hoboken, NJ: John Wiley & Sons.

Stoddard, J. A. & Afari, N. (2014). *The Big Book of ACT Metaphors: A Practitioner's Guide to Experiential Exercises and Metaphors in Acceptance and Commitment Therapy.* Oakland, CA: New Harbinger Publications.

Walser, R. D. & Chartier, M. (2010). Laying out in anxiety: Acceptance and commitment therapy for values-based living. In G. W. Burns (Ed.), *Happiness Healing Enhancement: Your Casebook Collection for Using Positive Therapy* (pp. 176–189). Hoboken, NJ: John Wiley & Sons.

Walser, R. D. & Westrup, D. (2007). *Acceptance and Commitment Therapy for the Treatment of Posttraumatic Stress Disorder and Trauma-Related Problems.* Oakland, CA: New Harbinger.

Chapter 5: On Being Mindful

Cayoun, B. A. (2011). *Mindfulness-Integrated CBT: Principles and Practice.* Chichester, UK: Wiley-Blackwell.

Cayoun, B. A. (2014). *Mindfulness-Integrated CBT for Well-Being and Personal Growth: Four Steps to Enhance Inner Calm, Self-Confidence and Relationships.* Chichester, UK: Wiley-Blackwell.

Fredrickson, B. L., Cohn, M. A., Coffey, K. A., Pek, J. & Finkel, S. (2008). Open hearts build lives: Positive emotions induce through loving-kindness meditation, build consequential personal resources. *Journal of Personality and Social Psychology,* 95, 1045–1062.

Hassed, C. (2010). Doing nothing, changing profoundly: The paradox of mindfulness in a case of anxiety. In G. W. Burns (Ed.), *Happiness Healing Enhancement: Your Casebook Collection for Using Positive Therapy* (pp. 164–175). Hoboken, NJ: John Wiley & Sons.

Jazaieri, H., Lee, I. A., McGonigal, K., Jinpa, T., Doty, J. R., Gross, J. J. & Goldin, P. R. (2016). A wandering mind is a less caring mind: Daily experience sampling during compassion meditation training. *Journal of Positive Psychology,* 11, 1, 37–50.

Kaplan, S. (2001). Meditation, restoration, and the management of mental fatigue. *Environment and Behavior,* 33, 480–506.

Kozak, A. (2009). *Wild Chickens and Petty Tyrants: 108 Metaphors for Mindfulness.* Somerville, MA: Wisdom Publications.

Malinowski, D. (2013). Flourishing through meditation and mindfulness. In S. A. David, I. Boniwell, & A. C. Ayers (Eds.), *The Oxford Handbook of Happiness* (pp. 384–396). Oxford: Oxford University Press.

Pernicano, P. (2011). *Outsmarting the Riptide of Domestic Violence: Metaphor and Mindfulness for Change.* Lanham, MD: Jason Aronson.

Siegel, D. J. (2007). *The Mindful Brain.* New York: W. W. Norton & Company.

Siegel, D. J. (2010). *The Mindful Therapist: A Clinician's Guide to Mindsight and Neural Integration.* New York: W. W. Norton & Company.

Yapko, M. (2011). *Mindfulness and Hypnosis: The Power of Suggestion to Transform Experience.* New York: W. W. Norton & Company.

Chapter 6: On Being a Reframer

Benammar, K. (2012). *Reframing: The Art of Thinking Differently.* Amsterdam, NL: Boom.

Carr, A. (2000). *Family Therapy: Concepts, Process and Practice.* Chichester, UK: Wiley.

Erickson, B. A. (2010). What's right with him? Ericksonian positive psychotherapy in a case of sexual abuse. In G. W. Burns (Ed.), *Happiness Healing Enhancement: Your Casebook Collection for Using Positive Therapy* (pp. 29–39). Hoboken, NJ: John Wiley & Sons.

REFERENCES

Madrid, S., Fernie, D. & Kantor, R. (2010). *Reframing the Emotional Worlds of the Early Childhood Classroom.* New York: Routledge.

Noelen-Hoeksema, S. & Davis, C. (2002). Positive responses to loss: Perceiving benefits and growth. In C. R. Snyder & S. Lopez (Eds.), *Handbook of Positive Psychology* (pp. 598–607). New York: Oxford University Press.

Perloiro, M. deF., Neto, L. M. & Marujo, H. A. (2010).We will be laughing again: Restoring relationships with positive couples therapy. In G. W. Burns (Ed.), *Happiness Healing Enhancement: Your Casebook Collection for Using Positive Therapy* (pp. 15–28). Hoboken, NJ: John Wiley & Sons.

Tedeschi, R. G. & Calhoun, L. G. (2010). A surprise attack, a surprise result: Posttraumatic growth through expert companionship. In G. W. Burns (Ed.), *Happiness Healing Enhancement: Your Casebook Collection for Using Positive Therapy* (pp. 226–236). Hoboken, NJ: John Wiley & Sons.

Tennen, H. & Affleck, G. (2002). Benefit-finding and benefit-reminding. In C. R. Snyder & S. Lopez (Eds.), *Handbook of Positive Psychology* (pp. 584–597). New York: Oxford University Press.

Yapko, M. D. (2012). *Trancework: An Introduction to the Practice of Clinical Hypnosis* (4th ed.). New York: Routledge.

Chapter 7: On Changing Patterns of Behavior

Biam, C. & Guthrie, L. (2014). *Changing Offending Behaviour: A Handbook of Practical Exercises and Photocopiable Resources for Promoting Positive Change.* Philadelphia, PA: Jessica Kingsley.

Carr, A. (2004). *Positive Psychology: The Science of Happiness and Human Strengths.* New York: Routledge.

Heard, H. L. & Swales, M. A. (2016). *Changing Behavior in DBT: Problem Solving in Action.* New York: Guilford Press.

Lankton, S. R. (2010). Inspiring change: How to use tools of intention for positive outcomes. In G. W. Burns (Ed.), *Happiness Healing Enhancement: Your Casebook Collection for Using Positive Therapy* (pp. 279–290). Hoboken, NJ: John Wiley & Sons.

Prochaska, J. O., Norcross, J. & Diclemente, C. C. (1994). *Changing for Good: A Revolutionary Six-Stage Program for Overcoming Bad Habits and Moving Your Life Positively Forward.* New York: William Morrow.

Chapter 8: On Learning from Experience

Jacobson, M. & Ruddy, M. (2004). *Open to Outcome.* Oklahoma City, OK: Wood 'N' Barnes.

Kolb, D. (1984). *Experiential Learning as the Science of Learning and Development.* Englewood Cliffs, NJ: Prentice Hall.

Mayer, R. (2004). Should there be a three-strikes rule against pure discovery learning? *American Psychologist,* 59, 1, 14–19.

Milton, N. (2010). *The Lessons Learned Handbook: Practical Approaches to Learning from Experience.* Oxford, UK: Chandos Publishing.

Seligman, M. (2011). *Learned Optimism.* North Sydney, Australia: William Heinemann.

Chapter 9: On Being Compassionate

Aussie Helpers, (2016). Accessed on November 20, 2016, from https://www. aussiehelpers.org.au

Dalai Lama. (1995). *The Power of Compassion*. London, UK: Thorsons.

Fredrickson, B. L. (2009). *Positivity: Groundbreaking Research Reveals How to Embrace the Hidden Strengths of Positive Emotions, Overcome Negativity, and Thrive*. New York: Crown.

Fredrickson, B. L., Cohn, M. A., Coffey, K. A., Pek, J. & Finkel, S. (2008). Open hearts build lives: Positive emotions induce through loving-kindness meditation, build consequential personal resources. *Journal of Personality and Social Psychology*, 95, 1045–1062.

Gilbert, P. (2005). *Compassion: Conceptualisations, Research and Use in Psychotherapy*. London, UK: Routledge.

Jazaieri, H., Lee, I. A., McGonigal, K., Jinpa, T., Doty, J. R., Gross, J. J. & Goldin, P. R. (2016). A wandering mind is a less caring mind: Daily experience sampling during compassion meditation training. *Journal of Positive Psychology*, 11, 1, 37–50.

Otake, K., Shimai, S., Tanaka-Matsumi, J., Otsui, K. & Fredrickson, B. L. (2006). Happy people become happier through kindness: A counting kindness intervention. *Journal of Happiness Studies*, 7, 361–375.

Post, S. G. (2007). *Altruism and Health: Perspectives from Empirical Research*. New York: Oxford.

Post, S. G. & Neimark, J. (2007). *Why Good Things Happen to Good People*. New York: Random House.

Schwartz, C. E. (2010). Can helping others help oneself? Reflections on altruism, health and well-being. In G. W. Burns (Ed.), *Happiness Healing Enhancement: Your Casebook Collection for Using Positive Therapy* (pp. 151–163). Hoboken, NJ: John Wiley & Sons.

Chapter 10: On Caring for One's Self

Carr, A. (2004). *Positive Psychology: The Science of Happiness and Human Strengths*. New York: Routledge.

Haybron, D. M. (2008). *The Pursuit of Unhappiness: The Elusive Psychology of Well-Being*. New York: Oxford University Press.

Keyes, C. L. & Haidt, J. (Eds.). (2002). *Flourishing*. Washington, DC: American Psychological Association.

Lyubomirsky, S. (2013). *The Myths of Happiness: What Should Make You Happy, but Doesn't. What Shouldn't Make You Happy, but Does*. New York: Penguin Press.

Malinowski, A. J. (2014). *Self-Care for the Mental Health Practitioner: The Theory, Research, and Practice of Preventing and Addressing the Occupational Hazards of the Profession*. London, UK: Jessica Kingsley Publications.

Malinowski, D. (2013). Flourishing through meditation and mindfulness. In S. A. David, I. Boniwell, & A. C. Ayers (Eds.), *The Oxford Handbook of Happiness* (pp. 384–396). Oxford: Oxford University Press.

Seligman, M. (2011). *Flourish*. North Sydney, Australia: William Heinemann.

Sykley, J.-A. (2012). *The Twilight Mind: Powerful Twilight Saga Psychology*. Alresford, Hampshire, UK: John Hunt Publishing.

Chapter 11: On Being a Positive Thinker

Burkeman, O. (2012). *The Antidote: Happiness for People Who Can't Stand Positive Thinking.* New York: Faber & Faber.

Carr, A. (2004). *Positive Psychology: The Science of Happiness and Human Strengths.* New York: Routledge.

Fredrickson, B. L. (2009). *Positivity: Groundbreaking Research Reveals How to Embrace the Hidden Strengths of Positive Emotions, Overcome Negativity, and Thrive.* New York: Crown.

Lankton, S. R. (2010). Inspiring change: How to use tools of intention for positive outcomes. In G. W. Burns (Ed.), *Happiness Healing Enhancement: Your Casebook Collection for Using Positive Therapy* (pp. 279–290). Hoboken, NJ: John Wiley & Sons.

Peale, N. V. (2003). *The Power of Positive Thinking.* New York: Fireside.

Robinson, M. D. & Compton, R. J. (2008). The happy mind in action: The cognitive basis of subjective well-being. In M. Eid & R. J. Larsen (Eds.), *The Science of Subjective Well-Being* (pp. 220–238). New York: Guilford Press.

Seligman, M. (2011). *Flourish.* North Sydney, Australia: William Heinemann.

Chapter 12: On Being Emotionally Positive and Engaged

Burns, G. W. (2007). *Healing with Stories: Your Casebook Collection for Using Therapeutic Metaphors.* Hoboken, NJ: John Wiley & Sons.

Burns, G. W. (2009). The path of happiness: Integrating nature into therapy for couples and families. In L. Buzzell & C. Chalquist (Eds.), *Ecotherapy: Healing with Nature in Mind* (pp. 92–104). San Francisco, CA: Sierra Club Books.

Burns, G. W. (2010). Sunsets and seashores: Nature-guided therapy in positive couple and family work. In G. W. Burns (Ed.), *Happiness Healing Enhancement: Your Casebook Collection for Using Positive Therapy* (pp. 239–251). Hoboken, NJ: John Wiley & Sons.

Burns, G. W. (Ed.). (2010). *Happiness Healing Enhancement: Your Casebook Collection for Using Positive Therapy.* Hoboken, NJ: John Wiley & Sons.

Burns, G. W. (2014). *Nature-Guided Therapy: Brief Integrative Strategies for Health and Wellbeing.* New York: Routledge.

Carr, A. (2004). *Positive Psychology: The Science of Happiness and Human Strengths.* New York: Routledge.

Conway, A. M., Tugade, M. M., Catalino, L. H. & Fredrickson, B. L. (2013). The broaden-and-build theory of positive emotions: Form, function and mechanics. In S. A. David, I. Boniwell, & A. C. Ayers (Eds.), *The Oxford Handbook of Happiness* (pp. 17–34). Oxford: Oxford University Press.

Emmons, R. A. (2008). Gratitude, subjective well-being and the brain. In M. Eid & R. J. Larsen (Eds.), *The Science of Subjective Well-Being* (pp. 469–489). New York: Guilford Press.

Emmons, R. A. & McCulloch, M. E. (2003). Counting blessings versus burdens: An experimental investigation of gratitude and subjective well-being in daily life. *Journal of Personality and Social Psychology*, 84, 2, 377–389.

Fredrickson, B. L. (2005). The broaden-and-build theory of positive emotions. In F. A. Huppert, N. Baylis, & B. Keverne (Eds.), *The Science of Wellbeing* (pp. 217–238). Oxford: Oxford University Press.

Fredrickson, B. L. (2008). Promoting positive affect. In M. Eid & R. J. Larsen (Eds.), *The Science of Subjective Well-Being* (pp. 449–468). New York: Guilford Press.

Fredrickson, B. L. (2009). *Positivity: Groundbreaking Research Reveals How to Embrace the Hidden Strengths of Positive Emotions, Overcome Negativity, and Thrive.* New York: Crown.

Larsen, R. J. & Prizmic, Z. (2008). Regulation of emotional well-being: Overcoming the hedonic treadmill. In M. Eid & R. J. Larsen (Eds.), *The Science of Subjective Well-Being* (pp. 258–289). New York: Guilford Press.

Lyubomirsky, S., Sheldon, K. M. & Schkade, D. (2005). Pursuing happiness: The architecture of sustainable change. *Review of General Psychology*, 9, 111–131.

Seligman, M. E. P. (2011). *Flourish.* North Sydney, Australia: William Heinemann.

Seligman, M. E. P., Rashid, T. & Parks, A. C. (2006). Positive psychotherapy. *American Psychologist*, November, 61, 774–788.

Seligman, M. E. P., Steen, T. A., Park, N. & Peterson, C. (2005). Positive psychology progress: Empirical validation of interventions. *American Psychologist*, 60, 410–421.

Chapter 13: On Being in Social Relationships

Burns, G. W. & Street, H. (2003). *Standing without Shoes: Creating Happiness, Relieving Depression, Enhancing Life.* Sydney, Australia: Prentice Hall.

Cacioppo, J. & Patrick, W. (2008). *Loneliness: Human Nature and the Need for Social Connection.* New York: W. W. Norton and Company.

Carr, A. (2004). *Positive Psychology: The Science of Happiness and Human Strengths.* New York: Routledge.

Demir, M. (2013). Introduction to relationships and happiness. In S. A. David, I. Boniwell, & A. C. Ayers (Eds.), *The Oxford Handbook of Happiness* (pp. 817–820). Oxford: Oxford University Press.

Demir, M., Orthel, H. & Andelin, A. K. (2013). Friendship and happiness. In S. A. David, I. Boniwell, & A. C. Ayers (Eds.), *The Oxford Handbook of Happiness* (pp. 860–870). Oxford: Oxford University Press.

Diener, E. & Seligman, M. (2002). Very happy people. *Psychological Science*, 13, 81–84.

Diener, M. L. & McGavran, M. B. D. (2008). What makes people happy? A developmental approach to the literature on family relationships and well-being. In M. Eid & R. J. Larsen (Eds.), *The Science of Subjective Well-Being* (pp. 347–275). New York: Guilford Press.

Fincham, F. D. (2015). Facilitating forgiveness using group and community interventions. In S. Joseph (Ed.), *Positive Psychology in Practice: Promoting Human Flourishing in Work, Health, Education, and Everyday Life* (2nd ed., pp. 659–679). Hoboken, NY: John Wiley and Sons.

Lakey, B. (2013). Perceived social support and happiness: Be role of personality and relational processes. In S. A. David, I. Boniwell, & A. C. Ayers (Eds.), *The Oxford Handbook of Happiness* (pp. 847–859). Oxford: Oxford University Press.

O'Connell, B. H., O'Shea, D. & Gallagher, S. (2016). Enhancing social relationships through positive psychology activities: A randomised controlled trial. *Journal of Positive Psychology*, 11, 2, 149–162.

Reis, H. T. & Gable, S. L. (2003). Toward a positive psychology of relationships. In C. L. M. Keyes & J. Haidt (Eds.), *Flourishing: Positive Psychology and the Life Well-Lived* (pp. 129–159). Washington, DC: American Psychological Association.

Reis, H. T., Sheldon, K. M., Gable, S. L., Roscoe, J. & Ryan, R. M. (2000). Daily well-being: The role of autonomy, competence, and relatedness. *Personality and Social Psychology Bulletin*, 26, 419–435.

Seligman, M. (2011). *Flourish*. North Sydney, Australia: William Heinemann.

Sheldon, K. & Hoon, T. (2007). The multiple determination of well-being: Independent effects of positive traits, needs, goals, selves, social supports, and cultural contexts. *Journal of Happiness Studies*, 7, 55–86.

Valliant, G. E. (2009). *What Makes Us Happy*. Accessed on May 5, 2016 from http://www.theatlantic.com/magazine/archive/2009/06/what-makes-us-happy/307439/

Valliant, G. E. (2012). *Triumphs of Experience: The Men of the Harvard Grant Study*. Cambridge, MA: Harvard University Press.

Chapter 14: On Improving Loving Relationships

Bao, K. J. & Lyubomirsky, S. (2013). Making it last: Combating hedonic adaptation in romantic relationships. *The Journal of Positive Psychology*, 8, 3, 196–206.

Burns, G. W. (2010). Sunsets and seashores: Nature-guided therapy in positive couple and family work. In G. W. Burns (Ed.), *Happiness Healing Enhancement: Your Casebook Collection for Using Positive Therapy* (pp. 239–251). Hoboken, NJ: John Wiley & Sons.

Cacioppo, J. & Patrick, W. (2008). *Loneliness: Human Nature and the Need for Social Connection*. New York: W. W. Norton and Company.

Carr, A. (2004). *Positive Psychology: The Science of Happiness and Human Strengths*. New York: Routledge.

Diener, E. & Seligman, M. (2002). Very happy people. *Psychological Science*, 13, 81–84.

Diener, M. L. & McGavran, M. B. D. (2008). What makes people happy? A developmental approach to the literature on family relationships and well-being. In M. Eid & R. J. Larsen (Eds.), *The Science of Subjective Well-Being* (pp. 347–275). New York: Guilford Press.

Gottman, J. (2001). *The Relationship Cure: A 5 Step Guide to Strengthening Your Marriage, Family, and Friendships*. New York: Three Rivers Press.

Johnson, S. M. (2004). *The Practice of Emotionally Focused Couple Therapy: Creating Connection*. New York: Brunner/Routledge.

Johnson, S. M. (2008). *Hold Me Tight: Seven Conversations for a Lifetime of Love*. New York: Little, Brown and Company.

Johnson, S. M. (2013). *Love Sense: The Revolutionary New Science of Romantic Relationships*. New York: Little, Brown and Company.

Perloiro, M. deF., Neto, L. M. & Marujo, H. A. (2010).We will be laughing again: Restoring relationships with positive couples therapy. In G. W. Burns (Ed.),

Happiness Healing Enhancement: Your Casebook Collection for Using Positive Therapy (pp. 15–28). Hoboken, NJ: John Wiley & Sons.

Reis, H. T. & Gable, S. L. (2003). Toward a positive psychology of relationships. In C. L. M. Keyes & J. Haidt (Eds.), *Flourishing: Positive Psychology and the Life Well-Lived* (pp. 129–159). Washington, DC: American Psychological Association.

Reis, H. T., Sheldon, K. M., Gable, S. L., Roscoe, J. & Ryan, R. M. (2000). Daily well-being: The role of autonomy, competence, and relatedness. *Personality and Social Psychology Bulletin*, 26, 419–435.

Saphire-Bernstein, S. & Taylor, S. E. (2013). Close relationships and happiness. In S. A. David, I. Boniwell, & A. C. Ayers (Eds.), *The Oxford Handbook of Happiness* (pp. 860–870). Oxford: Oxford University Press.

Chapter 15: On Finding Meaning and Wisdom

Buehler, E. (2006). *Bread Science: The Chemistry and Craft of Making Bread.* Carrboro, NC: Two Blue Books.

Carr, A. (2004). *Positive Psychology: The Science of Happiness and Human Strengths.* New York: Routledge.

Kunzmann, U. & Thomas, S. (2015). Wisdom-related knowledge across the lifespan. In S. Joseph (Ed.), *Positive Psychology in Practice: Promoting Human Flourishing in Work, Health, Education, and Everyday Life* (2nd ed., pp. 577–594). Hoboken, NY: John Wiley and Sons.

Myers, D. G. (2008). Religion and human flourishing. In M. Eid & R. J. Larsen (Eds.), *The Science of Subjective Well-Being* (pp. 323–343). New York: Guilford Press.

Reeve, C. D. C. (1992). *Practices of Reason: Aristotle's Nicomachaen Ethics.* Oxford: Oxford University Press.

Seligman, M. (2011). *Flourish.* North Sydney, Australia: William Heinemann.

Steger, M. F., Beeby, A., Garrett, S. & Kashdan, T. B. (2013). Creating a stable architectural framework of existence: Proposing a model of lifelong meaning. In S. A. David, I. Boniwell, & A. C. Ayers (Eds.), *The Oxford Handbook of Happiness* (pp. 941–954). Oxford, UK: Oxford University Press.

Sternberg, R. J. (2013). Teaching for wisdom. In S. A. David, I. Boniwell, & A. C. Ayers (Eds.), *The Oxford Handbook of Happiness* (pp. 631–643). Oxford, UK: Oxford University Press.

Ventura, M. (2001). Beauty resurrected. *Family Therapy Networker*, January/February, 30–35.

Chapter 16: On Being a Problem-Solver

Carr, A. (2004). *Positive Psychology: The Science of Happiness and Human Strengths.* New York: Routledge.

D'Zurilla, T. & Nezu, A. (1999). *Problem Solving Therapy* (2nd ed.). New York: Springer Verlag.

Haley, J. (1987). *Problem-Solving Therapy* (2nd ed.). San Francisco, CA: Jossey-Bass.

Heppner, P. & Goug-Gwi, L. (2002). Problem-solving appraisal and psychological adjustment. In C. R. Snyder & S. Lopez (Eds.), *Handbook of Positive Psychology* (pp. 288–298). New York: Oxford University Press.

Mayer, R. E. (1992). *Thinking, Problem Solving, Cognition* (2nd ed.). New York: W. H. Freeman/Times Books/ Henry Holt & Co.

Reivich, K. & Shatte, A. (2002). *The Resilience Factor: 7 Essential Skills for Overcoming Life's Inevitable Obstacles.* New York: Broadway Books.

Chapter 17: On Being Happy

Burns, G. W. (Ed.). (2010). *Happiness Healing Enhancement: Your Casebook Collection for Using Positive Therapy.* Hoboken, NJ: John Wiley & Sons.

Burns, G. W. & Street, H. (2003). *Standing without Shoes: Creating Happiness, Relieving Depression, Enhancing Life.* Sydney, Australia: Prentice Hall.

Carr, A. (2004). *Positive Psychology: The Science of Happiness and Human Strengths.* New York: Routledge.

Dalai Lama & Cutler, H. C. (1998). *The Art of Happiness.* Sydney, Australia: Hodder.

David, S. A., Boniwell, I. & Conley Ayers, A. (Eds.). (2013). *The Oxford Handbook of Happiness.* Oxford, UK: Oxford University Press.

Eid, M. & Larsen, R. J. (Eds.). (2008). *The Science of Subjective Well-Being.* New York: Guilford Press.

Huppert, F. A., Baylis, N. & Keverne, B. (2005). *The Science of Well-Being.* Oxford: Oxford University Press.

Joseph, S. (Ed.). (2015). *Positive Psychology in Practice: Promoting Human Flourishing in Work, Health, Education, and Everyday Life* (2nd ed.). Hoboken, NY: John Wiley and Sons.

Joseph, S. & Linley, P. A. (2006). *Positive Therapy: A Meta-Theory for Positive Psychology Practice.* New York: Routledge.

Klein, S. (2006). *The Science of Happiness: How Our Brains Make Us Happy—and What We Can Do to Get Happier.* Melbourne, Australia: Scribe.

Linley, P. A., Harrington, S. & Garcea, N. (2013). *The Oxford Handbook of Positive Psychology and Work.* Oxford: Oxford University Press.

Lopez, S. J., Pedrotti, J. T. & Snyder, C. R. (2015). *Positive Psychology: The Scientific and Practical Explorations of Human Strengths* (3rd ed.). Thousand Oaks, CA: Sage Publications.

Lyubomirsky, S. (2008). *The How of Happiness.* New York: Penguin Press.

Lyubomirsky, S. (2013). *The Myths of Happiness: What Should Make You Happy, but Doesn't. What Shouldn't Make You Happy, but Does.* New York: Penguin Press.

Niemiec, C. P. & Ryan, R. M. (2013). What makes for a life well lived? Autonomy and its relation to full functioning and organismic wellness. In S. A. David, I. Boniwell, & A. Conley Ayers (Eds.), *The Oxford Handbook of Happiness* (pp. 214–226). Oxford, UK: Oxford University Press.

Peterson, C. (2008). *What Is Positive Psychology, and What Is It Not?* Accessed on May 5, 2016, from https://www.psychologytoday.com/blog/the-good-life/200805/what-is-positive-psychology-and-what-is-it-not

Seligman, M. (2011). *Flourish.* North Sydney, Australia: William Heinemann.

Sheldon, K. & Lyubomirsky, S. (2007). Is it possible to become happier? (And, if so, how?). *Social and Personality Psychology Compass*, 1, 129–145.

Street, H. & Porter, N. (Eds.). (2014). *Better Than OK: Helping Young People to Flourish at School and Beyond.* Fremantle, Australia: Fremantle Press.

Sykley, J. (1997). *The Cognitive Determinants of Psychological Well-Being.* Darwin, Australia: Northern Territory University Press.

Valliant, G. E. (2009). *What Makes Us Happy.* Accessed on May 5, 2016, from http://www.theatlantic.com/magazine/archive/2009/06/what-makes-us-happy/307439/

Valliant, G. E. (2012). *Triumphs of Experience: The Men of the Harvard Grant Study.* Cambridge, MA: Harvard University Press.

A Guide to Creating Your Own Happiness-Enhancing Stories

Burns, G. W. (2001). *101 Healing Stories: Using Metaphors in Therapy.* New York: John Wiley and Sons.

Burns, G. W. (2005). *101 Healing Stories for Kids and Teens.* Hoboken, NJ: John Wiley and Sons.

Burns, G. W. (2007). *Healing with Stories Your Casebook Collection for Using Therapeutic Metaphors.* Hoboken, NJ: John Wiley & Sons.

Burns, G. W. (2010). Soaring to new heights: Outcome-oriented metaphor in a case of severe phobia. In G. W. Burns (Ed.), *Happiness Healing Enhancement: Your Casebook Collection for Using Positive Therapy* (pp. 315–327). Hoboken, NJ: John Wiley & Sons.

Pema Tshering's story, My Paralympic Dream. (2014). Accessed on October 14, 2016, from https://www.youtube.com/watch?v=0rShkVdJuUM

Tedeschi, R. G. & Calhoun, L. G. (2010). A surprise attack, a surprise result: Post-traumatic growth through expert companionship. In G. W. Burns (Ed.), *Happiness Healing Enhancement: Your Casebook Collection for Using Positive Therapy* (pp. 226–236). Hoboken, NJ: John Wiley & Sons.

Index